S0-CJE-213

Penguin Education

Marketing Research

Edited by Joseph Seibert and Gorden Wills

Penguin Modern Management Readings

General Editor

D. S. Pugh

Marketing Research

Selected Readings

Edited by Joseph Seibert and Gorden Wills

Penguin Books

Penguin Books Ltd, Harmondsworth,
Middlesex, England
Penguin Books Inc., 7110 Ambassador Road,
Baltimore, Maryland 21207, U.S.A.
Penguin Books Australia Ltd, Ringwood,
Victoria, Australia

First published 1970
This selection copyright © Joseph Seibert and Gordon Wills, 1970
Introduction and notes copyright © Joseph Seibert and Gordon Wills, 1970

Made and printed in Great Britain by
C. Nicholls & Company Ltd
Set in Monotype Times

Contents

Contents

Introduction

The use of marketing research in industry coincides with the emergence of discretionary incomes in the hands of potential customers. The research process is the way in which the seller reaches an understanding of his customers, and optimizes the operational behaviour he engages in to meet customer needs. It is vital, therefore, at the outset to place marketing research in its corporate context. Robert King has suggested a model of the marketing process (Figure 1) which shows the role of marketing research as the sensitivity monitor in the market place.

Our selection has been made with both the North American and British marketeer in mind. What is necessary now in the evolution of marketing research in the U.K. equally needs reinforcement in the happier marketing environment in the United States. We two editors, each with practical experience of each other's marketing scene, were quickly able to agree that the approach called for on both sides of the Atlantic was identical. Our basic aim has been to put technique, beautiful as it undoubtedly is, in its managerial context. Research in marketing is fruitless unless it illuminates an identified problem at a worthwhile cost. No amount of beautiful technique can compensate for answers to irrelevant questions, however well those questions may have been framed. Hence, we have divided this volume into two discrete parts. In the first we examine closely the managerial problems of marketing research; in the second we take an exhaustive look at the most regular tools and techniques.

The expertise which marketing researchers have developed in their own particular area has sometimes left them unaware of the possible overlap from other important areas of management development and research. The readings in Part One look in particular at the application of techniques such as PERT and cost-benefit analysis as well as the application of straightforward personnel selection procedures within the marketing research area. In addition, a range of rigorous approaches to regular

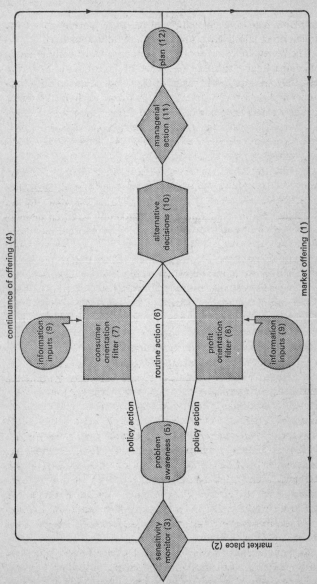

Figure 1 The marketing concept (after Robert King)

problems such as the selection of research contractors, or the design of an effective research brief, are fully considered.

The review in Part Two of marketing research techniques is, of course, unable to cover all aspects of the situation. Nonetheless, they are explored in terms of their application to both consumer and industrial markets and look once again at the rigour of the research methods involved and their applications specifically in the marketing area. They emphasize a multitude of aspects of research methodology which may often go by default in harassed commercial circumstances.

For the manager, therefore, these readings offer the opportunity to re-appraise the use which he is making of marketing research, if he is already deeply involved in this area. For the manager who is less familiar with marketing research methodology, and for the student of marketing research in graduate and undergraduate courses and on post-experience management training courses, the readings offer a wide ranging review of what is most valuable and well tried in marketing research.

A short list of 'suggestions for further reading' is provided at the end of the volume, based on the searching and sifting in which we engaged to make this selection. They are by no means second-rank contributions; if space had permitted many would have immediately won their way into these pages.

We have been aware and extremely conscious, indeed, in the preparation of these readings, of the substantially different marketing environments in which marketing research is conducted in Britain and the United States. British marketing research has a proud and successful history of development since the turn of the century. Marketing research is an activity which within the United Kingdom but not in the United States, has become an institutionalized profession, both in the Market Research Society, and the Industrial Marketing Research Association since the Second World War. In North America, the American Marketing Association has embraced both the marketing executives and the marketing researchers (and the educators as well).

There seems little doubt that the discrete existence of the Market Research Society in Britain has been one of the major factors explaining why U.K. marketing research is on a direct par with

North American standards, whereas in terms of operational marketing Britain obviously lags. The first phenomenon undoubtedly goes a long way to explaining the second. There has been a regrettable divorce in Britain between marketing research and marketing management. It has generally given rise to superb technical skills, even an obsession with technique on the part of the researcher, and a feeling of bewilderment in the operational manager.

When this division in Britain is compounded by the complete absence of any form of total education in marketing save the self-help begun in the professions at the end of the 1950s, and the addition of the Universities and Business Schools in 1965, the problem becomes acute.

Against the background of these general comments on both our selection and the thoughts which were in our mind when we made the choice, we hope most sincerely that the readings we have finally agreed upon and included in this volume will enable the constructive development and growth of effective marketing activity, wheresoever the process is required.

Part One
The Management of Marketing Research

The corner-stone of effective marketing research is classification of the marketing problem which calls for investigation. This Crisp (Reading 1) has done in classic style. Ehrenberg (Reading 2) discusses the form of brief which can be most usefully developed, and Mayer (Reading 3) offers a systematic procedure for choosing a contractor to conduct a study. The evaluation of the likely value of information from a research investigation and the programming of its activities are considered by Wills (Reading 4) and Harder and Lindell (Reading 5).

The final three readings in Part One, from Blankenship and Doyle (6), Haldane (7) and Rogers (8), look at the personnel problems of marketing research management. How can a research group be most creatively structured? How can marketing research staff be most carefully chosen? How can the researcher find a true identity at that interface between the area of real concern with objective research and the demands of speedy decision-making?

1 R. Crisp

Classification of Marketing Problems

Excerpt from R. Crisp, *Marketing Research*, McGraw-Hill, 1957, pp. 44–66.

A marketing research man is concerned not just with marketing research but rather with the entire broad area of marketing management. This does not mean that he trespasses on or intrudes into the provinces of others – of the sales manager, for example, or of the sales vice-president. It does mean that he must understand the problems his fellow executives face before he can apply his skills productively to the task of helping them by contributing the facts they need to aid them in arriving at key decisions.

This is an extremely important point. Marketing research cannot exist or function effectively in a vacuum, as something apart from marketing management. It is inseparably integrated with the broad base of common marketing problems that exist in most companies which have a product or service to sell. It is literally true that those common marketing problems form the base of all marketing research activities.

Although the number of marketing problems is limitless, those problems can be grouped into a relatively small number of *types* of problems. A useful framework for grouping the major types of marketing problems to which research can be and is profitably applied is needed at this point. Such a framework provides perspective on the specific activities marketing research men do and the relationships between those different activities.

There are many different ways in which marketing problems might be classified. For example, they might be grouped according to their scale, as into major and minor problems. Or they might be classified on the basis of their time component, thus separating short-term problems which require an almost immediate answer or decision from long-term problems. Or they might be classified functionally, thus distinguishing between sales problems and advertising problems, or between product problems and policy problems.

Operating Problems Versus Non-Recurring Problems

A classification base which provides a useful and practical framework for understanding marketing research activities is one which begins by dividing all marketing problems into two major types: *operating problems*, which are continuously present in almost every marketing-management situation, and *non-recurring problems,* which arise as a result of some specific development or circumstance.

Problems of the first type are found in all marketing situations. The second type of problems is frequently, but not necessarily continuously, present. A review of some of the major specific problems within each of these groups follows.

Major Types of Operating Problems

The outstanding characteristic of problems in this category is that they exist in every organization with a product or service to sell, even though their existence is not always explicitly recognized. Problems of this type are an inescapable element of a management job, as necessary to management practice as breathing is to life. To provide specific illustrations of problems of this type, consider an actual but anonymous company, Allied Products, Inc. At the time of this illustration, the company's annual sales volume was about ten million dollars. It employed about three hundred salesmen, with several levels of sales supervision between the salesmen in the field and the chief sales executive in the company's home office. It spent about $900,000 a year for advertising. It operated more than a dozen warehouses, strategically located in key markets in all sections of the country.

This company was in excellent corporate health. It was a sound, well-managed company. Its business had never been better than at the time of this illustration. This is a type of situation, in short, in which one might perhaps expect to find *no* marketing problems present. If you moved behind the desk of the sales vice-president of this healthy, vigorous business and peeked over his shoulder as he worked, however, you would find that he faced a constant flow of problems. In the course of a full year spent behind his desk, and in front of the desks of some of the executives of the company's major customers, this sales vice-president encountered the following types of operating problems.

Sales forecasting

Although this company's manufacturing cycle was relatively short – that is, only about three months elapsed between the release of a manufacturing authorization to the production department and the date when the merchandise was available on the shipping platform – the sales vice-president was responsible for the preparation of a *sales forecast* every six months. These forecasts covered a twelve-month period and were reviewed and revised every six months.

In developing estimates of company volume for each future time period, it was necessary to consider the trend of industry volume as well as trends in company volume and to weigh also various economic influences which might tend to stimulate or depress company sales opportunities. The sales vice-president did not have to prepare those sales forecasts personally. He delegated that responsibility to a group of subordinates. But the sales vice-president was personally responsible for reviewing the forecasts and accepting or modifying them.

He was also responsible for presenting those forecasts to the company's management committee, of which he was a member, for approval. He had to explain and justify the forecasts to that committee. Once the forecasts were accepted and approved by the committee as the foundation for the company's production and financial and sales planning, he became responsible for seeing that the volume of merchandise called for by the forecasts was actually sold.

Sales-expense forecasting

From the viewpoint of top management, a forecast of sales volume is only half the story. That forecast indicates what volume of merchandise the company may expect to sell. It therefore shows anticipated income for the time period covered. But management is concerned primarily with net income or profit rather than gross income. An operating profit results only when the income from sales exceeds the cost of making, financing, and selling the products sold.

With a staff of three hundred salesmen, Allied Products, Inc., obviously had a substantial amount of direct-selling expense, to which the $900,000 in advertising costs must be added. The sales vice-president was responsible for all sales costs, including advertising and warehousing expenses. He had to prepare a forecast of those expenses in detail, for the approval of the management committee, along with his forecast of sales volume. It is only when the forecast of sales volume can be equated with the estimated cost of achieving that volume that profit estimates can be made and the performance of the company's marketing management executives appraised.

Forecasts of production and financial expenses, prepared by the production and financial divisions of Allied Products, Inc., and submitted for management-committee approval by the vice-presidents who headed those divisions, were largely contingent on the sales forecast and were typically prepared after the sales forecast had been submitted and approved. This time relationship made it necessary for the sales forecast to be prepared a longer time in advance of the beginning of the sales period covered than would otherwise have been the case.

Comment. The intimate interrelationship of sales-volume responsibility and sales-expense responsibility is illustrated by this excerpt from the job description of the sales vice-president of Allied Products, Inc., as it appeared in the company's organization manual: 'The sales vice-president is responsible for determining sales objectives and budgets of sales and advertising expenses and for securing approval of those objectives and expense budgets by the management committee.' The process of making a carefully considered sales forecast is not a simple one.

Continuing control of sales volume and expense

Once forecasts of sales volume and sales expenses have been adopted, there exists a continuing need for a comparison of actual sales with planned-for or budgeted sales and for careful control of sales expenses to be sure those expenses do not exceed the forecast. The chief sales executive of any organization needs specific and detailed facts about sales progress at all times. Available data must be maintained in great detail. When actual sales begin to lag behind the sales forecast, such detailed data make it possible to *isolate the problem elements* in the situation quickly.

What individual products are failing to achieve anticipated volume? What territories, districts, or regions are lagging? What types of customers are failing to deliver the volume they were expected to contribute? The answers to questions like these are quickly available through sales-control machinery which ordinarily operates on the exception principle, requiring very little top-executive time.

The sales vice-president is responsible for the creation of that sales-control machinery. He must decide in advance what specific kinds of information he will require, and with what frequency, in order to maintain effective control over sales progress. Planning such control machinery is not a routine or clerical function. On the contrary, as a Stanford University study pointed out, it is 'one of the primary responsibilities of top management' to provide 'effective means of control, permitting top executives to delegate wide responsibility and authority, thereby freeing themselves of administrative detail in order to concentrate on broad planning and direction' (Holden *et al.*, 1951, p. 3).

It might be noted parenthetically that the sales vice-president of Allied Products, Inc., is a *divisional-management* executive, directly responsible for one of the major divisions of the company. He is therefore clearly included in the top-management group as defined in the Stanford study.

Appraisal of *territorial sales opportunities or potentials*

A national sales forecast for a company like Allied Products, Inc., is simply the sum total of 'a lot of little forecasts put together.' A detailed and current knowledge of the opportunity to make sales in individual sales territories, districts, and regions – and especially of the *relative* opportunities existing in different geographical units – is an essential element in developing sound

17

marketing plans. This is a continuing problem because territorial potentials change constantly and sometimes rapidly. Changes in territorial buying power and the revisions of a company's sales-territorial boundaries contribute to such changes.

The applications of such knowledge are numerous. You would find the sales vice-president of Allied Products, Inc., using them as a guide in determining how many warehouses his organization requires and where those warehouses should be located. He uses them constantly in planning sales-territorial assignments and in reviewing and revising sales-territorial boundaries. He uses them to help him determine the number of salesmen the company needs and in planning where those salesmen should be positioned for maximum productivity. Again note that the sales vice-president is not personally engaged in this activity, which he delegates to one of his subordinates. But he retains the responsibility for seeing that such appraisals are made and for using the detailed facts about territorial potentials in many aspects of his day-to-day work.

Comment. Because the term *potential*, or *sales potential*, is sometimes used in different ways by different writers, it tends to be confusing. As the term is used in this book, the potential of a territory or a market is *synonymous with the total industry volume* in that territory or market. It is therefore the total within which each competing individual company seeks to build volume. The success of these efforts is reflected in the *market share* achieved. Market share is a percentage figure which relates company sales – either nationally or in a territory – to industry volume nationally or in that territory.

To illustrate this further, one of the products in the Allied Products, Inc., line had industry volume nationally of ten million dollars at manufacturers' prices. The New York territory was estimated to represent 12 per cent of the national total on that product. The potential of the New York territory thus would be 12 per cent of ten million dollars, or $1,200,000. If sales by Allied Products, Inc., of that product in the New York territory were $300,000, that would represent a 25 per cent market share. In the relatively rare case of a company with a unique product and no competitors, company volume and industry volume would be synonymous and the company's market share would be 100 per cent. Occasionally the term potential is used to describe the total volume which an expanding industry may achieve at some future date. The term is here used in a more limited sense: to identify actual or estimated industry volume in a specific time period – usually this year or next year.

Measuring territorial variations in sales yield, market share, sales effectiveness

Facts about territorial sales opportunities provide a useful yardstick which can be used to evaluate the company's actual sales volume and performance, territory by territory. Measuring territorial sales performance and using analysis to find sales soft spots which represent inviting opportunities to achieve volume increases, is 'standard operating procedure' in well-managed companies like Allied Products, Inc. This type of analysis is usually executed *by* the marketing research director *for* the information and guidance of the sales vice-president and other sales-supervisory personnel. The analytical findings are used as guides in directing sales-supervisory attention where it is most needed and where it is likely to be most productive.

Sales-quota setting

Sales quotas, which are the individual sales objectives for a salesman or for a territory, are widely used as a tool of marketing management. Such quotas can be set much more accurately when they are built on a foundation of facts about territorial potential and the company's past success in each territory than when they are based on some arbitrary decision or on subjective judgement alone.

Measuring variations in individual salesmen's performance

With a sales force of three hundred individual salesmen, plus supervisory personnel, the sales vice-president of Allied Products, Inc., has a tremendous and continuous task of manpower management. In any group of three hundred salesmen, there are likely to be some good salesmen, some who are neither bad nor good, and some who are definitely below average in both ability and performance. Facts are needed to guide management in weeding out the weaker members of the sales organization and in identifying and rewarding the stronger members. Without some objective basis of evaluating the performance of individual salesmen, the sales vice-president would have to rely on judgement alone.

Suppose a sales-supervisory opening developed. Which one, if any, of the three hundred salesmen should be promoted? Suppose a competitive firm made one of the three hundred salesmen a 'better offer'. Should the firm meet the offer to retain the man's experience and ability or let him go? The decision requires, among other things, an appraisal of the salesman's abilities and performance. While actual appraisals of individual salesmen are likely to be made first by the direct supervisors of the salesmen, those evaluations must in turn be reviewed by other individuals higher in the sales organization. It is necessary to guard against the tendency of some supervisors to 'rate high' and of others to 'rate low'.

The task of evaluating salesmen's performance *objectively* is as difficult as it is important. Marketing research has made real progress in developing yardsticks which can be used, usually in conjunction with psychological yardsticks as well, to measure the contribution and potential of individual salesmen. Those yardsticks substitute objective measurement for the subjective likes and dislikes of sales executives.

Comment. The need for careful marketing research on this subject is apparent when you consider that there are many variables *other than the individual salesmen* which influence the total sales-volume contributions of two individual salesmen in two widely separated and quite different territories. The job of eliminating the influence of the other variables in so far as possible, so that the salesman's contribution may be evaluated fairly, is an extremely complex one. Differences in such factors as territorial potentials, past sales performance of the company in the territory, competitive weight and activities, and advertising emphasis must be recognized. Many sales managers long considered it impossible to eliminate such influences and to measure salesmen's performance objectively. That viewpoint is gradually being modified as more and more companies report that they have found acceptable ways to apply objective standards to this vital element in the marketing process. The responsibility of the chief sales executive is to see that the tools for such objective measurement are developed and used. He is unlikely to participate personally in this process other than in a supervisory way and by providing guidance and counsel.

Measuring industry trends and company position in industry

This activity is implicit within a carefully developed sales forecast, but it is so important that it merits individual attention. Its importance greatly increased in the years following the Second World War. The postwar expansion of total business volume found some industries growing at a slower and some at a more rapid rate than the economy as a whole. This variable rate of growth, combined with the rather general expansion trend in which most industries participated, led to some new and sometimes acute problems in management control. The danger that a company showing substantial sales-volume increases might actually be losing market position and market share in an industry expanding at a more rapid rate became an almost permanent addition to management's ever-present problems.

An acceleration of mobility in the consumer population and the sweeping changes in the nature of the consumer market in the postwar years also entered the picture. For example, consider the national total number of births each year from the 1920s down through depression-year lows, then up to peaks during and following the Second World War. That curve has tremendous significance as an industry-volume determinant in many industries. Among the beverage group of industries, sharp expansion in soft-drink sales could be confidently predicted as the bumper baby crop of the early 1940s moved into the teen-age bracket. Brewers of beer had to watch a decline in *per capita* consumption because the increase in total population became an increase in population of beer-drinking age only after a lag of eighteen or twenty years.

Product innovations were an additional major influence in industry trends requiring close attention. The increased importance of liquid-cream shampoos which followed the spectacular success of the Toni Company in introducing White Rain shampoo is an example of the impact of such innovations.

Product-quality and product-line review and evaluation

The chief sales executive of Allied Products, Inc., has the constant task of appraising and reappraising his company's line of products. He is concerned with the quality of the products and with the completeness of the line. If a product in the Allied line were inferior to a competitive product in quality, salesmen would lose orders to the competitor and the difficulty of achieving the company's sales objectives would be increased. If the line were incomplete, so that a major customer had to turn to a competitor for a product not available from Allied, that would ease the competitor's task in selling that customer other products.

Sometimes a product line is too complete, in which case salesmen may be overburdened with the task of selling a large number of small-volume products. This product-line responsibility includes packaging responsibility as well, if the products are packaged, and includes responsibility for exploring the opportunities inherent in ingenious packaging of non-packaged items. There is often a different viewpoint toward product quality in different divisions of a company such as Allied Products, Inc. The people who develop products – perhaps a research and development division, perhaps a part of the production division – have viewpoints which may differ from those of customers. The chief sales executive tends to reflect the customer's point of view in product matters. He wants his salesmen to be selling the kind of products customers want to buy, rather than the kind production executives think they *ought* to want to buy, because in the former case sales friction is reduced and the productivity of the sales force increased.

Comment. The extent to which sales executives have an opportunity to advance the customers' viewpoint in discussion leading to decisions dealing with the product, product line, etc., is increasing sharply. An unpublished study by *Business Week* magazine in 1953 among a group of industrial marketing executives revealed that by that date this trend had progressed to a point at which it was then unusual to find a sales executive who did *not* accept product responsibility and product decisions as part of his duties and responsibilities.

Evaluation of alternative promotion methods

Every sales executive has open to him a wide variety of different promotional methods. In the consumer-product field, for example, a manufacturer may choose to promote through straight product-selling advertising, or he may instead choose to rely on various types of promotional devices such as 'deals', premiums, special offers, etc., to move his merchandise into the hands of the final consumer. There are alternatives open even within the latter course. For example, should the deal be aimed at the final consumer or at some intermediate factor such as the retailer or wholesaler? Should promotional funds spent at the retail level be diverted into co-operative advertising, or would the same amount of money be more productive if spent as a commission (sometimes called a 'spiff', 'push money', or 'P M') for retail clerks?

Closely allied to decisions on alternative promotional methods are decisions as to alternative types of distribution channels: should a company sell direct to consumers, direct to retailers, or rely on wholesalers to sell to retailers and on retailers to sell to consumers? This is a continuing operating problem because of constant shifts and changes in the facts and factors on which decisions of this type are made. Re-appraisals of alternatives in the light of new circumstances developing from day to day, are frequently necessary. Every time a major competitor makes a change, a reappraisal is indicated. Marketing research contributes facts helpful in reappraising the desirability of alternative approaches in this area.

Appraisals of advertising effectiveness

Since Allied Products, Inc., spends $900,000, or nine cents out of each of its sales dollars, for advertising, it is obvious that the advertising responsibility in the company is of major importance. The sales vice-president is responsible for seeing that the advertising expenditures are made in that way which will maximize the company's sales and profit return from its advertising. This is a tremendously complex responsibility, a fact which becomes apparent when some of the major components are reviewed.

It includes an appraisal of the soundness of the story or message told in the advertising; a consideration of the relative productivity of different types of advertising media (for example, of magazine advertising versus newspapers or television or some combination of those or other media); decisions on the geographical or other allocation of advertising efforts; appraisals of different seasonal alternatives for peaking advertising as against an even, year-around program; and a dozen other basic and important decisions of vital importance to a company spending $900,000 a year for advertising. Primary responsibility for the development of sound advertising plans and recommendations rests with the company's advertising agency. Within the company, the advertising director works with the agency in formulating recommendations. The sales vice-president, to whom the advertising director reports, retains responsibility for the approval of all major advertising commitments. He must of course keep sufficiently well informed on advertising matters to appraise the soundness of the program developed for his approval.

Pricing policies and practices

Price policy is a key element in the chief sales executive's job. Decisions must be made on the final selling prices at which individual products will be offered to the company's customers. Where those products are sold for resale (as to wholesalers or retailers), those price decisions must take into consideration the normal operating margins of the distribution channels used. Decisions on other aspects of price policy, such as quantity discounts, are also necessary. When a company's costs rise or fall significantly (as when a new labor contract is negotiated which increases unit production costs), a decision has to be made as to whether the company's prices should be adjusted and to what extent. Where prices are changed, there are additional problems as to whether or not, or to what extent, orders will be accepted at the old price before an increase is put into effect, or whether stocks will be 'protected' in the case of a decline. A price change by a competitor may necessitate a review of company pricing. Changes in the relative importance of distribution channels or different customer types may make a re-examination of pricing necessary.

The dozen examples quoted above do not represent anything

like a complete listing of marketing problems of the current operating type which the chief sales executive of an organization like Allied Products, Inc., must face. These examples should suffice to illustrate both the general nature and the wide variety of such problems which are always present in a well-managed company.

Major Types of Non-Recurring Problems

Now let's consider problems typical of those in the non-recurring category. The primary characteristic of problems of this type is that they usually do not develop gradually and continuously out of the normal day-to-day activities of a business, but are instead typically created by some specific development or circumstance often from outside the company. Because there is usually a specific cause, circumstance, or company objective to which such problems can be traced or attributed, the task of identifying the major types is somewhat complicated. They could be identified by relating them to the types of causes, as well as to the types of effects or results. In the following discussion, an attempt is made both to indicate the nature of the situation out of which the problem developed and to suggest the nature of the action which is likely to be indicated.

Problems of competitive-product innovations

One of the most important types of marketing problems is the group which arises out of the necessity of appraising and adjusting operations to fit the changed marketing circumstances which develop when a competitor introduces a new type or modification of product which threatens to make serious inroads into a company's business. Such innovations occur rather frequently in some industries, less frequently in others. The threat of such an innovation is always present in every industry.

The dentifrice field is a classic example of an industry in which major innovations are the rule rather than the exception. Within a very brief period of time, innovations produced several sweeping changes in the nature and competitive division of industry volume. First there were ammoniated formulations, with decay-reducing advertising and promotional claims. The introduction of such products jolted the industry. Established brands with large market shares had to incorporate the ammoniated feature into their formulas and advertising in order to withstand the challenge of newly developed products. Then Lever Brothers introduced Chlorodent, with a newsy breath-purifying advertising story, and the industry had another fast job of product changing to cope with. The impact of chlorophyll as an ingredient is suggested by the fact that *Advertising Age* magazine reported on 10 August 1953, that 35 per cent of the total dentifrice market was then represented by tooth paste containing chlorophyll. There followed development of antienzyme formulations, and the entire industry had to make another product switch. Fluorinated formulas followed, to keep the brand- or market-share boat rocking.

Product innovations may range from the relatively minor influence of a minor product variant introduced by a relatively unimportant firm in an industry to the cataclysmic shock which results when a dominant firm in any industry introduces a product which threatens to make an entire industry's products obsolete. Consider the threat of turbine engines for automobiles to carburetor manufacturers. In adjusting to such innovations, there are many variable circumstances to which marketing research could be effectively applied.

There is always the problem of immediate and potential effect on existing inventories, including both those of the manufacturer which may be finished goods or in process, and those at wholesale and retail levels as well if the industry's distribution channels include them. The orderly liquidation of those inventories and a gradual transition to an improved product matching the innovation are sometimes possible; the threat that such a liquidation may be impossible, or that patent or other protection may prevent a duplication of the values present in the innovation, is one of the nightmares every sales executive must constantly face in a competitive industry.

There are dozens of potentially important innovations to each one that actually has a severe impact on an industry. Marketing research is used, in such cases, as a form of 'sales intelligence'. It permits an objective appraisal of each potential threat. When the innovation is significant, marketing research can sometimes provide a sufficient advance warning to permit management to act more promptly to meet and counter the threat than would otherwise be possible. If the innovation, however promising, is lacking in consumer or customer appeal, research can uncover that fact quickly in many instances. It can thus provide the basis for a confident prediction that what appears to be a competitive cloud on the horizon will fade without storming established industry patterns.

To illustrate, the makers of Servel refrigerators in 1953 introduced a product which made ice cubes automatically, eliminating the need for trays, for difficult ice-cube removal, etc. Was this development destined to revolutionize refrigerators as products? Consumer checks by a competitor indicated that consumer reaction to the new development was mixed to negative. Objections were focused on the fact that the ice-making mechanism took up so much space that it reduced the frozen-food capacity of the Servel units. Frozen-food storage space was more important to housewives at that time than the nuisance value of conventional ice-cube preparation and removal. With the consumer research before them, competitors could safely disregard the competitive threat of the Servel innovation.

Problems of changes in competitive forces

Not all competitive threats grow out of a product innovation. Sometimes the entry into an industry of a new and aggressive competitor, or a change in the operating approach of an established competitor, may be an equally grave threat to the competitive *status quo*. When the Kraft Foods Company began to build its own distribution facilities for handling such perishable commodities as margarine and salad dressing instead of selling them through independent distributors, the competitive climate in the margarine industry chilled suddenly. When the giant Procter & Gamble organization entered the ranks of makers of home permanents, the threat to Toni's long-dominant share of the market was greater than the addition of one more competitor in an industry including scores of brands would indicate. When Toni in turn moved into the lipstick business, Revlon and Hazel Bishop had to re-examine their own positions and plans in the light of the changed circumstances. Effective marketing

27

management requires constant study and appraisal of competitive activities. Marketing research contributes facts which aid such appraisals.

Problems posed by major price changes

Whenever a competitor introduces a major price change into an industry, the impact of that change must be appraised quickly. Often counter-measures must be taken without delay. When Kelvinator brought out its line of refrigerators in 1939, after all major competitors had already introduced theirs, at prices which were spectacularly lower than traditional in the industry, the result was the greatest shift in brand shares in a single year in the history of that dynamic industry. When the makers of Old English self-polishing floor wax changed their prices so that a pint container which had been selling for fifty-nine cents was priced to consumers at thirty-five cents, the makers of Johnson's Glo-Coat – still at fifty-nine cents – had to decide quickly what counteraction to take, if any.

When Procter & Gamble introduced a new home permanent at a price twenty-five cents higher than prevailing levels in the industry, the Toni Company faced a major problem. Marketing research was able to evaluate the test markets in which P & G had tested this move and guide Toni to the effective counteraction.

Problems created by changes in competitive sales methods or policies

The analysis of alternative sales methods was mentioned as one of the problems of the operating type in the preceding section. Where such analyses are being made continuously by many of the major firms in an industry, inevitably some shifts in the sales methods or policies of individual competitors develop. Every time such a change occurs, it becomes a new and relevant element in the reappraisals of competitors of the firm making the change. When one major firm in the food field introduced a warehousing discount which enabled chain-store organizations and other volume buyers to purchase at a substantially lower price than smaller customers, each competitor had to re-examine its own pricing and discount practices and policies.

Similarly, when the General Foods Corporation announced,

after extensive marketing research, that it would henceforth sell its Maxwell House Coffee through a separate selling organization selling no other product, the increased sales leverage on Maxwell House made it necessary for each competitive coffee marketer to re-examine the sales manpower picture. When the Avco Corporation announced the combined distribution of its two lines of appliances – Bendix and Crosley lines – that decision posed problems and opportunities for competitors and near competitors selling through the same distribution channels. When Avco discontinued the Crosley line and sold Bendix to Philco, reappraisal was again necessary.

Problems produced by shifts in consumption patterns

When the consumers or customers of an industry change, the result is likely to create opportunities for some sales executives and problems for others. For example, the calorie consciousness proved to be a bonanza for firms selling products accepted as low in calories (like Ry-Krisp and low-calorie carbonated drinks). In contrast, it was a major problem for organizations selling products thought to be fattening, such as candy, cake, flour, cookies and similar products. Such changes may occur quickly or gradually and may be temporary or permanent.

Problems involving changes in distribution channels

Changes in available distribution channels, or in the relative strength or weakness of various paths from factory to eventual consumer or customer, sometimes pose problems for the sales executive. Changes in types of retailers or wholesalers or in the relative importance of existing types fall in this category. For example, the development of supermarkets reduced the share of total volume moving through smaller outlets and led many manufacturers to shift from direct coverage of such stores by their salesmen to reliance on wholesalers for small-outlet coverage.

The broadening of product lines in supermarkets to include nonfood items like shampoos, dentifrices, and even soft goods like hosiery, necessitated reappraisals of distribution channels and of sales emphasis on different customer types. The introduction of drug-type items into supermarkets was stimulated by the development of a new kind of wholesaler known as a 'rack jobber', who specialized in servicing stocks of drug-type items in supermarkets. The growth in importance of movie theaters and vending machines as outlets for candy-bar volume illustrates a changed distribution pattern which candy-bar manufacturers had to make plans to serve.

Problems in developing and introducing a new product

New-product development represents one of the most important areas of marketing research application. The importance of research on new products is directly related to the cost-versus-results equation. Today the process of developing and launching a new product on a full scale may take years and may involve hundreds of thousands or even millions of dollars. Marketing research within this new-product area embraces a whole galaxy of closely related but individual marketing-research problems. These include estimates of demand for the new product; determination of the characteristics of the market for that product; identification of the product characteristics considered most desirable by customers or consumers, to guide product development; objective measurement of consumer acceptance of the proposed new product against established products of the same type if such products exist; determination of the most effective advertising or promotional approaches to be used; a test-market operation to reproduce on a small scale the planned introductory strategy; and finally, the all-out launching.

Problems of discontinuing major products or product lines

The reverse side of the new-product-development coin occasionally comes up, presenting the sales executive with major problems. This is particularly true when a decision to eliminate one or more entire product lines or major products from the company's marketing base is under consideration. Individual products and product lines often have their roots deep in the tradition and history of a company, and a decision to move out of an industry is rarely taken lightly. Thus when the makers of Johnson's wax decided to discontinue the production of a line of wax-fortified paints – thus abandoning a company-developed patent and writing off thousands of dollars' worth of developmental work – the detailed exploration of both sides of the decision required several years.

Problems arising from proposed changes in sales methods or policies

Whenever a major change in a company's sales methods or policies is under consideration, careful study of the possible consequences of the change is indicated. A decision to fair-trade the prices of a company's products, for example, or the decision by a militant supporter of retail-price maintenance like Westinghouse to discontinue fair-trade pricing, requires careful advance study. A contemplated change in distribution channels would fall in the same category. A change in the sales-compensation plan which involves a major policy shift warrants careful study and appraisal. When Max Factor & Company revised its price and discount policies, months of study on the effects of each proposed change on the company's volume and profit picture and of the likely effects on relative customer-type importance preceded the decision.

Problems created by advertising changes

The development of an important new advertising medium like television necessitates a complete reappraisal of a company's historic advertising activities. When the cost of advertising increases at a greater rate than the company's appropriation, a similar reconsideration of alternative possibilities is required. An illustration of the latter type of problem is provided by the experience of Congoleum-Nairn, Inc., which had been sponsoring a television program known as 'Garroway at Large'. When a contract expired, the cost of talent for the show was boosted sharply – reportedly from $7000 to $17,000 a *week* – which made it necessary for the company to re-examine its advertising program and eventually to decide not to renew the show at the higher rate.

The above list of ten different types of non-recurring problems is not intended to be exhaustive. Like the earlier list of examples of kinds of continuously present operating problems, these examples are intended only to illustrate in specific terms the types of marketing problems which management executives face and on which they make decisions – often with the aid of marketing research. These two major classifications of problems, as we shall see in the remainder of this chapter, together form *the marketing problem base of marketing research activities*.

Company Practices in Marketing Research

Upon that marketing-problem base there has developed a rather clearly defined structure of specific, interrelated marketing research activities. Information about the nature of those activities is provided by the A.M.A. research report entitled *Company Practices in Marketing Research*. We are concerned here with the portion of the study which deals with the specific marketing research activities performed and the relative importance of those activities.

In that survey, a check list of thirty-seven different specific marketing research activities was included in the questionnaire. After that list was developed, it was reviewed by six outstanding marketing research practitioners before it was converted into final form. In addition to the thirty-seven listed activities, space was provided for respondents to write in any additional activities omitted from the list. The specific list of activities was divided into three different groups, covering research on *products or services*, on *markets*, and on *sales methods and policies*. Table 1 reproduces the listing of the thirty-seven activities just as it appeared in the questionnaire, except that the three sets of blanks for writing in additional activities in each of the three areas have been omitted.[1]

1. In any check list of this type, some problems of communication are likely to develop. Instances in which a description of a specific activity means different things to different respondents are almost inescapable. This problem has a bearing on some of the findings of this study as discussed in this chapter. The sample of companies to which the questionnaire was sent included mostly manufacturers, but many service organizations and large retail organizations were also included. An attempt was made to use terminology that would span the interests and understanding of manufacturers and nonmanufacturers alike. Instead of the activity of *sales forecasting*, which would have been meaningful to manufacturers, the term *general business forecasting* was used in the questionnaire. This compromise was unsuccessful, with the result that the questionnaire failed to provide accurate data on the extent to which sales forecasting is carried

Figures 1, 2 and 3 show graphically the proportion of companies reporting that they performed each of the specific activities listed in the three major research areas. The base of the percentages charted is the total number of companies that do any marketing research. It has been necessary to condense the description of activities on these three charts to maintain legibility. It may therefore be helpful to cross-check between the full description in Table 1 and the capsule descriptions shown on the three charts.

Figures 1 and 2 show essentially similar patterns, with very high performance of the top-ranking functions. The activities in the sales methods and policies area charted on Figure 3 reflect a slightly lower level of activity in this area.

Table 1
Activities of the Marketing Research Function

Please indicate by a check mark those functions which are performed by the executives in charge of marketing research in your organization, or by your marketing research department. Please add to the list any other functions which are not listed.

A. Research on your products or services

.... 1. Determining consumer or customer acceptance of proposed new products or services.

.... 2. Comparing consumer or customer acceptance of existing products or services with similar competitive products or services.

.... 3. Determining present uses of existing products.

.... 4. Determining or exploring new uses of existing products.

.... 5. Packaging research, design, or physical characteristics.

.... 6. Evaluating new competitive products or competitive new-product developments or modifications.

.... 7. Studies aimed at product elimination or line simplification.

.... 8. Studies of the competitive position of company's products (market-share analyses, etc.).

.... 9. Studies of dissatisfaction with existing products or services, among present or former customers.

out. The relative importance of sales forecasting as a marketing research activity in manufacturing organizations is almost certainly considerably understated in the A.M.A. survey report.

....10. Market tests or test-market operations on new or improved products.

....11. Economic research (determination of industry trends, correlation of company sales with economic indicators, etc.).

....12. Determining advantages or limitations of proposed new products or services.

B. Research on markets

.... 1. Analysis of the size of the market for specific products.

.... 2. Analysis of characteristics of the market for specific products.

.... 3. Studies of the relative profitability of different markets.

.... 4. Estimating demand for new products.

.... 5. Studies of trends in market size by products.

.... 6. Studies of shifts in the nature of the market (examples: sectional changes, age-distribution trends, etc.).

.... 7. Studies of economic factors affecting sales volume and opportunities.

.... 8. General business forecasting.

.... 9. Analysis of territorial sales opportunities or potentials.

....10. Studies of changes in customer-type importance.

C. Research on sales methods and policies

.... 1. Studies of prices and their influence on sales volume.

.... 2. Studies of price policies, discount structure, etc., in relation to competition.

.... 3. Evaluation of existing sales methods.

.... 4. Appraisal of proposed changes in sales methods.

.... 5. Studies of distribution costs.

.... 6. Measuring territorial variations in sales yield, market share, sales effectiveness.

.... 7. Measuring effectiveness of individual salesmen.

.... 8. Analysis of salesmen's activities.

.... 9. Studies of effectiveness of promotional devices like 'deals,' premiums, etc.

....10. Studies of distribution of products.

....11. Establishment or revision of sales territories.

....12. Sales compensation.

....13. Advertising and selling practices of competitors.

....14. Selection of advertising media.

....15. Measuring advertising effectiveness.

Source: Crisp (1953).

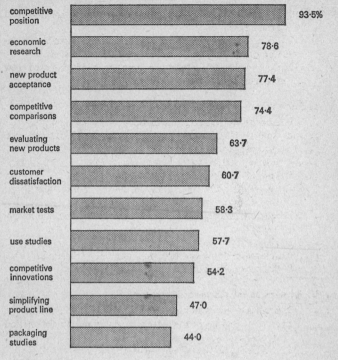

competitive position	93·5%
economic research	78·6
new product acceptance	77·4
competitive comparisons	74·4
evaluating new products	63·7
customer dissatisfaction	60·7
market tests	58·3
use studies	57·7
competitive innovations	54·2
simplifying product line	47·0
packaging studies	44·0

Figure 1

Versatility Clearly Indicated

The three charts reveal an important characteristic of marketing research which is not immediately apparent. That characteristic is the versatility with which marketing research is used in company practices. On each of the three charts, the percentages add to a total far higher than 100 per cent. For the product-services area charted in Figure 1 for example, the total is more than 700 per cent. This shows the extent to which multiple answers were recorded; that is, the extent to which companies reported performing more than one activity in each area.

Out of the total of thirty-seven activities listed on the questionnaire, the average (median) respondent company that reported

35

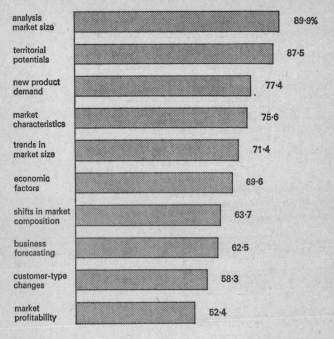

analysis market size	89·9%
territorial potentials	87·5
new product demand	77·4
market characteristics	75·6
trends in market size	71·4
economic factors	69·6
shifts in market composition	63·7
business forecasting	62·5
customer-type changes	58·3
market profitability	52·4

Figure 2

performing *any* marketing research reported performing *twenty-two of the thirty-seven listed functions, or 60 per cent of all of them*. Within the three major areas, the median firm performed almost three-fourths of the functions listed in the area of research on products and services; seven out of ten in the area of research on markets; but only eight out of fifteen, or 53 per cent, of the activities, listed in the area of research on sales methods and policies. Further, there is some understatement present in all of these figures because the performance of activities not listed in the questionnaire has been excluded from this summarization.

Relative Importance of Specific Activities

The three charts which show the proportion of companies performing specific activities provide a picture of marketing

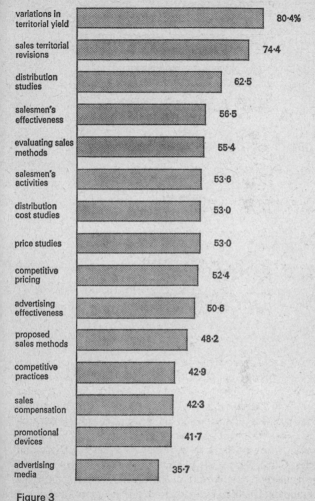

variations in territorial yield	80·4%
sales territorial revisions	74·4
distribution studies	62·5
salesmen's effectiveness	56·5
evaluating sales methods	55·4
salesmen's activities	53·6
distribution cost studies	53·0
price studies	53·0
competitive pricing	52·4
advertising effectiveness	50·6
proposed sales methods	48·2
competitive practices	42·9
sales compensation	42·3
promotional devices	41·7
advertising media	35·7

Figure 3

research in company practice which has the advantage of being specific, but the disadvantage of being somewhat lacking in depth; that is, they provide no indication of the relative importance of the specific individual activities listed. Without such an indication, the picture remains one-dimensional. There is no way to distinguish between the activity regularly performed and considered important and the activity which is performed infrequently and which is somewhat fringe in importance.

With the specific objective of providing a guide for organizations considering the addition of marketing research as a specialized function, or considering changes in the scope of their activities in this field, the A.M.A. study explored the relative importance of the specific activities listed. This was done by giving each respondent an opportunity to rate functions (including any he had written in as 'added starters') in five positions ranging from most important to fifth most important.

In filling out their questionnaires, some respondents indicated only the single function they considered most important, some indicated choices for only the first two positions, and so on. The proportion of respondents indicating a first choice was 85 per cent. That proportion declined with each succeeding choice until about 56 per cent designated the activity ranking fifth in importance.

These 'most important' designations have a significance so great that it should be underlined before the specific findings are presented.

The percentages of companies performing specific functions reflect a pattern which is partly influenced by the check list itself. Even though it was developed with great care, that list represented essentially an outside judgement. It provided each respondent with a ready-made list of what their marketing research activities *were expected* to include. By indicating their judgement as to the relative importance of the individual activities, the respondents in effect participated in the *creation of a new and much more significant list*. That list represented a distillation of their own experience with marketing research in practice. It is worth remembering also that each respondent had complete freedom to write in specific activities not included on the list and to designate such activities as 'most important' if he chose to do so. In point of fact, less than 6 per cent of all choices of activities as 'most important' were made from items which were not included in the printed questionnaire.

Figure 4 presents a graphic picture of the results of combining

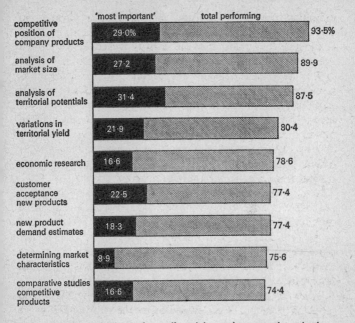

Figure 4 'Most widely performed' and 'most important' marketing research activities

two lists of marketing research activities. One is a list of those activities performed by the largest proportion of respondent companies. The other is a list of those activities voted most important by the largest proportion of companies. The charted list was made up, first by taking all activities performed by three-quarters or more of the companies, and then by adding to that list all activities named as important by one-sixth or more of the companies. (Those two cutoff points were arbitrarily chosen to provide a sharper picture of the top-ranking activities.)

Out of the thirty-seven listed activities, there were eight on the first list – performed by three-quarters or more of the companies. There were also eight activities included in the second list. Figure 4 shows only nine activities, indicating the extent of over-lap between these two lists. There was only one activity on each list which was not on the other. The remaining seven activities were duplicated on *both* lists.

Here are the highlights of this important chart:

1. Determining the competitive position of company products is the most widely performed of the thirty-seven listed functions and is rated as important by more companies than all but one of the listed functions.

2. Analysis of the size of the market for specific products ranked second in frequency of performance – 89.9 per cent – and third in frequency of selection as important.

3. Analysis of territorial opportunities or potentials was considered an important marketing research function by more companies than any of the other thirty-six listed on the questionnaire. This function was performed by almost nine out of ten – 87·5 per cent – of the companies that do marketing research.

4. Variations in territorial yield, market share, etc., were studied by eight out of ten companies, and this function was named as important by one-fifth of the companies.

5. Two different activities, both specifically concerned with new-product development, were included in this list of important functions. Determining customer acceptance of new products and preparing estimates of demand for new products were both reported performed by 77·4 per cent of the companies and named as important by 22·5 and 18·3 per cent, respectively.

6. Product research on existing products, involving comparative studies of company products against competitive products, were reported performed by 74·4 per cent of the companies and considered important by one-sixth of the respondents.

Current Operating Problems Predominant

Early in this chapter, the two major types of marketing problems – current operating problems which are continuously present and non-recurring problems – were illustrated. For a clear picture of the marketing-problem base of marketing research, this key question must be answered: Which type of problem absorbs the major share of marketing research attention? This question can be answered by reclassifying the nine functions illustrated in Figure 4 on the classification framework set up in this chapter.

The activity performed by the largest proportion of companies involves *studies of the competitive position of company's products (market-share analyses, etc.)*. Ranking second in frequency of performance is the *analysis of the size of the market for specific products*. These two closely related activities are both in the group of current operating problems.

Ranking third in frequency of performance, but first in the frequency with which it is considered an important activity, is the *analysis of territorial sales opportunities or potentials*. The activity ranking fourth in frequency of performance and fifth in mention as important is the function of *measuring territorial variations in sales yield, market share, sales effectiveness*. These two activities are also closely related. One is concerned with determining territorial potentials, and the other with applying the knowledge of territorial opportunities to evaluate the company's sales performance and to find sales soft spots. These two activities are also clearly examples of current operating problems.

Ranking fifth in frequency of performance is *economic research (determination of industry trends, correlation of company sales with economic indicators, etc.)*. This activity is another example which belongs in the current operating problem group. It is involved primarily in sales forecasting, although it has other applications as well. For example, economic analysis by individual territories is often used as an aid in determining territorial potentials or in interpreting cases of low territorial sales yields.

The sixth and seventh functions in frequency of performance are both in the area of new-product development: *Determining consumer or customer acceptance of proposed new products or services* and *estimating demand for new products*. Both are examples of the nonrecurring type of problems. (This is true in a strict sense, although increases in the extent of new-product development which are occurring in 1957 when this book went into production gave promise of making this a current-operating type of problem in the not-too-distant future.)

Analysis of characteristics of the market for specific products and *comparing consumer or customer acceptance of existing products or services with similar competitive products or services* are both examples of current operating problems.

References

CRISP, R. D. (1953), *Company Practices in Marketing Research*, American Management Association Research Report, no. 22, fig. 4, pp. 22–3.

HOLDEN, P. E., FISH, L. S., and SMITH, H. L. (1951), *Top-Management Organization and Control*, McGraw-Hill.

2 A. S. C. Ehrenberg

The Research Brief

A. S. C. Ehrenberg, 'What research for what problem?',
Research in Marketing, Market Research Society, 1964, pp. 46–66.

The paper opens with counter-arguments to the proposition
(Nowik, 1964) that the market researcher should be restricted
to 'describing the facts'. The question of the proper role for the
market researcher's judgement also runs through the remainder
of the paper, which concentrates on the adequacy of research
briefs. In the main, a selection of case histories in the third section
should illustrate how some very real problems for the market
researcher are reflected even by general exhortations such as, for
example, to ensure that the research brief 'means the same thing
to all concerned' or 'gives some indication of the required accuracy'. These problems call both for technical study and for
involvement in the marketing problem itself.

Preamble – A Matter of Controversy

The proposition that the researcher should restrict himself in his
reports to 'describing the facts' conflicts implicitly with much of
what I shall be saying later in this paper about ensuring an
adequate research brief. More important, it explicitly prejudices
the good functioning of research in general, and for this reason
I shall try to counter the proposition now, at the beginning of
my paper, rather than at various later points.

In moving for the dismissal of the proposition I enter for brevity
only three alternative pleas. First, I plead that the proposition
is impossible. Alternatively, I either plead that it would inhibit
good research or that it would not be in the public interest.

Firstly then, I base my case on that fact that much subjective
judgement and selectiveness is involved in reaching agreement on
a research brief, in devising the ensuing research procedures, in
carrying them out, and in analysing and condensing the final

results. To regard these final results as unadulterated objective facts is therefore impossible.

There is nothing intrinsically wrong as such with this built-in subjective element in research – it is unavoidable anyway. What would be wrong is to ignore it. Instead, the researcher must try to evaluate its significance; having exercised judgement at all the earlier stages of the research project, he must not pretend that no judgement was ever involved. He need therefore not particularly suppress his judgement at the reporting stage either.

It might now be argued that the only conclusions or opinions which the researcher need then give should be 'technical' ones. However, unless his conclusions – his judgements – are at all times closely related to the marketing problem itself, they will be arid and potentially misleading. In arguing against the (mis-)use of statistical significance tests, opponents frequently quote Sir Austin Bradford Hill's condemnation of 'the *mere* use of tests of significance' (my italics): it is the drawing of purely 'technical' or 'objective' conclusions which Hill deems 'meaningless'.

Good report writing means summarizing and condensing. In a recent product-test for a dog food, a like/dislike scale was supplemented by the opportunity to describe the response in a more specific, open-ended way. In summarizing the data, infrequent specific descriptions of dislike responses for example (possibly 'my dog would not eat it at all' – 2 per cent, 'he ran away from home for a week or more' – 1 per cent, etc.) might, would, or – in general – should be condensed into one broad category of 'Other Responses' – 7 per cent.

However, when one of these rare response categories was 'made my dog physically sick' – 1 per cent (or if two of the trials were not completed because the dogs had died), this might well be the most important finding of the whole product-test. The decision to report these numerically trivial results explicitly, and to emphasise them in his report as possibly meriting special attention, depends not only on the researcher's technical assessment of canine aetiology and morbidity and of the (human) interview situation, but also on his opinion of what might be important in terms of marketing – as indeed did his initial decision to include such an open-ended question in the survey at all.

This is perhaps a somewhat extreme example. Suitably detailed instructions from the marketing man could have been expected in the research brief. However, exactly the same considerations apply with all the less obvious and less extreme features of any research project; yet we can hardly expect the marketing man to draft the questions and tell us in detail how to code and analyse and report. It remains impossible therefore to avoid the research man's opinions and conclusions implicitly if not – and this seems preferable – explicitly.

My second counter to the proposition is that restricting the research man from drawing any conclusions is technically undesirable. As argued specifically later in this paper, it seems essential, for example when trying to ensure an adequate research brief in the first place, that he should exercise his judgement even on the marketing problem itself. This he can hardly do at all well unless he has been heavily involved in the drawing of conclusions from *previous* research projects. And probably his most effective experience would be gained where he himself suggests certain conclusions at the report stage, especially if some of these conclusions are then rejected by the marketing man – preferably on an explicitly argued basis!

It will be noted that I say that the researcher might *suggest* various conclusions, and that they might well be (rationally) rejected by the marketing man. I appreciate the fear here that the researcher's opinions might be (wrongly) thought to be as incontrovertible as his reporting of 'facts' (i.e., that 50 per cent preferred product A to B). However, this would indicate a fault on the marketing side, or in the liaison between the two sides generally, which must be remedied as such and not by pouring away the baby with the bath water. I agree of course that 'the *responsibility* for acting on a market research report ... is the prerogative of the marketing man' and that 'the technical research expert should not *dictate* the form of the action to be taken' (my italics), but it certainly does not follow that if the research man suggests some conclusions or gives vent to his opinions he must necesarily be 'usurping' the marketing man's functions. [...]

The third alternative plea against the proposed restrictive practice invokes the public interest. Quite briefly, there are still a number of market researchers whose main aim is to 'advance' to the marketing side, probably because they are unaware that some reasonably interesting technical problems exist in market research itself. Under a rigid demarcation rule, their latent marketing ambitions and talents might never burgeon nor yet be effectively recognised, much to the detriment of market research and hence of course against the public interest.

In concluding this preamble where I am arguing for the researcher not to eschew some involvement on the marketing side I would stress – bearing in mind the ease with which one can be misunderstood on the present subject – that the role of the market researcher in marketing is still to be a market researcher. This I hope will be substantiated by the remainder of the paper.

The Research Brief

In the remainder of this paper I concern myself with the briefing on which research has to be based. I make two assumptions, firstly that a marketing problem exists where research will be helpful, and secondly, since this paper is part of a symposium, that I can restrict myself to just one topic, i.e., the research brief.

Although I assume that a relevant marketing problem exists, some of the general features of such a problem may need to be noted:

1. *Research is usually instituted to aid more than one marketing problem at a time.* (The scientific textbook prescription of one experiment for one hypothesis is well worth bearing in mind, but we cannot always fly in the face of life as it is and must generally accept multi-purpose research.)

2. *Marketing problems are difficult to define precisely.* (Earlier research data about the market is usually insufficient and quantitative knowledge about the effects of various possible marketing procedures is usually lacking.)

3. *Some marketing problems do not actually exist when the research is commissioned.* (The research has then to provide general background information for future needs rather than to answer existing marketing problems now; much of continuous research is a typical example.)

4. *Research cannot usually give a direct answer to a marketing problem anyway.* (The consequent absence of a 'one-to-one' relationship between the marketing problem and the research brief creates, perhaps more than anything else, the difficulties found in formulating the latter.)

5. *Marketing problems are not easy to translate into research briefs.* (Those aspects of the problem which might affect the research and which should therefore be spelt out in the brief are not always obvious to the marketing man.)

6. *Research briefs have usually to be expressed in research terminology if they are not to be too vague.* (A marketing man can often do this most easily by specifying actual research techniques and procedures which he happens to know of, but this may well prejudice the issue.)

7. *The marketing man is not a research man.* (He may have neither the research expertise nor usually the time, nor yet perhaps the responsibility, to think through the research implications either of his marketing problem or of the research brief which he is formulating.)

None of the above remarks are meant as criticism of marketing men.

Marketing and marketing research imply different technical knowledge and expertise, and the problem is to bring the two effectively together, by way of an adequate research brief in the first instance.

If our endeavour then is to aim at an adequate research brief, could one not produce a 'check-list' of items which such a brief should satisfy? Such a list might begin as follows:

Ensure that, in relation to the marketing problem, the research brief:

(a) means the same thing to all concerned,
(b) does not ask for irrelevant information,
(c) defines the relevant population(s) to be sampled,
(d) states the right variable(s) to be measured,
(e) gives some indication of the required accuracy of the main results,

47

(f)   gives at least an order of priority for the required accuracy of the various specified breakdown analyses,

(g)   does not prejudge the selection of research techniques and procedures.

Obviously, one could add further items of this kind, but all – I suggest – to little purpose. Who is going to engage in an agonising reappraisal of his research brief so as to 'ensure that it means the same thing to all concerned' rather than automatically check that item on the list? And similarly for the next three items? Again, do we not all pay lip-service to the remaining three items listed above, but then religiously ignore them in practice? An effective checklist cannot be formed from such general exhortations telling us to be better.[1]

Indeed, the real problem as I see it is to be much more aware in practice that such apparent platitudes *are* important to the kind of research briefs which we normally handle. I believe that this is a problem more for the market researcher than for the marketing man, and that we as market researchers too often fail to follow-through during the briefing stage the technical implications of what we are asked to do.

Some Case Histories

The purpose of this section – the main part of the paper – is to give some fairly concrete illustrations of the practical importance of achieving an adequate research brief. The illustrations are in terms of real case histories rather than artificial examples. They are chosen to cover a fairly wide but no means comprehensive range of problems which can be discussed without getting too involved in specific detail, and are assembled under the seven 'checklist' headings which were suggested above, so as to show that such apparently self-evident advice does reflect some very real problems for the market researcher.

(*1*) '*Ensure that the research brief means the same to all concerned*'

The implications of this exhortation are by no means restricted

1. The contrast is with a checklist composed of highly specific items, as in starting some complex machinery, i.e., Pull switch A, Check dial B, Push button C, etc.

to loose wording or the apparent stupidity (or lack of expertise) of everybody other than oneself.

Consider our general practice of classifying informants for 'break-down' or cross-analysis purposes. The lack of sufficient classificatory variables (other than straightforward demographic ones) led to the 1963 Roy Thomson Gold Medal problem, namely 'for the best method of classifying informants in media studies, having regard to the end usage of such studies for marketing purposes'. The Thomson brief elaborated this problem in some further 500 words. (See Belson, 1963 and Sissors, 1963.)

Now one might have thought that the *meaning* of such a brief would be unambiguous, and that all that was required were solutions. However, in his award-winning paper Belson (1963) briefly and dogmatically gave one interpretation of the purpose of classificatory variables, whilst in the other printed submission for the award Sissors (1963) outlined a completely different interpretation (along fairly standard lines). The only relevant point here is to note heuristically the sheer *existence* of these different interpretations of the given brief.

Indeed, it does not matter here whether one or other or both writers were 'wrong' in their interpretation of the brief, and even if both were somehow 'right'. The fact that neither of them were led to refer to the possibility (or the existence) of interpretations of the brief radically different from their own underlines the need 'to ensure that the research brief means the same to all concerned'.

(2) '*Ensure that the research brief does not ask for irrelevant information*'

The danger of asking for information which is not relevant to the marketing problem can be well demonstrated in generalized terms, namely by referring to the areas of attitude, motivation and image research. (Initially I had a specific illustration in mind here also, but it seems simpler and perhaps more effective in this instance not to cling to it.)

Thus it is fairly common practice to approach research into attitudes or motivations or images by attempting to assess *all* the important attitude dimensions or the like which anybody can think of. Indeed, if we had standard textbooks, they would probably tell us to engage in preliminary research by way of depth interviews and/or group discussions to unearth even those attitude dimensions (if any) which no one had thought of in the first place.

Now I would suggest that a research brief which requests such *comprehensive* attitude or image research is often likely to be wrong, because most of the results would be irrelevant to whatever marketing problem is involved. In other words, the 'standard textbook' approach would be wrong just because it is standard, instead of being tailored to the specific marketing problem. I do not want to suggest here that a research brief requesting 'comprehensive' attitude or related research is *always* wrong. (Even less do I want to suggest that it would be wrong for the researcher – and for the marketing man – to get the 'feel' of his subject matter through depth interviews, etc.) However, researching attitude dimensions just because they are there, and irrespective of their relevance to the marketing problem, is a waste.

The actual waste of money in absolute terms is perhaps not very large, because research budgets are so limited anyway. However, by crowding an attitude or image survey with irrelevant matter, the few dimensions which *are* relevant to the marketing problem tend of necessity to be assessed very superficially only, with tragically little understanding of their reliability and validity, and indeed of their *quantitative* relevance to the marketing problem. Yet the follow-up research which would then be called for on these important dimensions is rarely carried out either, just because of our budget (and time) limitations.

Taking the area of attitudinal and related research as an example, researchers should therefore query strenuously any research brief which requests 'comprehensive' research, so as 'to ensure that irrelevant information is not asked for'.

(3) 'Ensure that the research brief defines the relevant population(s) to be sampled'

The specification of the population(s) of informants to be covered by the proposed research may be considered as a special case of ensuring that irrelevant information is not requested.

A recent research brief concerned the market for a durable product with a fairly long purchasing cycle and also a fairly strong second-hand market. The client's own product – or 'brand', as it were – lay at the relatively expensive (but not luxury) end of the product spectrum. Examples of the kind of product in question might be housing, motor cars, and certain industrial goods.

The initial research brief was a relatively full and, in the textbook sense, a good one. In terms of the proposed questionnaire content for example, it fitted also under (2) above in requesting 'comprehensive' attitudinal, etc., information. In terms of sample design, it specified three population sectors to be covered:

(a) *The existing market*, i.e., owners of the relevant brand.

(b) *The immediate potential market*, i.e., owners of 'brands' directly competitive in product formulation and price.

(c) *The less immediate potential market*, i.e., those non-owners of any of these more expensive 'brands' or of the product altogether who might all the same be regarded as potential buyers according to certain *matching* criteria, such as being 'large' enough in the case of industrial firms or sufficiently 'affluent' in the case of private consumers.

All the possibly relevant sectors of the population were thus properly covered, in the textbook sense, by the research brief. The reasons for interviewing (i) owners of the 'brand' in question, and (ii) owners of directly competitive 'brands', presumably require no comment here. The request to cover the remaining market potential as well, i.e., (iii) sufficiently 'affluent' non-owners of *any* of the more expensive (and directly competitive) brands, should however be queried by the researcher.

The immediate question should be whether the client is contemplating any effective marketing action to increase the present market by inducing such 'affluent non-owners' to buy *and* action to ensure him of an adequate share of any such market increase. If not, what is the marketing value of covering the 'affluent non-owners'?

In raising such a *marketing* query, the researcher should also, I think, raise two *technical* research queries. Firstly, it is easy enough to exclude certain ('poor') sectors of the total population which 'obviously' constitute no potential market at all. However, the precise demarcation of the supposed 'potential' – to be made up of sufficiently 'affluent' non-owners by some as yet undefined matching criteria – is necessarily arbitrary and technically inconclusive. 'Matching' is, to say the least, rather a loose concept and no very firm conclusions could be based on the results obtained by any particular matching procedure (Ehrenberg, 1963a). In other words, the research brief is technically insufficient to do a good job here anyway.

Secondly, the researcher should point out that by questioning owners in categories (i) and (ii) about the product (if any) which they owned *previous* to their most recent purchase, information about the size and even the nature of the potential market in category (iii) would be obtained anyway. The information would relate to an earlier time-period, and the possible import of that would have to be considered for the particular market in question. However, this source of information would be much cheaper, and would bypass the technical matching problem altogether.

Further discussion of these queries might lead to their being rejected by the marketing man (as indicated in the section 'Improving the Research Brief', see p. 64), but even so they would serve 'to ensure that the research brief defines the relevant population(s) to be sampled'.

(4) '*Ensure that the research brief states the right variable(s) to be measured*'

In a survey, a variety of variables can be measured, and often are. In assessing a given market, one can for example try to establish whether informants have *ever* bought the product in question, or in some stated period of time. Again, one can assess how much was bought, either on the last purchasing occasion, or again in some stated period, or 'on average'. Some of these variables will be more relevant to the marketing problem than others. Apart from simply seeing to it that the relevant variables are included at all, the researcher should ensure that the most important variables are actually measured with the maximum available accuracy – research designs and procedures do differ in the relative accuracy with which they measure different variables.

However, it is, I believe, unusual for research briefs to spell out which variables are most important for the marketing problem in this sense. Even when a research brief *does* specify some accuracy limits for a particular variable, the variable picked may well not be the most relevant one for the marketing problem in question. To illustrate this I turn to a well-known area of industrial marketing, namely the buying and selling of advertising time on television.

In television audience research it is now becoming fashionable to give some consideration to the sampling errors of one or two of the variables that tend to be measured. However, the present discussions of future industry research for I.T.V. (and earlier the (1961) Interim Statement of the Market Research Society's Working Party on Intermedia Comparisons) seem to concern themselves with the sampling accuracy of individual ratings (for homes or for individuals or for both). Yet I believe it to be true that in general nobody buys a single commercial spot. Subject to correction from any organised industrial market research into media planning and buying procedures (as posed as a problem for the 1963 Thomson Silver Medal – see Belson (1963) and Sissors (1963)), I believe instead that advertisers and agencies buy *schedules* or groups of commercial spots.

It can then be readily demonstrated (in terms of decision theory, if one likes to be formal) that it is the sampling errors of *groups* of ratings not of *individual* ratings, which have to be considered in planning television audience research.

The available research techniques fall into four broad categories, i.e., Coincidental Interviewing, One-day Aided Recall, Seven-day Aided Recall, and Panels. For any single spot, all four techniques would give approximately the same sampling accuracy with a given sample size in the case of *housewife* ratings (some differences in sampling accuracies do occur for other types of single-spot ratings). However, for assessing groups of spots, sampling errors increase quite drastically as we follow the above listing – coincidentals have much the lowest sampling errors for assessing ratings over a group of spots, then comes one-day aided recall,[2] and so on.

Now in deciding on a research technique, sampling accuracy must of course be related to costs (by which coincidentals would almost certainly still be ruled out, despite being the optimum in terms of sampling accuracy for schedules). Furthermore, the accuracy of other media marketing and programming requirements has to be allowed for also (such as comparisons within a day, a week, or a longer time-period, trend measurements over various lengths of time, audience build-up, audience composition, etc.). In practice, a balance sometimes has to be struck between technically conflicting desiderata. However, it seems unlikely that anything like the best balance will be struck without in the first place 'ensuring that the research brief states the right variable(s) to be measured'.

(5) 'Ensure that the research brief gives some indication of the required accuracy of the main results'

As already implied, most research briefs still do not in practice specify the accuracy level required. Even when an indication of a required accuracy level is given, it is not usually based on anything very solid in terms of the marketing problem. Thus to continue for the moment with the earlier illustration of television audience research, the Market Research Society's Working Party Interim Statement (1961) which has already been referred to, specified that individual ratings (the variable chosen) should have a sampling error of not more than 5 percentage points at the 50 per cent level.

This recommendation was based on judgement (Market Research Society Working Party, 1961). However, a tremendous welter of data exists to show what sort of variation in ratings do occur in practice. An adequate analysis is therefore possible to determine what sampling accuracy *is* required to pick up the kind of differences which actually occur. What is more, it should be possible here to work along 'decision theory' lines so as to estimate for any given sample size the losses in wasted advertising

2. For example as carried out by the B.B.C., whose marketing problems do *not* however seem to include anything technically equivalent to the buying of schedules!

expenditure due to making wrong decisions. By balancing the estimated losses due to sampling errors at various sample sizes against the cost of the research, a research budget (and sample size) could be determined to maximise overall profitability in some sense.[3]

Now in general, we can hardly expect the marketing man to specify by himself the statistical accuracy levels required to answer his marketing problems. Instead, we must give some technical assistance ourselves. Doubts however arise whether we can effectively assist in this way at the briefing stage, since we seem at present to have little practice in planning our surveys with sampling errors in mind (or even in thus evaluating our results).

How in fact do we plan our sample survey designs? Firstly, we decide that the sample size should be 2000 informants say, on some judgement basis. Next, knowing that multi-stage sampling as well as sheer sample size affects the sampling error, we carefully consider the choice of our first stage sampling units. As a result, we decide to use *administrative districts*, because we do not somehow quite like *constituencies* for this purpose (or vice versa). For our second-stage units we choose wards, perhaps *two* per administrative district because that should reduce sampling errors – by some unkown amount and at unknown extra cost. We then cluster our sampling a little more to reduce fieldwork costs, by selecting one polling district per ward, but have again no idea of how much this will actually reduce the fieldwork costs (and *increase* the sampling errors).

Finally, we have to decide upon the size of the cluster of informants in each polling district; here we recognise that if we chose eighty administrative districts, the survey would be spread over 160 polling districts, which seems quite a nice number. This then determines a cluster size of twelve or thirteen individuals per polling district and apart from somehow choosing between various forms of pre-selected, random route, area or quota

3. The media industry is in the relatively fortunate position of having available quantitative information on losses of advertising expenditure on which some such O.R. determination of research expenditure could be based. Admittedly, the most relevant measure of loss – lost sales of the advertised products themselves – is not to hand, but since the sales losses should in this case exceed the advertising losses, at least a minimum level of research budget could thus be 'scientifically' estimated.

selection of the individual informants, the sample design is complete.

This description of how we determine our sample designs may be unfair. Perhaps we no longer always pull the total sample size of 2000 out of the air like that, or even by dividing the available money by the likely cost per average interview. Instead, the total sample size is often determined much more 'scientifically', by ensuring that the smallest sub-sample in any of our required breakdown categories will be at least one hundred informants, or two hundred, or whatever minimum one personally happens to think of. But how *do* we happen to think of any such number? After all, as shown in a recent paper in *Commentary* (Ehrenberg, 1963b), if in a market survey the average number of units bought per buyer is ten times as large as we had thought (if we had thought about it at all), *fifty* times as large a sample would be required for the same accuracy level. To achieve the required accuracy in our smallest breakdown category (supposing that we had actually thought in terms of *accuracy* rather than simply *sample size*), we would require not 100 but 5000 informants in that breakdown category.

It seems clear that we as market researchers could contribute greatly to 'ensure that the research brief gives some indication of the required accuracy level of the main results'.

(6) '*Ensure that the research brief gives at least an order of priority for the required accuracy of the various specified breakdown analyses*'

Consider the standard type of research brief which simply asks for an assessment of the size and the brand shares of a given consumer market, with certain specified breakdown analyses (e.g., by age, social class, regions). With a directly representative sample of the relevant population, these various breakdown analyses will then have varying sampling accuracies, depending on the size of the breakdown categories (as well as on the buying patterns within each category – see (5) above). The varying accuracy levels are therefore arbitrarily determined when using a straightforward sample design and may be quite inappropriate to the marketing problem.

The potential pay-off from taking into account those breakdown categories which really have to be measured adequately can be illustrated by an outline research proposal developed from a very sparse initial research brief – essentially to measure the markets for three somewhat related branded product-groups.

On examination, the product-groups had the following characteristics:

(a) Each had a rather low market penetration and a fairly long re-purchasing cycle.

(b) Each market was subject to a marked summer/winter swing and to a slow secular trend.

(c) None of the markets had in the past shown any other very dynamic changes, and none appeared likely to respond particularly fast to dynamic marketing.

(d) There was some past research information on each market.

Very briefly, the research design put forward to meet the brief was to carry out sample surveys throughout the later part of the peak season of each year, in three successive years, as follows:

First Year. A sample of 6000 housewives, with the older age-groups however fairly heavily under-sampled in the actual field-work.

Second Year. Re-interviewing a balanced half of the initial sample, with initial non-buyers under-sampled.

Third Year. Re-interviewing the remaining half of the initial sample similarly.

This proposed design – and particularly for example, the decision to re-interview informants at all and to do so in the proposed proportions – was based on somewhat detailed technical considerations appropriate to the particular markets *and* to what was thought to be – by the researcher – relevant to the marketing problems. Thus the research design represents an elaboration of the initial research brief by way of suggesting priorities for various breakdown categories. For example, where the need for repeated assessments of a market is relevant to the marketing problem, time itself should be allowed for as an 'important' breakdown variable. More specifically, the following other technical considerations applied:

(i) The initial sample size of 6000 gave statistically sensitive measurements of the *kind* of brand share and profile differences, and trends, that had occurred in the past.

(ii) The large size of the older age-group in the population together with their particular purchasing patterns in these markets allowed them to be under-sampled as proposed, without reducing the accuracy of *any* breakdowns below the limits indicated by (i).

(iii) Repeat-purchasing patterns were such that trends in market size and in brand shares could be measured as accurately, or if anything slightly more accurately, by re-interviewing both in the second and third years half the initial sample of 6000 informants, rather than by interviewing new, independent samples of 6000 in each year.

(iv) Consumer profiles in these markets had in the past changed relatively slowly and there appeared therefore no need to assess them fully every year. Minor trends would not, it was thought, affect marketing policy and major changes, if any, would still be picked up by the reduced sample sizes.

(v) The precise quantitative nature of the summer/winter swings appeared also unlikely to affect marketing decisions and was therefore not covered at all; fieldwork however was deliberately to be spread over the later part of the peak season, so as to establish an annual benchmark of the market, unaffected by short-lived fluctuations. (Fieldwork in the *later* part of the peak season was specified because with the fairly slow re-purchasing cycle, outline purchasing information for a longer memory-period – e.g., three months – as well as more detailed information regarding more recent purchases was deemed necessary.)

(vi) With the slow purchasing cycle, the available evidence on repeat-purchasing levels, and the limitation of *ad hoc* survey questioning on events in the more distant past, the repeat-interviewing feature of the proposal was also seen capable of determining 'heavy buyers' (i.e., over two- or three-year periods) more precisely, thus improving an important breakdown category for cross-analyses with data on consumption habits and attitudes which were also to be obtained.

(vii) Again using calculations regarding repeat-purchasing tendencies in these low-penetration markets, it was found that the necessarily very large number of non-buyers could be somewhat under-sampled in the second and third years without any *relevant* loss of statistical accuracy.

(viii) Sampling was to proceed by well-controlled quota-sampling for the first year, and by using the resultant pre-selected addresses in the subsequent two years; in this way the under-sampling of older age-groups initially and of initial non-buyers subsequently would also bring about the largest cost savings.

(ix) The three-year duration of the design was determined by various technical features of these particular markets. For a more continuous operation, a repeat of the design itself was envisaged, subject to such technical changes as the new data *and* changing marketing needs might indicate.

It will be noted that what has been outlined here is not a research *brief* elaborating on breakdown priorities, etc., but a research *proposal*. The direct relevance of this to achieving an adequate research brief as such will be taken up again (in the section on 'Improving the Research Brief', p. 64).[4] The initial research brief could be met with a research design which would yield information statistically equivalent to annual surveys of 6000 informants each at an average per interview cost of up to £2, for an average annual cost of £2500 to £3000 by 'ensuring at least an order of priority of the required accuracy of the various breakdown analyses'.

4. It may be mentioned that in the outcome, the client used thi proposal to bring down the price of a competitive retail audit project and suggested that the present proposal should be presented as a technical paper, which had not been precisely the intention in preparing it. However, the implicit permission to publish has been verified and is gratefully acknowledged!

(7) 'Ensure that the research brief does not prejudge the selection of research techniques and procedures'

A research brief which is not to be technically vague and woolly must probably always be formulated, implicitly if not explicitly, in terms of certain research techniques and procedures, rather than just as a marketing problem. This however makes it easy to prejudice the selection of the most appropriate procedures. An obvious example which we must all have come across is when the research brief already lays down a certain sample size almost certainly without adequate technical consideration. Again, a particular research procedure such as an *ad hoc* survey may be requested when a retail audit might actually be a much more appropriate procedure (or vice versa).

More specifically, I return for simplicity to a problem-area which I have already touched upon once or twice and where the background information is fairly generally known, namely television audience research. Here there has recently been some discussion whether to use TAM-meters or Recordimeters as monitoring devices for diary panels.[5] This formulation of the problem does, I believe, prejudge the research issue.

Thus the evidence of the TAM Comparison Survey (Television Audience Measurement, 1961) is that these two monitoring methods lead to virtually identical diary panel results in a two-channel situation. The lesson to be drawn from this is *not* that one can simply choose between these two procedures on grounds such as cost, but that there is scope for developing still different monitoring procedures, possibly more economical or suitable in other respects (see next paragraph). Thus if it is immaterial to the diary results whether or not the monitoring device precisely checks if the set was on at any time, *and* whether or not each diary has to be marked not only with who was viewing when but also with the choice of channel, then the precise form of monitoring device has been shown to be so immaterial as to provide scope for developing other devices.

The potential attractiveness of a new monitoring device for diary panel procedure would lie not only with some marginal

5. The availability of minute-by-minute ratings as such, which are produced by TAM-meter panels only, has not been relevant to these discussions.

savings in annual operating costs of some x hundreds of thousands, but especially also with a view to the coming complications of a poly-channel (three or more) situation. Thus whilst Recordimeters with the current diary form performed well in the two-channel situation of the TAM Comparison Survey, any failure to do so in a poly-channel situation might be avoided by a new and still economical diary panel procedure, such as for example the use of a diary form in which (some) programme information would also have to be recorded.

Indeed, the tendency to prejudge a technical issue can also be illustrated in terms of the relative appeal of the two *existing* diary-panel techniques for a poly-channel situation. Thus it is sometimes argued that the risk of relying on Recordimeter control is great, because household members *do* have to record the viewing channel and this might (or indeed would) be beyond their capacity with *more* than two channels.

Now if it were a question of *one* person per household filling in a weekly diary *once* only, general research experience might well support this *a priori* judgement. However, the Recordimeter diary panels as operated by TAM are *not* run in this way and have in fact two self-correcting devices built-in. Firstly, *all* household members' viewing has to be entered and this has to be done by each person individually. Even without necessarily assuming perfect operation of the latter feature in practice, incorrect entries of the channel viewed would tend to lead to controversy within the household. This in turn would lead to the entry being corrected and would also motivate increased attention to accurate recording in the future. The latter point is relevant because of the second self-correcting feature in the TAM-type of diary panel which is due to its continuous nature. For people who belong to a continuous diary panel, the only way to do the task without undue effort and with some satisfaction is to try at least to do it properly, and certainly to avoid repetitive family controversy over what channel was viewed. Panel-members become 'educated' in their task, and this does not necessarily involve any biasing effects, as has been shown for the choice of channel in the two-channel situation by the TAM Comparison Survey (Television Audience Measurement, 1961), and by experimental results for the Attwood Consumer Panel (Ehrenberg, 1960) in the case of frequency of purchase and brand choice information.

Whilst it is not suggested here that Recordimeter diary panels would *necessarily* work as adequately in a poly-channel situation as they did in the two-channel situation of the Comparison Survey, the above technical analysis of why they might work adequately serves to stress the need for 'ensuring that the research brief does not prejudge the selection of research techniques and procedures'.

Conclusions

Many other kinds of technical problems can of course arise with research briefs, but the limited selection of specific instances discussed above should demonstrate in hard terms how a research brief can fail to determine adequately the kind of research that is required, namely because:

1. The research brief is not related closely enough to the specific marketing problem (which may itself not yet have been adequately specified).

2. The brief does not state technical requirements clearly enough.

3. The research implications of the brief are not studied sufficiently to determine whether or not the brief *is* inadequate.

As a result, any ensuing research may fail to provide any or all of the relevant information, or may provide wrong information altogether. Even if the research is on the right lines, it may be insufficiently accurate or reliable on the most relevant points and it will almost certainly be more costly than it ought to have been.

These faults are serious because in market research we seldom learn from our mistakes – or have a chance to do so. If we could follow up unsatisfactory research with further work, the situation would not be quite so serious. But in practice, we seldom can undertake follow-up research, for a number of reasons:

(a) There may be no time for further work, since many marketing decisions have to be taken *now* (and even the initial research was probably started too late).

(b) There is no money for further research, because market

research has so far failed to generate sufficient management confidence – and probably rightly so – to attract the theoretically appropriate budgets.

(c) Often nobody actually *knows* that the research results obtained are inadequate, because neither the research man nor the marketing man has enough time to do the technical work and thinking which would be required.

(d) Even when somebody does know that the results are inadequate, there tends to be a conspiracy of silence – partly because nothing much can be done about it anyway (see (a) and (b)), and partly because of the general atmosphere of doubt surrounding market research which makes it difficult – by a natural inversion – to admit a mistake without running the risk of sapping the user's confidence altogether.

The fact that we have therefore in general to do the best possible research *now*, together with the – I hope – sufficiently forceful nature of the case-histories outlined above, means that we cannot pharisaically shrug off the need for improving our research briefs either as applying only to the other chaps or by admitting that of course things are not quite as good as they ought to be but that no doubt we will do better in future. No, the problem concerns us *now*. Let us have a long second look at the research briefs which are sitting right on our desks.

When I myself now take even just a quick 'second look' at the above case-histories, I feel that whilst they probably *do* demonstrate superficially the scope for technical study at the briefing stage, they fall very much short of the mark as effectively illustrating the mechanics of fitting research to the marketing problem. For this failure it would be easy enough to blame a fear of making this paper even more long-winded, since explicit discussion of all the combinations and permutations of each given marketing problem and its research implications would certainly have been laborious. However, the true reason for this failure is much simpler, namely that I now have found how woefully little I know about the marketing problems even in these case-histories which I myself happily selected only a little while ago. For me at least, that is the main lesson I have learned in trying to prepare this paper.

Improving the Research Brief

To ask for a simple rule for improving our research briefs is like asking how to be good – at best one can attempt to set down some do's and some don't's.

Firstly, I would regard it as generally wrong to accept the initial research brief as if it were gospel and simply try to produce a research proposal to fit it. Instead, there must be *interplay* between the research man and the marketing man to try and reach an adequate research brief. The marketing man should expect queries and suggestions from the research man and the latter should have the courage to make these. The struggle should go on until agreement can be reached. It follows *inter alia* that the *initial* research brief need not necessarily be a very full one, as long as its detailed marketing and technical implications are in fact brought out in the subsequent 'interplay'.

In thus striving for an adequate *final* research brief, the research man must however recognise that the apparently best research procedures will sometimes not be feasible, for nontechnical reasons. Thus it was suggested on page 60 that the available evidence demonstrated ample scope for developing research procedures somewhat different from either of two existing ones. Whilst the research man should certainly point this out (supposing that he were given a research brief expressed in terms of the *existing* procedures only), he should not necessarily seek to persevere with such a technical argument if there are other grounds for not making any radical change in the existing techniques (such as lack of time or a desire for an easy life). The precise line of demarcation between pigheaded perseverance and professional irresponsibility may of course not always be easy to draw.

Secondly, the 'interplay' between marketing and research men need not necessarily take the form of producing revision upon revision of the initial research brief as such. This *might* be the best procedure in an ideal world, but would not necessarily be so in one which is governed by considerations of time, of money, and of the various individuals who are involved.

Thus on page 57 the response to the initial research brief (a very sparse one) did not take the form of a revised brief at all, but already that of a *suggested* research proposal (in outline form). Such a response can serve quite effectively to bring various assumptions and judgements about the supposed marketing problem into the open and can therefore provide a good basis for the next stage of interplay, i.e., the marketing man's comeback as to what information he really requires.

Thirdly, the research man must not be afraid to 'stick his neck out'. Even if his counter-suggestions turn out to be wrong, their very rejection will probably have helped to clarify the marketing man's research needs and it will also have helped the research man himself to a clearer understanding of these needs – no mean achievement.

On page 51, for example, the research man's first comeback to the initial research brief (here a rather full, textbook one) was to argue that one of the initially specified sub-populations should be excluded from the research. This argument was wrong in the event, because the marketing problem concerned not only the existing product, but also a certain area of *product-diversification*. However, this aspect of the marketing problem had not been mentioned in the initial brief. Without bringing it into the open, no proposed research based on the initial brief would have been very adequate.

As a fourth point I would stress that the research man must not only 'stick his neck out' in terms of suggestions and queries of a technical research kind, but he must do so also in terms of *marketing* aspects of the research brief. In doing so he is not trying to usurp the marketing man's function, but simply aiming at an adequate research brief which can only come by a full joining together of marketing needs and technical research possibilities. Just as the marketing man in formulating his research brief will necessarily tend to use research terminology and may even perhaps already specify (or, preferably, suggest) actual research procedures, so the research man need not be backward in stepping over the boundary into the marketing man's domain.

A simple illustration arose in the case-history on page 51 which was just referred to, where the researcher queried whether *any* results to be obtained from a certain sub-population would affect any contemplated marketing action, and if so, how. A more detailed illustration is given by the research proposal outlined on page 57 as a comeback to the initial research brief. The researcher's comeback here contained many judgements and assumptions about the marketing problem, for example about the need to measure the trends of market size and of brand shares but *not* trends in consumer profiles, about the relative lack of importance of measuring seasonal swings, about the importance of isolating and describing heavy buyers, and so on. None of these items were contained in the initial research brief – nor perhaps even in the formulation of the relevant marketing problems themselves. But *some* such assumptions and judgements have to be made in planning research – if not in marketing also – and the purpose of the outlined research proposal was simply to provide the first explicit opportunity to examine them.

The fifth and final point is to suggest quite generally that there can not be, and should not be, any prescribed, formal rules and regulations governing this interplay between marketing and research men – a point already touched on in the first section (page 43). As long as we recognise the need for such interplay and try to understand its nature, procedural implementation must be adapted to the actual situation (e.g., whether the discussions have to take place between departments within one company or with an outside research agency) and to the particular technical expertise and personalities of the people involved.

The important thing seems to be effective *rapport* between the various parties. There must be sufficient mutual confidence, and self-confidence for that matter, to dare to put a foot wrong in the search for an adequate brief. Whilst such *rapport* may be somewhat lacking even within a single organization, because of departmental and/or personal rivalries, and protocol and the like, it is likely to be particularly absent when outside research agencies are commissioned on a purely *ad hoc* basis, so that the commercial considerations of 'getting a low price' on the one hand and of 'getting the survey' on the other may unduly interfere with getting the research which is right for the marketing problem.

References

BELSON, W. A. (1963), 'The best method of classifying informants in media studies, having regard to the end-usage of such studies for marketing purposes', *The Roy Thomson Medals and Awards for Media Research*, Thomson Organisation Ltd.

EHRENBERG, A. S. C. (1960), 'A study of some potential biases in the operation of a consumer panel', *Applied Statistics*, vol. 9, p. 20.

EHRENBERG, A. S. C. (1963a), 'On matching and experimental design', *New Developments in Research: Proc. 6th Ann. Conf. Market Research Society*, Market Research Society.

EHRENBERG, A. S. C. (1963b), 'Verified predictions of consumer purchasing patterns', *Commentary*, vol. 10, p. 16.

Market Research Society Working Party (1961), 'Interim statement on television audience research', Market Research Society.

NOWIK, H. (1964), 'The role of market research in a marketing orientated company', *Research in Marketing: Proc. 7th Ann. Conf. Market Research Society*, Market Research Society.

SISSORS, J. Z. (1963), 'A discussion of a media audience classification system', *The Roy Thomson Medals and Awards for Media Research*, Thomson Organisation Ltd.

Television Audience Measurement Ltd (1961), *Comparison Survey of Audience Composition Techniques*, Television Audience Measurement Ltd.

3 C. S. Mayer

Choosing the Research Contractor

C. S. Mayer, 'Evaluating the quality of the marketing research contractor', *Journal of Marketing Research*, vol. 4, 1967, pp. 134–41.

Increased awareness of the potential of marketing research, combined with fluctuating demand for it, is prompting a large number of companies to turn to outside contractors for their research needs. Relying on outsiders for accurate marketing information can be puzzling and frustrating for the research buyer. The buyer usually knows what information he needs and may even specify the particular study design before asking contractors to bid on it. He has more trouble, however, deciding which contractors should bid on a study, how he should evaluate the quality of the supplied research, and consequently, whether he should accept the lowest bid.

Without any guide lines, the research buyer may be tempted to select his suppliers on the basis of personal acquaintance, intuition, or established reputation. Moreoover, he may accept the research findings without questioning the quality of the data collection and processing. Under such circumstances, high quality research suppliers find themselves in the difficult position of either relaxing some of their quality standards or of not being able to compete effectively against the less quality conscious suppliers.

A fair system of contractor evaluation would be useful to buyers and contractors. From the buyer's point of view, he would be in a much better position to select the appropriate suppliers for a particular study. The same system could also be used to evaluate their work. From the contractor's point of view, research competition would be more equitable if competitors were proposing to supply work of the same quality. The purpose of this article is to present such a system of evaluation.

The Evaluation Concept

To evaluate the quality of research supplied by a contractor, it was decided to conduct a thorough audit of his operating procedures. Such an audit could only be done by visits to his base of operation – usually the home office.

During these visits, every attempt was made to keep the evaluation as objective as possible. Instead of relying on verbal reports of quality control throughout the operating procedures, evidence of such quality control was sought. For example, instead of accepting the Field Director's word that an up-to-date file system was kept on all interviewers, an examination of the interviewer files was conducted to see what kinds of information were kept and how current the last entry was.

An attempt was also made to talk with the operative personnel, as well as the senior researchers. The researchers knew the proper operating procedures while the personnel were more likely to say what they were doing. The propriety of this approach was often borne out by conflicting statements obtained from the senior researchers and their technicians.

Objectivity in evaluation was also attempted by breaking the research function into as many small components as feasible. Any evaluation of this sort eventually becomes subjective, but by constraining subjectivity to a small range, an essentially objective procedure was developed. This approach accounts for the need for great detail in the procedure.

Another feature of the evaluation procedure was the recognition that a supplier could produce high quality work without performing every conceivable check. For example, if a supplier validated interviews by telephone from both the home office and the field, there was no need for postal validation. This concept of redundancy of controls is also reflected in the evaluation system.

Developing the Evaluation Procedure

Four well-known and reputedly high quality research agencies were asked to suggest what factors determined quality in contracted research. On the basis of their suggestions, plus talks with research executives responsible for buying outside research, a detailed questionnaire was constructed.

Armed with this questionnaire, uniform data were gathered from several contractors. To permit comparison of total quality among these contractors, a system of weights for the various components of data collection and processing had to be devised. A rating scale, totalling two hundred points, was selected. The points assigned to each component reflect the writer's assessment of its contribution to total quality.

It must be emphasized that the particular weights reported here refer to typical surveys carried out for many research buyers – product placement tests, preference tests and usage patterns in one or more metropolitan markets. It is also assumed that the research buyer bears the responsibility for the study design and the analysis of the results. For different kinds of surveys or research requirements, new weights would be necessary.

The Contractor Rating System

The contractor rating system is designed to evaluate the quality of surveys that rely on personal interviews with consumers in the household, using a probability sample design. To facilitate the evaluation, the research function is segmented into seventeen different components. Each component is given a weight that reflects its importance relative to the others. The way in which a contractor is awarded points is specified in detail, so that several evaluators will similarly rate the same contractor.

To simplify the job of making an evaluation, the contracted research job is first broken into three main categories. The two hundred total points are distributed among these sections as follows:

1. General assessment of physical and technical capabilities (thirty)
2. Sampling and field (eighty-five)
3. Coding and tabulating (eighty-five).

Each section is then further subdivided, and points are awarded to each subsection for various quality-producing components.

Each subsection has a total number of points allocated to it.

These points can be earned in a variety of ways, not all of which are likely to be performed by the same contractor. Accordingly, it is possible to earn more points in a subsection than are allocated to that section. If this occurs, the contractor is limited to the total points assigned to that subsection, showing that he has adequate quality control.

For example, a contractor can earn points through validating field work by mail, by supervisors in the field, by telephone from the home office, or by analysis of responses obtained by the interviewers. Each of these earn some points. Since one method might make another unnecessary, the components making up the subsection on validation carry more points than the total value of that subsection. However, should a supplier use several of these methods, he would still be limited to that total. No additional points would be awarded for what could be designated as 'overcontrol' on one phase of the operation.

Special mention should also be made of a subsection (Section Q) that is more subjective than the rest. It was recognized that the total quality of any organization is more than simply the sum of the individual components that make it up. For this reason, twenty-five points were reserved to reflect the evaluator's subjective judgement about the intangibles in the research contractor's operation.

	Points assigned
General Assessment	30

A. Study design

How will the supplier assist with the study design?	5
1. Will the contractor suggest alternative study designs if he thinks that the problem can be solved better than the way the buyer is approaching it?	1
2. Who is responsible for the layout of the final questionnaire? Are past questionnaires easy to follow? (Note: When possible, actual forms were obtained for these judgements).	1
3. Are interviewer's instructions written by the contractor; are they easy to understand?	1

4. Are supervisor's instructions written by the contractor; are they easy to understand?   1

5. Are rotation patterns routinely followed when a list of items is presented to a respondent, or only if the client specifically asks for it?   1

6. If the questionnaire is precoded, are these precodes clear? How are precodes established?   1

Q. Subjective assessment

Although this assessment is made as the last step in supplier evaluation (hence the designation Q), it is included under the General Assessment section because of its general nature.

An attempt was made to keep the grading system objective. However, 25 points were allotted for the evaluator's assessment of the less tangible aspects of the supplier's operation.

1. Is there a well-balanced and cohesive group of professional researchers? Are all functions covered competently?   10

2. Is the physical set-up conducive to good work? Are machines modern and up-to-date? Are there any essential pieces of equipment missing? (e.g. keypunches, verifiers, tabulating equipment, calculators, etc.)   5

3. Does the layout of the office make it easy to find components of a study at any time? Could some data get lost? Are the offices quiet? Is there good morale in the office? What is the general atmosphere?   10

Sampling and Field   *85*

B. Sample selection and implementation

Does the contractor obtain a reliable probability sample?   *10*

1. Who is responsible for drawing the sample? What are his qualifications?   3

2. What materials are available for drawing the sample? Are they the most current documents?   2

3. Are the sampling instructions clearly written? How specific are they?   1

4. Are callbacks only used at the client's request? How many callbacks are authorized? When are the callbacks made?   1

5. Is it possible to substitute for a sampling point? Who makes the decision to substitute? How are alternates selected?   2

6. Does the interviewer have any element of choice in selecting the respondents? (For example, is the interviewer given a specific address as a starting point, or is she told what page, column and line in her phone book represents the starting address?)   2

7. Are any checks performed to ensure that the interviewer actually followed the sampling plan? Could the interviewer visit addresses of her choice without detection?   2

C. Field control

What ensures that the work flows smoothly to the field and back? Are there sufficient controls to detect problems before they become costly?   *15*

1. How are interviewers alerted that a job is coming? How much lead time is given, and how are acceptances made? When are turndowns apparent?   2

2. What controls ensure that complete materials are mailed to the field?   2

3. Does the home office know that the materials have arrived safely, or could a packet get lost in the mail

without any signal to the home office? (A materials
received postcard is the usual way of acknowledging
receipt.) 2

4. How is completed work checked in? Is it compared
with any list that shows what should be coming in?
How soon after receipt is the work checked in? 3

5. Is there a call record form, and is it being used?
Does the home office know why an interviewer
was late with an assignment, or the reason for a low
completion rate? 3

6. How soon will the home office learn about potential problems? How often is the work mailed in? 3

7. If problems occur in the field, how are they resolved? Are interviewers or supervisors encouraged
to telephone the home office? Is there evidence that
telephone calls are made regularly? 3

D. Field supervision

It is the writer's opinion that the field cannot be
properly controlled from the home office – local
supervisors are necessary for a workable span of
control. The grading system reflects this belief. *15*

1. How were supervisors hired and trained? Do
they have personal contact with the home office, or
are they simply names in a file? 3

2. Do the supervisors know what is expected from
them? Is there a supervisor's job description? 3

3. Can the supervisors control their interviewers
properly? What control forms (listing sheets,
time sheets, interviews, etc.) are available to them?
What material is sent by the interviewers directly
to the home office? 3

4. How are supervisors paid? Will their own pay be

reduced if they detect interviewer padding (percentage fee system?) 3

5. Do the supervisors know the quality of their interviewers' work? Are they asked to edit and validate work? 3

6. What controls does the home office have on the supervisors? Do the supervisors complete reports showing that their supervisory work was done? 3

7. Does the company have travelling supervisors who check the quality of the work in the field? Is there evidence of such travel? 3

E. Field interviewers

The quality of the data collected is affected by how well the interviewers are selected, trained, and instructed. *10*

1. What information does the home office have about the interviewers? What kind of information is given on the application forms? Is this information readily available? 2

2. What initial training does the interviewer receive? (Initial training refers to such things as how to gain rapport, to interview, to probe, to follow sampling instructions, etc.) Is there a training manual, and how good is it? 2

3. Are briefing sessions held routinely, on difficult studies only, or never? 2

4. What personal contact is there between home office personnel and interviewers? (evidence). 2

5. Do the interviewers receive special instruction occasionally, (e.g. how to probe effectively, how to reduce the refusal rate, etc.)? Is training an ongoing effort? 2

6. Do the interviewers receive special communi-

cations from the home office, such as newsletters, Christmas cards, etc.? Can they identify with the company?   2

7. How are the interviewers paid? This refers both to the level of pay and the method of distribution (from company or through supervisor).   2

F. Field quality checks

The contractor can take a number of internal steps to ensure that the quality of fieldwork is acceptable.   *20*

1. Are there any checks on the quality of interviewing, (e.g. complete responses, skips followed, no blank questions, etc.)? How is this done and by whom? Is the evaluation structured or unstructured?   3

2. What are the controls on interviewer costs? Are interviewers with atypical costs questioned?   3

3. What records are kept on costs and quality? Can an interviewer be marginal on several surveys without detection? Are these records current? (Check files).   5

4. Are interviewers told about results of quality and cost checks? Are suggestions for improvement routinely made? Does the interviewer know that she is being checked on?   5

5. Is skill in interviewing rewarded? Are there incentives to do a good job?   3

6. What are the qualifications of the people directing the field in the home office? Are they familiar with field problems? Are they likely to get interviewer loyalty?   3

G. Validation

What methods ensure the validity of the interviewer's work?   *15*

*Points
assigned*

1. Some firms use postcards (letters) to validate interviews. How effective postcard validation is depends on how conscientiously the method is used. Even at best this method is not very effective. 7

2. Often the supervisors are asked to validate. What proportion do they validate? Do they make validation reports? Who selects the questions to be validated? Are there checks on the supervisors? 8

3. The method of validation preferred by the writer is a number of telephone interviews from the home office. What proportion is validated? How? What records are kept on validation? 12

4. Some companies also attempt to validate by looking for divergent trends in the answers of interviewers. Such validation can be done during coding or by a special analysis of results. It necessitates processing data separately for each interviewer. 5

Coding and Tabulating 85

H. Editing

Is editing a separate function? What is done? 5

1. What types of editing are done? 2

2. Who does the editing? What are their qualifications? Are there checks on the editors? 2

3. Are editing instructions written, spoken, or other? 2

I. Code building

How are the codes built? 10

1. How large a sample is used, and how is it selected? 3

2. How are codes developed? Are answers recorded verbatim? Where does the code collapsing occur? 6

	Points assigned

3. Who is responsible for approving the codes? How are they approved?   2

4. Are codes checked by a representative of the buyer?   1

J. Coding

How well is the coding done?   *15*

1. What are the qualifications of the coders? How are they selected? What proportions of them are temporary and permanent?   2

2. How are the coders trained? Is there a training manual?   2

3. Are coding instructions spoken, handwritten or typed? Are the coding instructions easy to follow?   2

4. Are specific coding supervisors assigned to each job? Are these supervisors always available? Are questions asked as they occur, or are questions saved until several can be asked together?   2

5. What are the qualifications of the coding supervisor? Does he have the confidence of the coders?   2

6. Are the questionnaires coded by one question at a time, groups of questions, or the complete questionnaire?   2

7. What happens to the 'all other' category? How large can it get? Is it easy to assign a code to some items in the all other group? Are the all other answers recorded verbatim?   3

8. Is the physical layout for coding conducive to good work? Can the coders see the codes easily from where they work (pin-up boards?) Is the lighting good?   2

*Points
assigned*

K. Coding control

What control ensures accountability for coding?　5

1. Are questionnaires numbered before or after coding? Are questionnaires identified individually or in batches?　2

2. Does a batch control form go with each bundle of questionnaires? Does the form show who edited, coded, and checked the work?　5

L. Coding verification

Is the coding verified? To what standard is coding held?　*10*

1. What percentage of the work is verified? Is verification continuous, or done only at the beginning?　4

2. What are the qualifications of the person responsible for verifying the coding?　2

3. What records are kept on coding errors? Are coders retrained or discharged if errors occur repeatedly?　3

4. What action is taken if more than the maximum number of coding errors are found? Is all of that coder's work recoded?　2

M. Keypunching

How well is the keypunching done?　5

1. What are the keypunchers' qualifications? Are they trained to punch marketing research data?　1

2. Are the facilities and equipment conducive to accurate punching?　2

3. What control and supervision is given to the keypunchers?　3

N. *Keypunch verification*

Is the punching verified? To what standard is
punching held?   *10*

1. Is keypunching verified by a verifier, reproducer,
or sight check?   4

2. What proportion of the work is verified?   4

3. Are records kept of punching errors? What
action is taken if errors reach a maximum limit?   3

O. *Cleaning procedures*

How are the cards cleaned?   *10*

1. Is the person specifying the cleaning procedures
familiar with both the questionnaire and machine
capabilities? How are cleaning instructions given?   1

2. Are there checks for illegal punches, multiple
punches in single punch columns, blank columns,
etc.?   2

3. Are several columns cross checked for logical consistency?   2

4. How are errors corrected – by using an automatic
program or by referring to the questionnaires?   5

5. Are records kept of how much cleaning was
necessary? Are these available to the client?   2

P. *Tabulation*

What effort is made to give meaningful and accurate
tables? At what cost can further tables be requested
after the data are analyzed?   *15*

1. Who orders the tabulations? How are specifications
given?   2

2. What equipment, such as computer or sorter, is

	Points assigned
used to produce the tables? Are qualified people responsible for producing the tables?	3
3. What efforts ensure that the data are accurate? How are numbers recorded? How are tables annotated? What checks prevent typographic errors? Does a senior researcher inspect tables before they are released?	10
4. How long are data stored?	1
Total	*200*

While the total number of points is meaningful, it is not a sufficient measure of contractor quality. An additional rule has to be added that if a contractor scores too low on a major section, he is automatically disqualified. For example, if the fieldwork of a contractor is questionable, it does not matter how good the subsequent processing is, the adage 'garbage-in, garbage-out' will hold.

At this stage, the reader may wonder how points are assigned for each component. It is a relatively simple task when two features are emphasized. First, at each decision level, the number of points to be allocated is few. Of the eighty-one decisions which must be made from section A to P, twelve are worth one point, thirty-four are worth two points, twenty-two are worth three points, eight are worth four or five points, and only five are worth over five points. Second, most contractors either perform a particular function well, not at all, or partially. The point allocation is easy at the extremes. While some subjectivity does enter into rating the ones between, the scope of this subjectivity is greatly restricted by the range of points.

Where several questions are asked for a particular component, they are interrelated to give detail of a single function. One example is sufficient to illustrate this point. Under field supervision, the questions 'Do supervisors know what is expected from them? Is there a supervisor's job description?' are weighted with three points. If the audit turns up a clear supervisor's job description, three points are awarded. If supervisors are notified of what is expected of them through occasional instructions or briefing sessions, one or two points are assigned. If no evidence is found that there are specific requirements made of supervisors, no points are awarded.

One test of the extent of subjectivity in the evaluations is whether different evaluators make similar assessments of the same contractors. While admittedly an insufficient test, four independent assessments by two experienced evaluators came extremely close.

The System Demonstrated

To illustrate the system, five hypothetical contractors are evaluated in the table. These contractors do not represent actual operations; they were created by combining features of a large number of contractors.

Company A

Company A has the highest quality operation. Its only weakness is that it does not have local supervisors, but attempts to control the field from the home office and through a few travelling supervisors.

It relies on the integrity of individual interviewers and does little validation. A postcard is sent to 25 per cent of the respondents, but the returns are not checked in a systematic way. In the past, but not in the last year, interviewers' answers were checked for divergent trends by processing results separately for each interviewer.

Company B

Company B is another high quality operation. An interesting feature of its procedures is that all fieldwork is validated from the home office, using WATS lines (Wide Area Telephone Service). Supervisors receive a detailed report on the results of the validation.

Company B's main weakness is its subcontracting of keypunching and tabulation. Coded work is shipped to a tabulation house and returned as computer-produced tables. During the past year the prime contractor, Company *B*, did not visit the offices of its subcontractors.

Unless the prime contractor ensures through personal checks that the subcontractors are in fact supplying the quality requested, no credit is given for the quality of subcontracted work. This stand is taken to protect the research buyer. Quality of subcontracted work, which may have been high at one time, does not necessarily stay high.

Cleaning procedures are specified. The subcontractor is told exactly what cleaning is to be done and is supposed to change incorrect cards after referring to the questionnaires. Coding problems are resolved by telephone calls to the coding supervisor. However, no cleaning report is submitted, and Company *B* cannot know how the cleaning was really done.

Company C

Company *C* entered the business as a supplier of field interviewing. Its design and sampling capabilities are limited. In sampling, it relies on an outside consultant.

Its field operation is impeccable with the exception of validation. Ten per cent of the work is validated by a general postcard; the same postcard is used for all studies; and 10 per cent of the work is validated by supervisors' telephone calls. However, no validation procedures are prescribed, and the supervisors do not turn in validation forms. Supervisors have not reported invalid work during the last six months.

Company *C* performs editing, coding, and keypunching, but sends the decks to a tabulation house. Cleaning is performed by an automatic program, and Company *C* does not know what proportion of cleaning is necessary. The computer produced tables received from the tabulation house are given a cursory check and then sent to the research buyer.

Company D

This company evolved from a high quality tabulation house into a full line research supplier. Its expertise lies in machine processing and not study design. Also, the company has outgrown its present space; the overcrowding produces inefficiencies.

An attempt is made at probability sampling. For instance, supervisors are given randomly selected page, column, and line numbers in their telephone books. These serve as starting points for a cluster of households. The identification of the starting points is determined by the local supervisors.

Fieldwork is handled by local supervisors or supervisory services (the same group that many researchers use indiscriminately today). No contact is made with interviewers. Validation is performed by the supervisors, who are required to validate 10 per cent of the work and submit validation reports. An additional 5 per cent of the work is validated by evening telephone calls from the home office.

Company E

Company E is an independent opportunist acting as a marketing research broker. It has only three officials and some secretarial help. All field and tabulation work are subcontracted. Fieldwork is subcontracted by a secretary who keeps a file of available local supervisors and supervisory services.

Material received from the field is sent in bundles to one of several tabulation houses. Finished tables are received back with no further intervention by Company E.

The officials are busy and have little time or interest in checking the quality of work.

The Use of the Rating System

While the writer is the first to acknowledge the weaknesses of the check-list approach proposed in this paper, the fact remains that a research buyer makes either implicit or explicit evaluations in his choice among market research contractors. An explicit method is preferable as it is consistent and communicable.

The system of contractor evaluation in this article is for a particular kind of outside research requirement.

Similar systems could be set up for any research requirement. Weights among subsections would change, but the explicitness of the system would remain.

The highest quality research is not always necessary. Since high

Table 1
A Hypothetical Set of Contractor Ratings

	Assig-ned values	Company				
		A	B	C	D	E
A. Study design	5	5	5	4	2	3
Suggests alternative designs	1	1	1	0	0	1
Questionnaire layout	1	1	1	1	0	1
Interviewer's instructions	1	1	1	1	1	0
Supervisor's instructions	1	0	1	1	0	0
Rotation patterns	1	1	1	1	0	1
Clear precodes	1	1	1	0	1	0
B. Sample selection and implementation	10	10	10	6	3	4
Qualifications of sampling head	3	3	2	2	1	1
Sampling materials on hand	2	2	2	0	0	0
Sampling instructions	1	1	1	1	1	1
Callback procedures	1	1	1	1	0	0
Substitution schemes	2	2	2	1	0	1
Interviewer's role in selection	2	2	2	1	1	1
Check on adherence to sampling plan	2	2	2	0	0	0
C. Field control	15	12	13	15	9	5
Alert	2	2	2	2	1	1
Mail-out controls	2	2	1	1	1	0
Materials controls	2	1	2	2	1	1
Check-in procedures	3	3	2	3	2	0
Call record control	3	3	1	3	1	0
Trouble detection	3	0	2	3	1	1
Method of problem resolution	3	1	3	3	2	2
D: Field supervision	15	3	12	15	4	3
Hiring and training of supervisors	3	0	2	3	0	0
Supervisor's job description	3	0	1	3	0	0
Control forms available to the supervisor	3	0	3	3	3	2
Method of payment	3	0	1	2	0	0
Validation by supervisor	3	0	3	3	1	1
Controls on supervisor	3	0	2	2	0	0
Travelling supervisors	3	3	0	3	0	0
E. Field interviewers	10	10	8	10	2	0
Information on application	2	2	2	2	0	0
Initial training	2	2	2	2	0	0
Briefing	2	2	1	1	1	0
Personal contact	2	2	1	1	0	0
Special instructions	2	1	1	2	0	0
Newsletters, Christmas cards, etc.	2	2	0	2	0	0
Compensation	2	1	1	2	1	0
F. Field quality checks	20	20	20	20	7	2
Quality control	3	3	2	2	0	0
Cost control	3	3	3	2	1	1
Records	5	5	5	5	2	0

	Assigned values	Company				
		A	B	C	D	E
Feedback to field	5	5	5	5	2	0
Individual merit incentives	3	2	3	3	1	0
Personnel qualifications	3	3	3	3	1	1
G. Validation	*15*	*6*	*15*	*5*	*11*	*3*
Postcard (letter)	7	4	0	2	0	0
Supervisor	8	0	0	3	5	3
Home Office (telephone)	12	0	12	0	6	0
Other, e.g., computer analysis	5	2	3	0	0	0
H. Editing	*5*	*3*	*4*	*4*	*4*	*0*
What is done	2	1	1	1	1	0
Who does editing	2	1	2	1	2	0
What are instructions	2	1	1	2	1	0
I. Code building	*10*	*9*	*10*	*9*	*10*	*1*
Sample size and selection	3	3	3	2	2	0
Method	6	4	6	4	5	0
Responsibility for code	2	2	2	2	2	0
Checked by buyer's representative	1	0	1	1	1	1
J. Coding	*15*	*15*	*15*	*13*	*14*	*3*
Personnel (temp/perm)	2	2	2	2	2	0
Training	2	2	1	1	1	0
Instructions	2	2	2	1	1	0
Supervision (problem solving)	2	2	2	2	1	0
Qualifications of code supervisor	2	2	2	2	2	0
Method	2	1	2	1	2	0
Process of 'all other'	3	2	3	3	3	3
Physical layout	2	2	1	1	2	0
K. Coding control	*5*	*5*	*5*	*5*	*5*	*0*
Questionnaire identification (when)	2	1	2	2	2	0
Batch control form	5	5	5	3	5	0
L. Coding verification	*10*	*9*	*8*	*8*	*10*	*0*
Percentage	4	4	3	3	4	0
Who	2	2	2	2	1	0
Records	3	1	2	1	3	0
Action taken	2	2	1	2	2	0
M. Keypunching	*5*	*5*	*0*	*5*	*5*	*0*
Personnel	1	1	0	1	1	0
Layout	2	2	0	2	2	0
Supervision and control	3	2	0	2	3	0
N. Keypunch verification	*10*	*6*	*2*	*9*	*10*	*2*
Method	4	2	0	4	4	0
Proportion	4	4	2	4	4	2
Record of errors	3	0	0	1	3	0
O. Cleaning procedures	*10*	*10*	*7*	*0*	*10*	*0*
Whose responsibility	1	1	1	0	1	0
Illegal punch checks (blanks)	2	2	2	0	2	0
Logical consistency check	2	2	2	0	2	0

	Assigned values	Company A	B	C	D	E
Error correction procedure	5	5	2	0	5	0
Record of errors cleaned	2	1	0	0	2	0
P. Tabulation	15	15	8	7	14	6
Specifications	2	2	2	1	2	2
Equipment/personnel	3	3	0	0	3	0
Accuracy checks	10	10	5	5	8	3
Data storage	1	1	1	1	1	1
Q. Subjective	25	25	22	18	16	10
Staff capability	10	10	10	7	6	4
Physical equipment	5	5	2	3	5	1
General layout, flow and atmosphere	10	10	10	8	5	5
Total	200	168	164	153	136	42
General	30	30	27	22	18	13
Sampling and field	85	61	78	71	36	17
Coding and tabulating	85	77	59	60	82	12

Note: The contractor is held responsible for the whole job even if he subcontracts part of it. Even though the quality of the subcontracted work may be high, the prime contractor is given no credit for it unless his personnel were sufficiently involved in the subcontracted work to certify its quality.

The number of points in each subsection adds up to more than the total points assigned to that subsection. If the sum of points earned by a contractor is higher than the total assigned, he is awarded only the total assigned to that subsection.

quality and high costs usually go hand in hand, a research buyer may at times settle for less than the highest quality work. He should recognize the trade-off that he is making. Having decided on a specific level of research quality, he should invite tenders only from those contractors who can supply that level. With specific reference to the rating system, only contractors with comparable ratings (within a twenty point range) should be asked to bid on the same job.

Contractor operating procedures change through time – high quality operations may become lax, and low quality operations may improve. Evaluation must be viewed as a continuous process, with periodic re-evaluations. Only in this way can a system of evaluation stay current – and only a current evaluation system is useful to the research buyer.

4 G. Wills

Cost-Benefit Analysis of a Test Market

G. Wills, 'Cost-benefit analysis of a test market', *Effective Test Marketing*, revised version, B.I.M. Information Notes, 1968. First appeared in *Management Decision*, vol. 1, no. 1, 1967, pp. 17-21.

One of the most intractable problems facing marketing managements today is to know when to buy marketing research to enhance their understanding of the probability of success. Conversely, when will the expenditure and resultant delay outweigh the benefits from a reduction in uncertainty? Nowhere is this problem more keenly felt than in new product development.

Launching new products is often vastly expensive, and available evidence suggests that products fail more often than they succeed. However, well researched 'pilot' marketing and sequential launches give competition time to retaliate or imitate, thereby constituting risks of a different ilk. None the less, marketing managements are tending to carry out more and more test operations to attempt to assess the likely outcomes of broadscale operations.

This article provides an early report from part of a research program carried out at the University of Bradford into methods of marketing experimentation. It offers an integration of Bayesian decision theory and network analysis which, in conjunction with D.C.F. techniques, provide a powerful tool of cost/benefit analysis.

Classical test-marketing theory is based on the assumption that it is possible to identify a representative microcosm of a broadscale market, and use it as a laboratory.[1] In its simplest form, the test market will be x per cent of a total market, so broadscale sales forecasts can be computed simply by grossing-up from test results.

---

1. For a fuller development of classical theory see Wills and Hayhurst (1966), partially reprinted (1967). The original paper includes an exhaustive bibliography and abstract of test marketing literature.

Although a wealth of unpublished, and some recently published (Davis, 1964; Gold, 1964), evidence bears witness that no such laboratory has yet been located, there is a booming industry in Britain and North America in the sale of test marketing facilities. Each test area produces sales literature which purports to demonstrate its representativeness on whatever particular dimensions can be discovered which are indeed representative. However, we cannot normally expect the purveyors of such test facilities to say whether the dimensions are relevant.

In the face of such complexities, there are two major courses of action open to the marketing manager. Either to buy the standard test facilities, but to take the research results with a pinch of salt, or not to test market at all. The purpose of this article is to examine precisely how big or small a pinch of salt should be involved, and at what point the marketing manager can safely dispense with a test market rather than doing so out of desperation from previous experiences. The choice is now becoming more complicated since a third alternative, qualitative, course of action is emerging.

Qualitative Approaches

The blatantly unsatisfactory nature of the conventional test market as a truly scientific laboratory has led several researchers to rethink the laboratory approach. To get the bugs out of the marketing operation, the straightforward mechanical aspects of pilot-marketing can easily be taken care of by a sequential launch program. In contrast the predictive component cannot, without incurring considerable cost.

The new approach, which can be broadly described as qualitative, seeks to identify the determinants of buyer-response in the laboratory situation away from the test market. One direction currently being pursued is to seek a relationship between the results of product placement tests and eventual sales levels. A second[2] seeks to test market new products through mail

2. This approach is common to Jack Gold and the Research Programme in Marketing Experimentation at the University of Bradford. For a partial description of Gold's new method see the National Industrial Conference Board (1967).

order panels, or through direct mail promotion and severely limited distribution.

In both these approaches the researcher hopes to establish an understanding of the reasons why a buyer behaves in the way he/she does and that this will provide the basis for a quantitative assessment of the broadscale market before any national launch takes place.

However, significant results from these new directions do not seem imminent. Furthermore, they cannot meet the need of the marketing manager who has to rush his fences in order to beat his competitors. But what they can do, as can the decision theoretical approach outlined below, is take the cant out of the sales talk about test-marketing today, and hold out hope for more effective deployment of company resources.

What is Decision Theory?

The term decision theory represents a group of theories developed in their present form only in the past decade. They are prescriptive, which means that if the decision taker accepts the assumptions they make, he should adopt the course of action which appears as optimal. We are concerned with using these theories in order to decide which of a variety of possible courses of action to take when each possible course is shrouded in uncertainty. In particular should we test market our product, go ahead and launch it directly onto the broadscale market, or junk it. For each of these three possible courses of action, there will be outcomes or payoffs, which decision theory treats by means of what is termed a payoff-matrix.

The first published approach to this type of analysis of test-marketing in the U.K. was made recently by John Davis (1967). In the two matrices reproduced in Tables 1 and 2, he analyzed, against forecast, the level of profit and loss involved in actual market outcomes and the relative losses arising from taking the wrong decisions.

He concluded that computing these two matrices assists the manufacturer in the following way in deciding whether or not to test market.

If all the available evidence points very firmly to a level of forecast

Table 1
Absolute Levels of Profit and Loss*

Forecast sales ('000s cases)	Actual sales achieved ('000s cases)					
	100	120	140	160	180	200
100	−33					
120	−49	−17				
140(Ei)	−63	−31	0	6	13	19
160	−83	−45	−14	17	26	33
180	−91	−59	−28	3	35	44
200(En)	−103	−71	−40	−9	23	54

Table 2
Relative Losses Through Taking the Wrong Decision*

Forecast sales ('000s cases)	Actual sales achieved ('000s cases)					
	100	120	140	160	180	200
100	0	0	0	(−17)	(−35)	(−54)
120	0	0	0	(−17)	(−35)	(−54)
140(Ei)	0	0	0	11	22	35
160	−83	−45	−14	0	−9	−21
180	−91	−59	−28	−14	0	−10
200(En)	−103	−71	−40	−26	−12	0

*The manufacturer is assumed not to launch unless expected sales are at least Ei (break even).

(sales) far removed from Ei (break even) towards En, and the matrix shows this to be a profitable position, and is surrounded by profitable situations within all likely levels of expectations, then there is little point in test marketing, because a (broadscale) launch will yield at least some level of profitability.

The (relative loss) matrix also contributes to the solution of the problem of whether to test market or not, particularly where the expected forecast is near to En.

If the relative losses shown in the bottom right corner of this matrix are small compared with the absolute gains shown in the profit and loss matrix, then there will be little point in spending time and money to predict where one will sell in the right hand corner. In his numerical example, however, this is not the case. Deviations of actual sales from forecast can give rise to losses upwards from 25 per cent of potential profit. This, Davis suggests, may well make it 'less expensive to undertake test marketing in order to more closely define (the broadscale forecast of sales) than run the risk of greater losses through either over or under-estimating potential'.

This example brings us to the crux of the problem in test-marketing: *How much more accurate can our sales forecasts be made as a result of the conduct of a test market?* Clearly the answer depends on how certain we are before we test market, and how much credence we are prepared to give to the test market findings we obtain. I know no businessman who would take the results of a test market as gospel. I know surprisingly many who do not take them into account at all, even when they have spent considerable sums to collect them. I know even more who take decisions on the basis of an intuitive assessment of what they really mean – with a varying size pinch of salt depending on their past experience in a market.

The Bayesian Approach

We are, of course, talking about the subjective probabilities businessmen attach to various possible outcomes in launching a new product. It is a form of problem which has taxed the intellect of many over the ages, but of none with greater effect than the Rev. Thomas Bayes in the eighteenth century. During the past decade his work has been turned into a practical and operational approach to decision making under uncertainty (Schlaifer, 1959). His approach can be summarized in three main steps:

1. *Prior Analysis* involves choosing amongst alternative courses of action where no data exists for evaluation. The marketing manager is called upon to use his prior judgement (based on his experience and other research) to attribute probabilities to the range of alternatives occurring given each possible course of action. Payoffs reflect the expected financial value of each outcome deemed possible.

2. *Posterior Analysis* enables the marketing manager to inter-

pret data as it becomes available in order to revise his prior judgements.

3. *Preposterior Analysis* enables the marketing manager to evaluate the worth of additional information before he purchases it, in terms of its anticipated effect on reducing the costs associated with uncertainty. Further, this approach can be used to evaluate relative efficiencies of differing research plans and sample sizes. Preposterior analysis can also be extended to provide the means of pursuing an optimal present course of action where a sequential set of decisions are involved. It provides a way of interpreting the interaction of present decisions on future choices.

Whenever the time dimension is present in such analysis, the expected present value of the various courses of action must be arrived at by discounting from the expected future values. To take an example, a marketing course of action which yielded £100,000 over two years, half at the end of each year, for an expenditure of £75,000, could be compared with a similar operation which yielded only £25,000 at the end of year one and £75,000 at the end of year two. We assume that the cost of capital to our company is 10 per cent.[3]

		Operation 1	Operation 2
Cost of capital (per cent)		10	10
Cost of operation		£75,000	£75,000
Actual income:	Year 1	£50,000	£25,000
	Year 2	£50,000	£75,000
Discounted value of income:			
	Year 1	£45,500	£22,500
	Year 2	£41,500	£62,250
Present value of operation:		*£87,000*	*£84,750*

For the sake of simplicity, in the subsequent workings in this article all expected profits are shown discounted to the present (time period t).

3. The application of D.C.F. to marketing decisions is well treated in Winer (1966).

The specific pattern of network analysis known as the decision tree can fruitfully be employed in exposing the alternative courses of action open to marketing management and demonstrating the probabilities and expected values of each. Networks have been extensively used in project analysis, and were originally developed to hasten the U.S. missile programme. Their use in the form of decision trees is much more recent, and the application has usually been in terms of establishing new plant (Archibald and Villoria, 1967).

The New Products

Let us now examine two new products (A and B) which manufacturers have developed through the various stages of research up to and including a placement test with a sample of users. Neither product is going to make a millionaire of its developer overnight, but both are felt to have pleasant prospects of success, B more so than A. If it were a straightforward choice for a manufacturer between which to market and which not, B would be preferred. In Tables 3 and 4, marketing management has set out what it feels is the probability of each product achieving broad-

Table 3
Forecast Broadscale Brand Shares, Implicit Profit Levels, and Prior Probabilities of Achievement for Product A

Forecast broadscale brand share per cent	Implicit profit discounted to t	Probability of achievement	Profit consequences
(i)	(ii)	(iii)	(ii) × (iii)
15 (BS_1)	£8m.	0·2	£1·6m.
10 (BS_2)	£2m.	0·4	£0·8m.
5 (BS_3)	− £4·3m.	0·4	− £1·72m.

Expected value of introduction of Product A without test market.......................... £0·68m.

Expected value of perfect information: £1·72m.

Table 4

Forecast Broadscale Brand Shares, Implicit Profit Levels, and Prior Probabilities of Achievement for Product B

Forecast broadscale brand share per cent	Implicit profit discounted to t	Probability of achievement	Profit consequences
(i)	(ii)	(iii)	(ii) × (iii)
15 (BS_1)	£30m.	0·3	£9m.
10 (BS_2)	£12m.	0·5	£6m.
5 (BS_3)	−£23m.	0·2	−£4·6m.

Expected value of introduction of Product B without test market.......................... £10·4m.

Expected value of perfect information: £4·6m.

scale market shares of 15, 10 and 5 per cent. For the sake of this illustration these are deemed the only possible outcomes, although it will be readily appreciated that the method could evaluate any share from 0 to 100 per cent.

On the assumption that such shares are rapidly obtained, and maintained throughout the products' lives ($t + n$ months if test marketed for six months, $t + (n − 3)$ if launched broadscale after a three month sell-in period) the accountants have calculated the present value of profits accruing. It will be seen that product B will make a greater loss if it gains only 5 per cent of the broadscale market than A, but a substantially greater profit if it gains 15 per cent. Overall, the expected value of immediately introducing product A is £0·68m. and of product B, £10·4m., values obtained by summing the profit consequences of each level.

But what would be the expected value of perfect information for each new product to marketing management?

With product A, marketing management could avoid launching if it knew a 5 per cent broadscale share would materialize, and could therefore save £1·72m. For product B, the similar saving would be £4·6m. Hence under no circumstances should marketing management contemplate spending sums exceeding £1·72m. for product A, or £4·6m. for product B. For lesser sums than these, however, marketing management may be able to obtain test marketing information which could improve on the expected values of introduction given in Tables 3 and 4.

How Credible are Test Marketing Results?

In Table 5, the marketing manager has set down what he considers to be the probabilities that if he carried out a test market, tests shares would materialize if the true outcome was reflected in the broadscale shares shown. We have assumed once again that only three levels of sustained test market are possible, but the method can of course deal with any number. This particular marketing manager has had extensive experience of test marketing, and is prepared to spend £250,000 on a six-month test market. With such an expenditure, he believes the probabilities shown in Table 5 to be right.

Table 5
Probabilities of Test Market Penetration in the Light of Given Broadscale Brand Shares

	Sustained test market penetration		
Broadscale brand share per cent	over 15% (TS$_1$)	10–15% (TS$_2$)	below 10% (TS$_3$)
15 (BS$_1$)	0·9	0·05	0·05
10 (BS$_2$)	0·1	0·8	0·1
5 (BS$_3$)	0·0	0·15	0·85

These probabilities represent the size of the pinch of salt for the particular marketing manager we are working with. They indicate the extent to which he feels that if the broadscale shares are a true state of nature, test market results as shown will occur. Many would not be prepared to formulate so bold a matrix of probabilities on the basis of their understanding of test markets in the past. Apart from the representativeness of data from a test area of the true state of a broadscale market, the whole armoury of potential interviewer, coding and tabulating errors must be taken into account at this stage, if they occur, in the collection of test marketing data. Brown (1962) has suggested a method of credence analysis which is appropriate.

Bass (1963), in one of the earliest papers examining the use of decision theory in marketing research expenditures, suggested a much less optimistic matrix than that given in Table 5. He placed no greater reliance on test data accurately reflecting a true state of nature in a broadscale market than $0 \cdot 6$ probability where the broadscale figure was 10 per cent. (The reader could well set out his own probabilities in Table 5 and make the subsequent workings, in the light of his own experience in his own markets.)

The choice of the maximum credibility for test marketing results in terms of their ability to reflect true states of nature in the broadscale market has been deliberately made here to demonstrate the maximum likely value in the most favourable circumstances after an investment of £$0 \cdot 25$m. on the test.

Likelihood of joint occurrence and posterior probabilities

The next computational stage required yields the probabilities as shown now (at time *t*) of the joint occurrence of given test and broadscale shares. From these the posterior probabilities are calculated. The results are given in Tables 6 and 7 for products A and B.

The probabilities of joint occurrence are the product of the prior probability and the conditional probability. Hence, in Table 6, $0 \cdot 18$ probability of the joint occurrence (TS_1 and BS_1) is the product of $0 \cdot 2$ (BS_1 Table 3) and $0 \cdot 9$ (TS_1/BS_1 Table 5). The marginal totals are equal to the prior probabilities in Table 3.

Posterior probabilities are then computed by dividing each probability of joint occurrence by the column totals, i.e. the likelihood of the test market brand shares materializing. In Table 6, posterior probability $0 \cdot 818$ (BS_1/TS_1) is the outcome of:

$$\frac{0 \cdot 18 \ (BS_1 \text{ and } TS_1)}{0 \cdot 22 \ (\sum TS_1)}.$$

Expected Value of Information

We have already noted that the expected value of perfect information would be saving the losses which would be incurred if BS_3

97

materialized for either product A or B. These were £1·72m. for product A and £4·6m. for product B. The final computations are designed to establish whether the discounted value now (at time t) of test market information, is increased to a greater extent than the £0·25m. the test market will cost.

Posterior and preposterior analyses, which yield this information, are demonstrated in Tables 7 and 9. Table 7 for product A shows an increased value of introduction now, if test market data is acquired, of £1·983m. − £0·68m. = £1·303m. at a cost of £0·25m. If we abide by the decision rules implicit in our analysis then the test market should be undertaken.

For product B, Table 9 shows an increased value of introduction with test market information of £13·27m. − £10·4m. = £2·87m. Once again, if the probabilities provided in Table 5 were credible for a test marketing cost of £0·25m., a test would clearly be optimal.

Tables 7 and 9 are derived by posterior and preposterior analyses, which can be illustrated as follows in Table 7.

Column (i): £6·544m. = 0·818 (posterior probability Table 6, BS_1/TS_1) × £8m. (implicit profit of BS_1 Table 3)

likewise, columns (ii) and (iii). Column (iv) is the sum of the implicit profits of any test market share being achieved. When this is multiplied by the probabilities (derived from Table 6 as $\sum TS_1$ etc.) it provides the profit consequences which when the optimal course in each case is summed, indicates the expected value of introducing product A with test market information. For each test market share observed, marketing management will have the option of continuing or junking the product. If TS_3 materializes the loss of £3·337m. will be avoided in favour of junking product A. With TS_1 and TS_2, however, broadscale marketing would go ahead.

Figure 1 uses a decision tree to describe the alternative courses of action, and their profit consequences, for product B. This is a more comprehensible version of the data given in Tables 8 and 9.

Table 6

Product A

Broadscale brand shares	Probability of joint occurrence of test and broadscale brand shares			Marginal total	Posterior probabilities taking cognizance of test data		
	TS_1	TS_2	TS_3		TS_1	TS_2	TS_3
BS_1	0·18	0·01	0·01	0·2	0·818	0·026	0·026
BS_2	0·04	0·32	0·04	0·4	0·182	0·820	0·102
BS_3	0·0	0·06	0·34	0·4	0·0	0·154	0·872
	0·22	0·39	0·39	1·0			

Table 7

Posterior and Preposterior Analysis of Expected Profits on Product A in the Light of Given Test Market Shares (£m.)

	Posterior			Preposterior		
Observed test brand share	BS_1	BS_2	BS_3	Implicit Profit	Probability	Profit consequences
	(i)	(ii)	(iii)	(iv)	(v)	(iv)×(v)
TS_1	6·544	0·364	0·0	6·908	0·22	1·520
TS_2	0·208	1·640	—0·662	1·186	0·39	0·463
TS_3	0·208	0·204	—3·749	—3·337	0·39	0·0

Expected value of introducing Product A after test market research ....£1·983m.

Conclusions

Some critics of the Bayesian approach to decision theory have suggested that it oversimplifies the decision situation. Certainly the illustration given here oversimplifies the situation in relation to a test market. However, it is my contention that formalizing the process of assigning probabilities and of computing the likely

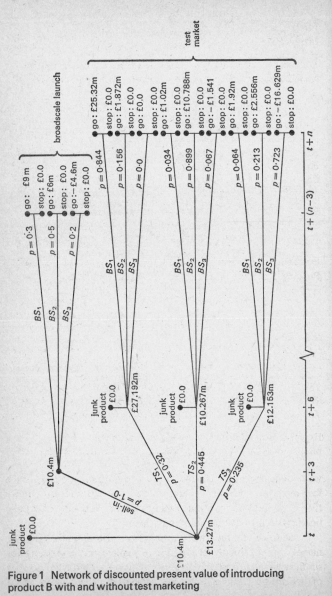

Figure 1 Network of discounted present value of introducing product B with and without test marketing

Table 8

Product B

Broadscale brand shares	Probability of joint occurrence of test and broadscale brand shares			Marginal total	Posterior probabilities taking cognizance of test data		
	TS_1	TS_2	TS_3		TS_1	TS_2	TS_3
BS_1	0·27	0·015	0·015	0·3	0·844	0·034	0·064
BS_2	0·05	0·4	0·05	0·5	0·156	0·899	0·213
BS_3	0·0	0·03	0·17	0·2	0·0	0·067	0·723
	0·32	0·445	0·235	1·0			

Table 9

Posterior and Preposterior Analysis of Expected Profits on Product B in the Light of Given Test Market Shares (£m.)

	Posterior				Preposterior	
Observed test brand share	BS_1	BS_2	BS_3	Implicit Profit	Probability	Profit consequences
	(i)	(ii)	(iii)	(iv)	(v)	(iv)×(v)
TS_1	25·32	1·872	0·0	27·192	0·320	8·701
TS_2	1·02	10·788	−1·541	10·267	0·445	4·569
TS_3	1·92	2·556	−16·629	−12·153	0·235	0·0

Expected value of introducing Product B after test
market research ....£13·270m.

value of any research undertaken can do nothing but good in the face of the complexities inherent in test marketing. Furthermore the method allows for a much more substantial degree of sophistication than I have demonstrated here.

In addition to the two courses of action deemed possible, namely going directly broadscale as against test marketing for six months at a cost of £0·25m., many other possible courses of action can, and should, be evaluated. The possibility of sequential regional launches must be included, so too must various levels of test marketing activity. There will be a research expenditure, for instance, which gives us the optimum increase in the expected value of introducing a product. There is also, of course, the possibility of modifying the product to enhance the probability of success after test results begin to emerge.

In all its sophistication, therefore, such an approach to evaluating additional information will require using computers. Indeed, the most desirable analysis will look at the whole life cycle of a proposed new product and discount the expected values of various courses of action to meaningful time intervals throughout its life.

Part of the current programme of research in marketing experimentation at the University of Bradford, involves constructing such a model on the basis of company data. As currently presented, the application of Bayesian decision theory, allied to D.C.F. and network analysis, offers marketing management an opportunity to compare the benefits of test marketing against its cost. This is accomplished by comparing the discounted expected values of the various courses of action open. In so doing it affords the opportunity for marketing management to formally recognize the inability of test marketing techniques to afford absolute predictability of the broadscale outcome of any marketing mix. It also offers the opportunity of evaluating the optimum research expenditure in any given situation once the marketing manager has indicated how he would interpret any results he received.

Finally, by tying the analysis of research expenditure in closely with the use made of research data, a better understanding of each other's standpoint emerges for both marketing executives and researchers.

References
ARCHIBALD, R. D., and VILLORIA, R. L. (1967), *Network-Based Management Systems*, Wiley, pp. 330–67.
BASS, F. M. (1963), 'Marketing research expenditures: a decision model', *Journal of Business*, vol. 36, pp. 77–90. Reprinted in E. A. PESSEMIER, *New Product Decisions*, McGraw-Hill, 1966, pp. 119–40.
BROWN, R. (1962), 'Measuring uncertainty in business investigations', *Journal of Management Studies*, vol. 1, no. 2, pp. 143–63.

DAVIS, E. J. (1964), 'Test marketing: an examination of sales patterns found during forty-four recent tests', *Research in Marketing*, Market Research Society.

DAVIS, E. J. (1967), 'Test marketing – or pilot marketing', Paper presented to graduate marketing students at the University of Bradford.

GOLD, J. A. (1964), 'Testing test market predictions', *Journal of Marketing Research*, vol. 1, pp. 8–16.

National Industrial Conference Board (1967), 'Market testing consumer products', NICB. New York, pp. 77–9.

SCHLAIFER, R. (1959), *Probability and Statistics for Business Decisions*, McGraw-Hill.

WILLS, G., and HAYHURST, R. (1966), 'Is there a future for test-marketing as we know it?', Market Research Society Seminar on Test Marketing.

WILLS, G. and HAYHURST, R. (1967), 'Are test markets necessary?', *Advertising and Marketing*, vol. 3.

WINER, L. (1966), 'A profit-orientated decision system', *Journal of Marketing*, vol. 30, pp. 38–44.

5 V. E. Harder and F. R. Lindell

Using PERT in Marketing Research

V. E. Harder and F. R. Lindell, 'Using PERT in marketing research', *Business Horizons*, vol. 9, 1966, pp. 97–102.

The basic methodological aspects of marketing research are readily available. Any good marketing research text, for example, offers a 'list' of items that must be investigated if one is to properly research a given basic marketing objective. When a researcher tries to use this list, however, certain practical problems face him.

To structure the problems in a meaningful way, the following question is posed: How can a marketing department (or investigator) provide systematic order to the research methodology when determining the feasibility of producing and marketing a new product? How well that question is answered depends upon how well the department or investigator determines:

1. The areas (task objectives) to be researched.
2. The sequence of interrelationships of the areas.
3. The cost of researching each area.
4. The time schedule for researching each area.

A workable body of methodology exists whereby one can determine the areas to be researched. The other aspects of the marketing research program, however, are not yet as well set forth in the literature. The element lacking is a means for integrating the various methodological aspects of the research program into some sort of system or network[1] that allows for control of:

(a) *When* (in terms of time) *what* (the task objectives) shall be done by *whom* (in terms of resources).
(b) *When* (in terms of quality) *what* (the task objectives) is complete.

1. For a general discussion of systems theory in business, see Johnson *et al*. (1963).

Controls are necessary if one wants to make efficient allocation of resources, funds, and so on to the various task objectives. In addition, feedback is needed to permit measurement of performance against the task objectives, budget allocations, and time allocations. Thus, a desirable addition to existing marketing research methodology would be a technique that allows the integration of sequence, time, and feedback with the various task objectives. The result would be a system or network of established schedules for the marketing research program. Such a technique already exists – PERT (Program Evaluation and Review Technique). The purpose of this article, therefore, is to illustrate how PERT can be used in marketing research as a technique to integrate the various task objectives into a network or system. Selections can be made from many marketing objectives – for example, determination of the feasibility of moving into a new market or new area with an existing product, or attempting to increase share of market. The selection of a particular marketing objective for illustration and elaboration in this article is, therefore, purely a device of convenience in order to make the discussion more meaningful.

The Potential of PERT

PERT is based on the concept that in any program there are three variables: time, resources, and technical performance (United States Air Force, 1963, p.I-I). Since its inception by the armed services (during the development of the Polaris missile), the technique has won prominence as a useful tool in development of prototype items such as ships, airplanes, and missiles. Much credit has been given PERT for the successful completion, in compliance with an established schedule, of many production items. If PERT can be successfully used as a technique in the area of production, then such a technique should offer potential for similar use in marketing research – since the principal difference is mainly the form of the end product.

Successful use of this method depends upon integration of the various research task objectives into a sequential system. The investigator must arrange the task objectives into a sequential order – into a network. To illustrate the mechanics of this network-building procedure, a PERT program for a hypothetical product is used in this article. The objective is to build a network of task objectives (in sequence) that are necessary in evaluating the feasibility of producing and marketing a new product. After the mechanics for using the technique have been explained, it will then be possible to visualize how portions of the network or system can be eliminated and other portions expanded to adapt the procedures to studies with varying degrees of complexity.

The Mechanics

Before detailed PERT networks can be developed, a general program plan must be devised that consists of the large and most important phases of the marketing study. These broad areas are set up schematically in Figure 1, which is a broad picture of the scope, sequence, and anticipated schedule for completion of the study. More detailed supplementary PERT programs are then designed for each of the broad phases. For the moment, however, the implications and mechanics of the PERT program are limited to the general program as illustrated in the figure.

The arrows on the joining lines (called activity lines) indicate the sequence required for satisfactory completion of the study. Boxes (or circles, or triangles, or the like) indicate events – the culmination of activities. As the chart indicates, it is not necessary to complete all events in the order shown. For example, acquiring options on raw materials does not constrain the completion of the patent requirements event. Therefore, no activity arrow is shown between events III and IV. Instead, event II (the availability of financing) is shown – with an activity arrow – as governing the completion of event IV. The same is true of event V, since the acquisition of options on neither raw materials nor patent rights restrains the geological study.

Two phases of the market study could be conducted simultaneously. Activity arrows from events VII through X indicate the comprehensive path for conducting the product-market study. Results of the preliminary market study should reveal the feasibility of conducting a preliminary production study. Should the results of event VIII indicate that the item could be produced at a reasonable price, the signal would be given for a more comprehensive market review. The feasibility of investing the money required for a full-scale production study would be based upon the outcome of event IX.

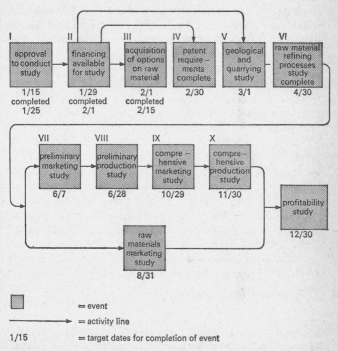

Figure 1   General P E R T program for a new-product study

While the product study is being conducted, it is possible to study the marketing of other materials obtained from the ore deposit. Such simultaneous study could include the feasibility of selling by-products from refining processes or raw materials in pit-run condition. This market study could be conducted with two possible end goals under consideration. Should the product study look promising, income could result not only from marketing the finished goods, but also from marketing various extracted raw materials or various refined by-products or both. Since simultaneous market studies of this type, or others which involve one or more unrelated products, do not depend upon the outcome of each other, they are graphically shown by parallel activity lines – such as that shown for event XI in Figure 1.

Completion of both the product study and the raw materials study is shown as a constraint on completion of the profitability study. This is the case because the former would provide sufficient information to consider alternate courses of action before making final recommendations.

Other information of value to management is readily available from Figure 1. The dates immediately below each event box indicate the desired schedule date for completion. Events I, II, and III are shown as having already been completed (with cross-hatched lines). The date of completion is shown below the schedule dates. Thus, managers are able to evaluate quickly whether the program can be expected to remain on the proposed schedule. Event I was finished ten days later than originally planned. In an attempt to prevent the whole study from lagging behind, however, financing (event II) was provided more rapidly than originally anticipated. Although event II was only two days late, event III slid fourteen days beyond the scheduled date. Since event III does not constrain any downstream activity, a delay at this point will not affect other portions of the study.

Suppose management is reviewing this chart on 15 March. Since events IV and V are scheduled for completion on 30 February and 1 March respectively, visual inspection immediately reveals that events IV and V are both behind schedule. Concern over the delay should be concentrated on event V because it has direct impact on the proposed schedule dates for all other portions of the study.

Detailed planning

Once the PERT chart for the broad plan is completed, the investigator then prepares detailed charts for each activity line shown on the master plan. As an example, the required activities between events VI and VII are portrayed in Figure 2. In this chart the various activities that must be conducted to complete the preliminary market study are shown.

Figure 2 provides at a glance an immediate picture of the interdependency between events. For example, the activity line tying events VII–1 and VII–2 indicates the need for knowledge of where products will be moved before the appropriate channels of distribution can be properly evaluated. The sequencing of events VII–6 and VII–7 points out the importance of evaluating competitive reaction before the annual sales can be intelligently evaluated for purposes of completing the necessary accounting studies.

Location of all the events on the chart is such that the sequence of completion for a well-conducted study is shown. Figure 2 is only a suggested format; for most studies, a more complete and detailed description would be desirable.

More information possibilities

A PERT chart can be expanded to provide marketing management with useful tools in addition to the descriptive pictures of the sequencing of events. As an example, consider the activity line in Figure 2 between events VI and VII–9. Here a description of the activity being conducted is given below the line, which in this case covers the approximation of production costs. Above the line and within parentheses is the number 2, which in this example denotes the number of employees involved with this phase of the program. The number could be altered to show man-hours, days, weeks, or even the name of the responsible individual.

Financial information pertaining to each phase of a study can also be shown on the chart. The amounts shown in Figure 2 are in the form of budget estimates, established before the study started, to serve as a guide for the responsible individual. By adding a budget figure for each activity, it is possible to visualize the way the expenses are allocated; this in turn facilitates the development of a realistic total budget for the complete study. If, upon completion of each phase of the study, the actual cost is entered on the chart, the marketing department has a ready reference of expenditures in relation to allocated budget. This systematic feedback permits management to detect problem areas as they occur. This accessibility to allocation and costs also facilitates the control function, which management must exercise in bringing the study to a successful culmination.

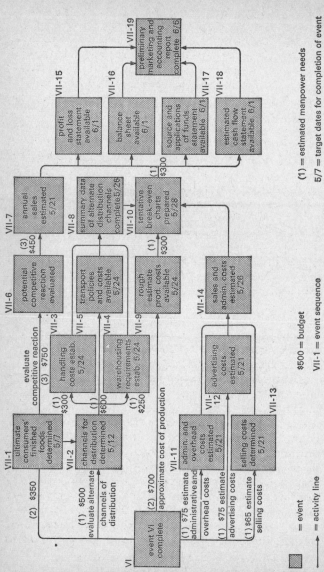

Figure 2 The achievement of event VII (from Figure 1)

110

PERT provides the marketing department of any firm or investigator with a useful tool for planning studies of varying degrees of complexity. In addition to providing a pictorial network of the method for conducting the study, this approach offers a versatile tool for evaluating the status of a program at any time. A well-organized and well-maintained PERT chart can provide rapid answers (feedback) pertaining to schedule status, financial position, and expenditure of manpower.

Only the most basic and elementary PERT principles have been set forth in this article – deliberately, so that the discussion is not cluttered with technical jargon. The PERT technique has been refined to the point where complex, specialized 'language' of application can be used:[2] likewise, the technique has been the springboard to more complex systems, such as CPA (critical path analysis).[3] One need not learn all the technical language in order to apply the PERT technique, although some, such as that set forth in this article, is helpful.

The charts used in this article have likewise been kept relatively simple. The more complex and/or detailed the marketing study, the more complex and detailed must be the charts (system). And the more complex the system, the greater the need for a technical language. Thus, the basic PERT concept is flexible and easily adapted to expansion or reduction to meet specific marketing task requirements, but, as expansion takes place, the need for a larger technical vocabulary is more pressing.

Success in the use of the PERT technique depends not so much upon learning the mechanics as upon achieving a state of mind. In other words, PERT is based on a concept – the concept of *integrating*. One can integrate only sequence (first this, then that), or cost (budget, manpower, and so on), or time (this by such-and-such a time, that by so much later than this). Or, one can integrate the several variables simultaneously – probably the more desirable objective. The PERT technique has already been well crystalized with a language to facilitate its use. Thus, its adaptation to marketing research problems should be fairly simple – if one does not let himself become cowed by the technical sophistication and complex jargon which is available but not necessary to its

2. See, for example, Federal Electric Corporation (1963).
3. See, for example, Wong (1964) or Levy *et al*. (1963).

successful application. It can be used in simple format; it is so used. Most important of all, it is and can be used effectively in marketing research.

References

FEDERAL ELECTRIC CORPORATION (1963), *A Programmed Introduction to* PERT, Wiley.

JOHNSON, R. A., KAST, F. E., and ROSENZWEIG, J. E. (1963), *The Theory and Management of Systems*, McGraw-Hill.

LEVY, F. K., THOMPSON, G. L., and WIEST, J. D. (1963), 'The ABCs of the critical path method', *Harvard Business Review*, vol. 41, pp. 98–108.

United States Air Force (1963), PERT-*Time System Description Manual*, vol. 1.

WONG, Y. (1964), 'Critical path analysis for new product planning', *Journal of Marketing*, vol. 28, pp. 53–9.

6 A. B. Blankenship and J. B. Doyle

Organization of the Marketing Research Activity

Excerpt from A. B. Blankenship and J. B. Doyle, *Marketing Research Management*, American Management Association, 1966, pp. 42–61.

The organization is the backbone of marketing research; sound organization is as important to any corporate operation as bone structure in an animal. Just as poor bone structure can make an organism ineffectual or even lead to its destruction, so it is with organization of the research group.

Unless the organization is properly constructed, it will not allow for the right job functions. It will not be properly staffed to handle marketing research effectively. It will not be useful. It will make few or no contributions to the improvement of marketing, its overall objective.

Organization Structure as Affected by Research Activity Requirements

Because research work takes so many various forms and pursues so many diverse activities, we are not surprised to find that the organization structure of the manufacturer's research department and that of the research firm are necessarily quite dissimilar. Ford Motor Company, as well as other manufacturing firms of like size, must carry out many different kinds of research yet cannot afford the facilities to provide all of them on its own. Its research department needs are centered around a research and planning group with marketing orientation. It must buy processing from some outside source.

A research firm such as National Analysts, on the other hand, must be able to turn out the complete product, including processing, if it is to meet its buyer's needs. Its organization structure, of course, reflects the fact that its activities must cover the entire range of research from the construction of questionnaires to the processing of replies and other data collected. The structure of the two types of research groups varies also according to the nature and use of the data they generate and the breadth of the research they carry on, as we shall see.

Nature and use of data generated

The nature and use of the data generated by research show considerable variation from one manufacturing firm to another. One firm will be primarily interested in having marketing research contribute to the activities of its technical research and development group by consumer testing of potential products; for example, a tobacco company which had long ignored marketing research turned to it for help when it became convinced that the cancer scare meant it should look for product diversification. In that firm the marketing research manager reports to the technical research group, and his major contribution is to new product development and testing.

Another company will want a small marketing research group that handles only sales analysis. One dairy, operating in several cities, wants only this sort of contribution. Its research is really a sales analysis department, analyzing sales by type of product, by store type, by customer location, by socio-economic group and by season.

A third company will want to make the broadest possible use of its marketing research group, letting it contribute wherever it can to help improve marketing efficiency and even to help nonmarketing departments when it can do so profitably. This attitude marks the marketing-mature firm which thoroughly accepts the marketing concept and depends heavily on research for guidance in its behavior. The Scott Paper Company is a good example.

Each concept of the nature and use of the data generated has somewhat different implications for the organization of the manufacturer's research department.[1] The work of the department that is, dictates its organization structure.

But now let us consider the research firm to see how its structure differs from that of the manufacturer. If its purpose is to

1. An interesting discussion of this point can be found in American Management Association (1960, see especially pp. 6 and 7).

operate in one small area – such as measuring television audiences – certain organization practices are dictated so that processing can be set up efficiently. It will have units, separately organized and managed, to handle field work, coding, and data processing, for instance. If it decides that it also needs 'presenters' – executives who review and stress the implications of data in group meetings with clients – another layering of the organization is necessary. If it decides that it will handle only processing, it has no need for analysts. But when the custom-tailored research end of C. E. Hooper, Inc., decided to write interpretive reports for clients who wanted them, it had to staff for the new function, and its organization was changed accordingly.

Another aspect of the data generated in the nonresearch firm (the advertiser medium, advertising agency, retailer, and so on) is whether its research department is to be oriented primarily toward problem-solving research or toward conducting research for long-range policies and planning. The two approaches call for somewhat different organization structures. In the former the department will have to be staffed primarily with technicians, and the research manager may establish a project director type of organization in which the technicians simply accept problem assignments and see that they are executed competently. Since the emphasis of the latter type of department is on the long range, it must stress a marketing orientation, creativity, and breadth of vision. These requirements indicate a marketing-oriented generalist and could compel the manager to set up a staff of researchers, each of whom is responsible for research among a group of brands, augmented by some full-time consultants to provide creative guidance in psychology (or social science generally), statistics, and so on.

Breadth of research

Breadth of research varies considerably from one company to another and has a definite influence on the structure of the research organization. Procter & Gamble has many more individual products and product categories than Lehn & Fink, for instance. Audits & Surveys (which offers store audits and custom-tailored consumer studies) handles many more kinds of studies than does American Research Bureau (which specializes in audience measurement). The organization of the research group in each of these four companies reflects the quantity and areas of their operations. As the breadth of research in a company increases, we find an organizational demand for more specialists, either by brand or by technique. Audits & Surveys must have operating heads of many specialized kinds of technical groups within its shop. American Research Bureau can specialize in each stage of processing, since its product is a continuing, repetitive one.

Company Organization

The over-all corporate organization is often paralleled in the structure of the research department. General Foods Ltd is organized for marketing along brand lines and has a brand research management setup; that is, its researchers are assigned responsibility for individual brands. The typical advertising agency's research department has a copy research division, a media research division, or some other division paralleling departmental structure elsewhere.

If a company's research operation (we are not now discussing the research firm) has been established for many years, its structure is likely to be firmly entrenched. It is usually sound, but we sometimes find that it has evolved because of the dominance of one or two top managers whose careers are approaching an end. The research and marketing managers should review critically any historical influence upon the department's organization and judge whether it is proper. If they discover an imbalance, they must take steps to correct it.

The executive to whom the research manager reports also influences organization. In one sense he is the most important influence, for it is he who has to agree (or disagree) with the organizational form recommended by his subordinate. The strengths, weaknesses, and predispositions of the superior influence his reaction to the organizational format suggested by the manager.

The research manager must go through several successive steps in organizing his operation: defining its philosophy, determining its major functions, fixing its basic form of organization, deciding its degree of centralization or decentralization, and creating the necessary special facilities. The rest of this chapter discusses these steps in detail.

Defining the Research Philosophy

Basically, the best research philosophy is to operate in such a way as to provide management or customer with the finest possible research at the lowest possible cost. This statement contains many hidden implications of a twofold nature: one concerns the research manager's responsibility to his management or customer, the other his responsibility to the whole field of marketing research.

The research manager should be marketing-oriented if he is to do the best possible work. The only excuse for marketing research is to help improve marketing. If he is incapable of designing or conducting research which helps, at least partly, to achieve this, he is performing no conceivably useful service. One marketing research manager, whose work was primarily in the field of medicine cabinet products, recently suggested to his management a study to determine which products could and which could not be stored in a normal-size medicine cabinet. He showed little appreciation of practical marketing problems; this sort of study might make a lot of sense for new products, but it was completely valueless for existing products, since any change in size to fit a medicine chest might well dispel the consumers' favorable reaction to them. Furthermore, consumer studies had yielded no clue that people were objecting to size.

Also implied in this basic research philosophy is practicality. The research manager must stress results rather than techniques. He owes it to his customer or management. In the past he was often drawn from a speciality background: psychology, sociology, statistics, or survey research. His orientation was toward technique, and he was little concerned with being practical. As his function grew in importance, it came to need a practical manager, not a theoretical one.

Practicality is beneficial in other ways, too. A completely defensible in-home consumer product test, with five hundred cases, may be priced at $9000. But if the brand cannot afford such an expensive consumer test, the research manager who insists on maintaining high standards instead of seeing what he can do for a more restricted budget simply is not being practical. Not every study can be letter-perfect.

Our simple statement of a research philosophy also implies service from the manager. Wherever his function is located, he must remember that the only reason it exists is to provide service. The reputation of a service function is based upon day-to-day activities – the small, time-consuming, often dull projects – and not just upon the glamorous, intriguing, challenging major undertakings. Providing good service requires constant vigilance; it is not a 'sometime thing'. It is part of the built-in implications of the research philosophy.

Recently a research buyer was dealing with a supplier which did not meet its time commitments. Its contact executive was chided, gently but positively, for the delay. He took a casual view of the entire affair and showed no understanding that the lateness was causing his client considerable pain. Nothing could shake him from this nonchalant attitude. While his delivered project was sound, his firm is no longer a source for the buyer.

The research manager must be ethical in representing the interests of his management or customer. This is so obvious that it seems foolish to reiterate it, but too many researchers are loose in their talk and reveal competitive secrets. Worse, we hear of cases in which a buyer demands kick-backs from his suppliers or a supplier offers such a bribe to a buyer.

A less obvious implication of this stated philosophy is that the marketing research manager also has a professional responsibility. While his primary responsibility is to his company, he cannot operate in splendid isolation. Regardless of whether his management or his customers appreciate his problems, it is his professional responsibility to keep up with what is going on in his field, with new developments, new techniques.

Further, he must make sure that whatever research he designs, buys, or conducts is of the highest possible quality within budgetary limits. If these restrict the quality of the research, he must point them out, even though his doing so may not always be appreciated.

This last point raises an interesting question: what should he do if *ordered* by his management to handle a study in a particular way, even after he has made known all his objections to it? Or if his customer tells him he can either do the study the customer's way or some other firm will get the work? He doesn't have to resign his job or to forgo handling the study. He would be wrong to do either, for he then acknowledges that he has lost the war; he will never have another chance to overcome the opposing arguments and viewpoint. Instead, he should carry out the research in the manner directed but place it on record that in his opinion it is wrong. Such a statement should also be made in his report, so that it cannot be misused – that is, with the implication that the method has the blessing of the research manager or research firm.

Determining the Major Functions of Research

If we are ever to arrive at a workable list of the functions of the research department, we must first spell out clearly and distinctly its authorities and responsibilities. This statement is true equally of manufacturers, advertising media, agencies, and research firms.

Let's dispose quickly of this authority–responsibility discussion. If marketing research is to be well handled within the company, then a special department should be given *complete* responsibility for it and sufficient authority to implement the necessary actions to fulfill it. This means that it is the sole group responsible for developing, carrying on, and interpreting research within the firm. No compromise is possible without weakening its work. The delegation of the necessary authority from top management means that the research department alone is authorized to develop and submit research plans, to deal with, recommend, and perhaps select research sources, to spend research funds, to employ research personnel, to retain research consultants, and the like.

Again, however, the manager must be practical. He must remember that he cannot win all his points overnight. He must be willing to play a waiting game, to keep coming back to his management for support on some of his philosophy which it does not at first accept.

Putting together a list of research functions for any particular company is not simple. It isn't easy even to define the term 'function'. An inadequate synonym is 'job'. Our question then is, how can the jobs or tasks of the marketing research department be listed? They fall into three categories: the 'housekeeping' functions common to all parts of business, the types of research to be undertaken, and the administrative functions peculiar to research. Our discussion ignores 'housekeeping', since information on it is available from any general text on management.

The manager should determine the major types of research to be undertaken by his group. We cannot spell out all the possibilities, since they vary considerably among the many companies. However, the latest American Marketing Association study of marketing research lists some forty-three functions under four broad headings: market and sales research, product research, business economics, and advertising research (Twedt, 1963, see esp. pp. 41–4). This same study provides a few clues as to how functions vary by the position of a company within the marketing scene. Unfortunately it completely excludes marketing research firms.

The large manufacturer's research department has the broadest scope of activity. Procter & Gamble performs many more kinds of studies than the research department of an advertising medium, an agency, or even a research firm. While a typical advertising agency's research department performs almost every kind of research activity less often than a typical manufacturer's, it does more in media research. The advertising medium's research group centers its efforts on media research, development of market potentials, market share analysis, determination of market characteristics, and sales analysis. While these generalizations scarcely help us to write a list of the types of research called for in a specific company, they at least stimulate thinking about what a research department should be doing.

Another important aspect of responsibility is administrative in nature. Is the research management expected to develop research programs? In most cases the answer is yes, but we find occasionally a research group with an established routine which wants no help at all from its research management.

An expanding company that is just organizing a marketing research department may have very different requirements. The newly appointed manager may be asked to recommend an overall program. For instance, one company was expanding from the industrial field to the consumer, and its newly appointed marketing research manager for consumer goods recommended and obtained approval for Nielsen service that matched, in cost, the company's total annual spending on its industrial marketing research.

The marketing research group is usually expected to handle all its own administrative details. This means the manager must guarantee that his department's designs fall within his company's own and overall professional requirements. It means further that his department maintains control over all aspects of a study or facility. About control, which is the essence of management, we shall have much more to say.

Interpretation and communication of results are highly serious functions of the research department. No one else, no other group within the firm, should ever be permitted to take on these functions. They are so important, so easily distorted or minimized that they are crucial.

The research department has access to many data, some deliberately sought, others flowing in unsolicited. The marketing research groups of the advertiser and its agency are barraged with data about markets and media and with studies showing relative brand standing within specific product fields. By being sensitive to management needs, the research groups can be surprisingly helpful in circulating these and other secondary data. Articles or comments on population trends, on findings of experimental advertising research, and on the business climate may be of great interest to marketing and top management. Such communications are good internal public relations, too.

Organization Within the Group

The market research group can be organized in five ways: by the 'processing' of research, by its application, by brand, by other methods, or by various combinations of these four ways.

The processing organization

The main function of the research group which is organized along processing lines is to provide processed data to its customers. The organization chart in Figure 1 shows the typical structure of such an organization.

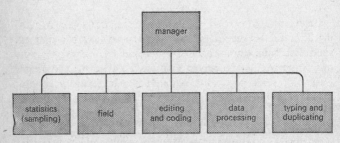

Figure 1 Organization of a processing department

Two forces hold it together. One is production, operating under the direction of the production manager or the office manager. The other is the project, which is a unit of production, operating under the direction of the project manager or director. [. . .]

Where work quantity and volume continuity are sufficiently high, efficiency is the greatest advantage of the processing organization. If a coder can keep busy full time, even if he has a minimum of experience, he will quickly become truly skilled, able to perform quality work at a high production level. But if that same man is forced, because of low volume, to work first in the field, next in editing and coding, then in card punching, and later in typing, his efficiency is at a far lower level. Efficiency through repetition is not too far from Henry Ford's idea of assembly-line production.

A concomitant advantage is that an organization which specializes in processing can set and maintain high quality and output standards. The firm which engages in processing only as a sideline, or at a low volume, cannot have high quality of output. Too much works against it.

A major disadvantage of the processing organization is that so few companies can afford it. The research firm *has* to be able to afford it; this is its stock in trade. But other types of companies with research departments rarely can, whether they are advertisers, agencies, media, or other kinds of marketers. Research volume must be high, the work must be repetitive, or process must be the primary activity of the research group; otherwise loss of efficiency results.

One man took over the research department of a manufacturing firm and discovered that he had inherited a processing organization complete with field control (and even a limited group of interviewers and supervisors within restricted regions of the United States), editors, and coders. This made little sense, but it did explain why it was tardy in getting out reports and why it was limited in the number of studies it could handle simultaneously. Under his reorganization, which is *not* processing-oriented, there is almost no limit to the volume of work it can handle, since outside firms do its processing. An advertiser who has his own research-processing facilities tends to 'force' projects through this production line, whether or not they can adequately be handled there.

If processing volume falls off somewhat, there is little probability that anyone will be dropped from the staff. Efficiency drops instead. The research firm, which is in business to make a profit from research, cannot afford such luxury; hence it is likely to operate a processing organization at a higher efficiency level.

The application-oriented group

The application-oriented group is often found as a partial system or division within the advertising agency's research department. It is set up according to the specialities which it researches: copy, media, and markets. Young & Rubicam's research department, for instance, has an application-oriented group for each of these three divisions in its research department.

Application orientation is often a reflection of management needs. If an advertising agency has a creative flair, its research department must be strong in copy testing. If it is strong in media planning, its research department should be strong in computerization. This paralleling of the basic structure of the company also means that the research department works far more effectively within its environment. It creates close co-ordination between the copy research division of an advertising agency's research department and its creative departments. The research organization is molded clearly to serve the needs of its corresponding department in the agency.

If research management understands that it is to operate within the broad limits of marketing, the chances of originality and skill in research are enhanced. The man with a background in copy research and psychology, who knows that his employer will benefit from his ideas about how to uncover buying motivations, and with a knowledge of audience reactions to advertisements, will find it easy to make a worthwhile contribution. One agency researcher, for instance, realized that the copy department was intensely interested in determining the relative merits of various mechanical features of print advertising. It was relatively simple for him to use Starch reports (scores on noting and readership of print advertising in various publications), to provide codes for various elements of the advertisements (space, size, their position in the magazine, position on the page, the amount of color, the type of caption, the type of illustration, and so on), and to program these findings into a computer. In very short order, results showing principles of print ads – in terms of Starch scores – were printed out.

Application-oriented organization, of course, has its disadvantages. With the maturation of marketing research, specialists expect to be – and are – paid well. It is not wise to have specialists on the staff unless there is a real need for them. It is often less expensive to employ consultants. The trained psychologist in advertising research, for instance, demands a high salary. A top senior advertising psychologist is worth $25,000 and up yearly – mostly up. So, unless the research group needs his services on a continuous basis, it is cheaper to hire him as needed, even though his per-hour rate is high. In this way the manager is not paying for idle or nonprofitable time.

If the department is so strongly oriented toward sales, media, copy, or the like that it is organized along one of these lines, the chance is strong that its manager has come up from a similar company department. The risk here is that his thinking is likely to be strongly colored. New ideas or approaches will be rare. One medium-size advertising agency, for instance, has not yet learned about the recent revolution in media research. Its research department, because of inbreeding, simply cannot accept the fact that the 'tried and true' measures of audience size are no longer the unquestionable statistics they were once assumed to be. This agency, needless to say, is losing volume, though its principals still do not understand why.

The brand-oriented department

This type of department is one whose employees, directly under the control of the research head, are organized by brand responsibility. The organization chart in Figure 2 shows Carter Products' brand-oriented research department.

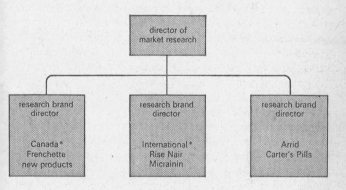

*Canada is handled as a 'brand' in marketing; international research volume is small, hence it is also handled as a 'brand' in research organization

Figure 2 Carter Products' brand-oriented research department

The central idea of brand-orientation is organization according to brand interests. The research brand director is responsible for all marketing research on his list of accounts. In the manufacturer's research department he may be called project director, assistant research director, research brand director, or one of many other titles. It is not his title which is important; it is the nature of his function.

Organization by brand (or account) is common in the larger advertising agencies, where the brand researcher may be known as a research account supervisor, research supervisor, research account executive, or the like. He is a member of the product (or account) group, which is composed of personnel from all the various departments, including research, assigned to work on a particular brand or account. The director of a small agency with a one-man research department simply puts on a different hat for each account. His orientation is still basically by account.

This method of organizing the research department has several advantages. One frequent limitation of research is that its manager takes the easy way out: he waits until he is called to do anything. In the brand-oriented department this is pretty tough to do since the research team is so committed to its own brands that it must produce. Let's put it another way. If the research department has a vague, overall assignment, it may turn out nothing of value. But if it must give planned and continuous attention to the brands' research needs, its work is likely to be better in quality.

It is desirable for any research man, regardless of his orientation, to be a functioning member of the marketing team and not merely to be consulted when marketing management thinks it sees a problem which he can solve. It is far better for him to participate in basic marketing meetings and, if he has sufficient marketing judgement, in the marketing decisions as well. This not only makes him feel that he is a member of a team and develops his basic interest in the brands and their success, it also means that he can foresee and recommend research work which ought to be done rather than sit back until someone else sees a need for it. He will be a more creative researcher, and his research will be better done, more aggressive.

This discussion raises an important point. Should the marketing research manager be primarily a marketing man, merely assigned to research; or should he be a researcher, assigned to a marketing task? Our feeling is that he should be foremost a marketing man, but with a professional research bent. If he combines these two qualities, his research will be professionally conducted and of maximum marketing value to his employer.

Establishing the research group on a brand-oriented basis doesn't achieve this goal automatically, but it at least sets the stage. Any other kind of group organization offers little or no chance for the research man to become a part of the marketing team.

Closely akin to this last point is that if he is assigned to a group of brands, he obtains far more background in and understanding of it. He will accumulate a good backlog of information and research on it, instead of having a new man act as project director each time some bit of research is carried out on any one brand. One advertiser's research manager first set up his department on the basis of project directors, and a new study was assigned to whoever had a light load at the time. The brand managers in the firm – after two years' experience with this departmental organization – insisted on its realignment by brands in order to obtain the continuity of background and effort they felt was essential.

The limitation to this sort of organization is the risk that the researcher assigned to a stated list of brands may become bored and stale. The range of problems can sometimes be small, and if it is too small, then a person capable of doing varied work, of displaying imagination, may be unable to stand the sameness. In fairness we must say that we have not seen this operate as a strict disadvantage. In our experience, even where the number of branded products handled by a single person is small, the problems and the techniques demanded are so diversified that boredom is not likely.

Other forms of departmental organization

Some research departments are organized on other bases than processing, application, or brands, but these bases can vary so much, and they occur so infrequently, that we can class them all in this miscellaneous pool. The two most often found are technique-oriented departments and respondent-oriented departments.

Technique-oriented groups, as their name implies, are organized according to technical specialities in either academic fields or marketing research. In the former category are groups which gather and process psychological, sociological, anthropological, mathematical or economic data. In the latter category, we find groups engaging in store audits, surveys, or panels. Market Facts, Inc., one of the larger U.S. research companies, has basically a custom-tailored consumer survey parent company, with a mail panel subsidiary, a market test subsidiary, and Canadian and international subsidiaries.

Respondent-oriented groups are organized according to the kinds of people they approach in investigations. Stewart, Dougall & Associates has both a consumer group and an industrial group, whose respondents are clearly implied. Other firms have retailing research divisions or executive research divisions.

The combination research group

Few research organization structures are 'pure'; they more often are chiefly organized along one of the lines we have discussed but are modified with one or more other lines. Manufacturers' research departments are almost always chiefly brand-oriented, but occasionally we find an application group or a small processing group. The advertising agencies' research departments are also most often brand-oriented, but if they are large enough, they almost always have overtones of application. The research companies are chiefly organized along processing lines, but some large ones also have overlays of technique.

Basically, the reason that such combined organizations so often occur is that they meet particular situations. This same point is their greatest advantage. If the manufacturer (whose interests, we remember, almost always dictate a brand-oriented department) has distinct ideas on the proper way to conduct consumer product testing, its research department might well attach a consumer product testing group to its staff. If a consumer research firm decides to offer psychological testing facilities, it is reasonable for it to set up a separate psychological group.

One manufacturer, for instance, firmly believes that consumer panels – questioning of the same group of people – have no value because their members are aware of being 'respondents'. It does not use panels; each study is undertaken with a completely new group of respondents.

A research group organized according to a single method may suffer from ingrowth. Its sights are constantly along the same lines. It is not exposed to new experience. But the group that has more than a single basis for organizing has an opportunity for more cross-fertilization, more exchange of ideas, since its approaches will be richly interrelated. For example, the coding department may know, from much experience, that only 2 per cent of the population falls into a given educational level. When the psychological department suggests an analysis at this level – since it doesn't know how few people make up its population – the coding department can save it the trouble of carrying out a study. Or the psychological department can assist the coding department. The coding department may be instructed only in how to handle the nine or ten total categories of occupation. But the psychological department may provide clues as to how to code on a total socio-economic scale, such as the Vaughn, which credits the type of telephone ownership, ownership versus rental of home, type of automobile ownership, education, and occupation. On this scale, for instance, a party-line telephone gets one point, a private-line telephone two points, no telephone zero points. By allowing point credits for each kind of variable answer within the categories indicated, it is possible to get a socio-economic score of anywhere from 0 to 15 points for any one family. This means that socio-economic categories can be established objectively and families classified according to where they fall in the scale. The coding department would probably not know about the Vaughn scale, but the psychological department surely would.

With more than a single basis of organization, however, operating efficiency may drop. If a department is essentially brand-oriented, the divergent interests of a technique-oriented group are likely to suffer. To achieve the greatest efficiency of the whole, all its parts should be put together according to the same basic design structure.

The brand-oriented research manager is basically interested in the total picture of marketing; the application-oriented manager has more interest in the marketing pieces going into the total; and the processing-oriented manager is more interested in the costs and quality of the various research steps and in trying to make a profit. When we ask a research manager to show capability and interest in more than one of these basic types of structure, we are demanding a highly unusual mix of interests and skills.

Centralization versus Decentralization

Sometimes, as the next organizational step, we must decide whether to centralize or decentralize the research group. This question normally applies only to manufacturers, advertising media, advertising agencies, and retailing, and it is not always an easy issue to resolve.

The problem does not arise until two conditions occur. One is that a major corporation exists, and the second is that it has separately organized divisions. Under centralization a single department is responsible for all the divisions' marketing research. Under decentralization each division has its own marketing research unit which usually reports functionally to the divisional management; in matters of technical standards it reports to central research management, if there is any.

Pretty much the same factors which affect the basic organization structure of the marketing research department also affect the centralization–decentralization issue. If a heavy volume of research is to be done, centralizing provides greater efficiency. A light volume favors decentralization, with perhaps only one person in each location or division handling research as a sideline.

Homogeneity also influences the decision. If a company is in diverse product fields – say, industrial chemicals *and* fast-moving consumer goods – decentralization may be logical. Socony-Mobil Gas is an example. If the company is in a field of closely allied products, all in a single mass market, centralization makes sense, as with Procter & Gamble. While it is usually less expensive to conduct a centralized than a decentralized operation, economy may be shortsighted if specific needs are sacrificed.[2]

Company organization is also a key. Decentralization in General Electric affected not only its marketing, sales, and product departments but its marketing research as well. If the general management policy is to centralize, the research department's structure will almost surely centralize too, and vice versa. But it depends on company size; in a small company with several decentralized divisions the marketing research group may well be centralized, depending on the geographic locations of the divisions.

2. See the discussion by the National Industrial Conference Board (1955).

The executive to whom the research manager reports is also an influencing factor, as we have seen. If he reports to the president or to some other executive representing central management, the department is likely to be centralized. If research reports to a divisional executive (not a marketing executive for the entire company), then it is likely to be decentralized, with separate research managers reporting to each division head. But this is not necessarily the case. In some companies of several divisions the marketing research manager *reports* to an executive of one division but *works* for several other divisions as well. He is sometimes placed on loan, as it were, to other departments. This practice is occasionally so extensive that the manager is working constantly for several departments other than his own, even though he still reports only to the head of his own department.

The nature of the department's organization is itself an influence on whether or not research is centralized. A processing-oriented department with sampling, field, editing–coding, data processing, and typing–duplicating units will usually be centralized because of the need for close co-ordination of effort and the economy of a single office. Also, the researchers are more flexible when their work is centralized. If four people are in a central location instead of each in a separate location, they constitute a task force that can concentrate on specific and immediate problems. If these same people are scattered in assignment, they are not so flexible.

Co-ordination, flexibility, economy – these are the reasons so few research firms *are* decentralized. Note that there is a distinction between true decentralization and having branch sales offices. Numerous research companies have regional sales offices, but few perform any processing work in them.

While its environment fairly well dictates either centralization or decentralization of any individual research function, we find advantages and disadvantages in each. When different divisions of a company face similar problems, a centralized research operation is an advantage. Where divisional efforts are so unique as to eliminate similarity, the advantages all favour decentralization.

The centralized operation is usually the less costly, for centralization leads to specialization, which means that it is less expensive to conduct a particular operation (National Industrial Conference Board, 1955). While four separately operating individuals must all be *generalists* in research, it is possible – if desirable – to place specialists under a single generalist at a central location. The direction of their specialization may take any of the forms we have been discussing.

While the centralized research department has the major advantages – at least potentially – of specialization, at least one point favors decentralization. Decentralized researchers have the advantage of their own types of specialization. They tend to specialize to meet the particular needs of their territory. The man who works within a specific geographic region far better understands its demands and requirements than any centralized research manager. He probably visits retail outlets frequently, a thing which the national marketing research manager cannot easily do except within his own area. Nor is any economy lost in decentralizing a department organized along brand lines. If the marketing manager for one of a company's brands is located in New York and another in Chicago, a different brand research man may work in each location. This is what happens in many large advertising agencies, for instance.

The decentralized researcher is closer to the firing line, but this may mean that he is not well equipped to see the importance of an overall centralized policy, research or otherwise. It could also mean that he is in a far better position to handle day-to-day research. For example, one central sales management did not realize the importance of a local brand in a product field which the national company was entering. The local product's importance lay not so much in its share of the market as in its consumers' sentimental attachment to it. When the new product was introduced, it was a miserable failure. Research showed that it was the sentiment, not the new product, which caused the failure. A researcher in a centralized department might never have stumbled onto this fact; it came out only after very subtle questioning of consumers by people who were accepted within the business community.

Special Department Facilities

Research departments have special facilities: a library (or 'information service', as it is now sometimes euphemistically called), business machines, a charting group, a duplicating group, or a product storage facility. The manufacturer's marketing research department may require special additional facilities.

The library consists of reference books, government-sponsored statistical reports, trade-published statistics, and the like. It may also include active research, comprising the department's own reports. At best, it is headed by a librarian competent not only in library work but expert at seeking out, first-hand, published and unpublished information.

The offices of the manufacturer, the advertising agency, the advertising medium, and – if it is a large chain – the retailer almost always have libraries, but the usual research firms do not. In all the research firms we have visited (and we have seen many) wc havc comc across nothing approaching a true library. A few volumes on research methodology, statistics, and the like; if sampling is a function of the firm, then a liberal sprinkling of government statistical sources – that is all. One type of library most research firms do have is a filing system that makes it easy to locate any of their past studies. If a firm has been in business for years, the files take up a lot of space and require a lot of cross-indexing.

Charting is a worthwhile facility, largely because it is such a useful method of presenting research results. Charts are more often used to communicate research findings than in any other type of activity except the stock market. So it makes good sense to locate charting within the research group.

Business machines may or may not be included in the research operation. Here we're discussing, not single calculators, but installations of punched-card equipment, usually I.B.M. Since every large-size manufacturer, advertising agency, advertising medium, and retailer has D.P. equipment for accounting and perhaps other purposes, it is usually possible, if the research manager sees any advantage in it, to have the accounting department handle his machine processing. If he has trouble getting service of the nature and timing he requires, he may decide to have his own machines. However, few go this far, for there is difficulty in maintaining sufficient volume and hiring enough people to warrant the installation. The research firm – that's a different question. It must use punched-card machines, so it can choose whether it wants to have its own installation or to purchase service from an outside source.

Duplication is another process often heavily relied upon within the research group. It is usual to find the normal typing facilities and clerical personnel and such equipment (with its operating specialists) as mimeograph and photo-offset within the research department. Clerks usually process only their own requirements (questionnaires, field instructions, tables, reports), but they may process the requirements of other departments as well.

Product storage is another research-related facility often placed within the research department. One manufacturer has a policy of storing six samples of each product used in a consumer product test. They are intended as a check in case of some unexpected results or in case someone later raises questions about the characteristics of the product tested. Since all products show some deterioration over time, this sort of storage has limited usefulness. The research firm does need storage space for its own products: completed questionnaires, punched cards, and other job materials, all classified on a project basis.

Should there be any special facilities within the company? This question must be answered about each facility of potential interest. There are three successive decisions to be made, as we shall see:

1. Is there a real need for the facility? It is valuable only if it will be used.

2. If there *is* a need for the facility, should it be handled within the company or outside? The answer is not always obvious. One large North American research firm, despite its volume, concluded that it should not have its own data-processing installation. It had many reasons for its decision, chiefly the rapidly changing machine technology, the growth in the number and variety of computers, and the tremendous investment. It

decided to deal with outside computer firms rather than to attempt to have its own – inferior – data-processing facilities.

3. Let's assume that the company can benefit from the proposed facility and that it will do better to handle it inside. It still has to answer the third question: should whatever the proposed facility achieves be a function undertaken by the research group? Obviously this discussion does not apply to the research firm. If the research firm has answered the two preceding issues affirmatively, the third question never arises; the facility has been taken on.

The facility and the operation to which it gives rise might be more logically located within some other department because of its workload, experience, other physical facilities, or even simply *desire*. If one group within the company has already started to collect the rudiments of a library and shows a desire to continue and develop it, it might be foolish for the research department to absorb it. Another consideration is qualification. If the group that is starting the library has little interest in marketing, it probably cannot effectively collect and manage a marketing library, while the research group can.

Another consideration is where the facility is most likely to be used. If a location other than the research department will encourage its greater use, this factor should be considered. Sometimes it can even be a question of physical location; if the research department is off the beaten track for the marketing executives, then it may be a poor place for a marketing facility (and perhaps a poor place for the research group as well).

Where the raw materials for the facility originate is another important consideration in its placement. If most raw materials originate somewhere distant from the research department, it makes little sense to gather them within it.

Finally, there is the question of costs. One location within the company may be less costly than another for processing work through a given facility. If it is to be placed within the research group, the costs of handling the facility there should not be markedly higher than for handling it elsewhere.

References

American Marketing Association (1960), *Market Research in International Operations*, A.M.A. Management Report, no. 53, A.M.A., Inc.

National Industrial Conference Board (1955), *Marketing Business and Commercial Research in Industry*, NICB, New York.

Twedt, D. W. (ed.) (1963), *A Survey of Marketing Research*, American Marketing Association.

7 I. Haldane

Selecting Marketing Research Staff

I. Haldane, 'The selection of market research executives', European Society for Opinion and Marketing Research, Conference Proceedings, paper no. 16, 1966.

The value of systematic personnel selection procedures has been recognised for a considerable time throughout industry, the Armed Forces and Civil Service (Fraser, 1962; Vernon and Parry, 1949; Adkins, 1956; Barrett, 1963), and the application of these procedures has resulted both in improved efficiency in the use of scarce human resources and greater satisfaction in work on the part of employees. The greater the labour-component which enters into the final product, the greater will be the benefits which result from the introduction of these procedures.

Human skills are the very essence of market research, as of any kind of research, and it is a curious fact that despite a fair amount of attention to the problems of recruitment, selection, training and payment of field staff, a search of the literature provides little evidence of any attention to the problems of research executive selection and development (see, however, Handyside, 1960). No doubt this reflects the relative importance of research and field time in cost terms, but is unrealistic in its lack of appreciation of the real importance of these elements in the total research operation.

Research skills are vital to our business: they are its motive force, and the efficiency of the research which we undertake depends upon them.

About three years ago the British Market Research Bureau decided to institute more formal and systematic personnel selection and training procedures. It is the purpose of this paper to describe the selection procedure – its rationale, its techniques and its results – not in order to provide a 'blue print' for executive selection for market research, suitable for any size of firm, conducting any type of operation in any country, since this would be an impossible objective – but to stimulate thought in this important area, and to suggest to other firms that advantages may be gained from similar analyses of their personnel needs.

Development of a Personnel Policy

Aims

The basic aim of B.M.R.B.'s personnel policy is to ensure an adequate supply of research executive manpower, potentially suitable for undertaking, after training, all the types of research on which we are engaged; and to provide within the organization and structure of the firm, opportunity for promotion in accordance with reasonable career expectations.

The growth of business and the introduction of new specialist operations may on occasion require the recruitment of senior staff from outside the firm, but it is our aim to fill most of our senior posts by promotion from within, and I shall therefore be considering only our selection procedures for new entrants to market research, recruited to the starting grade of 'research executive'. Senior staff require other qualities in addition to those which we try to assess; if recruited externally the sources from which they are recruited differ; we would not consider the selection procedure, as described, as adequate or suitable for these grades.

Since recruitment procedure is geared to B.M.R.B.'s needs, it may be desirable briefly to describe the company for those who are not familiar with it. B.M.R.B. is one of the larger British specialist market research organizations, providing a comprehensive range of client services and research operations, with the exception of retail audit services which are now provided by an associate company, Retail Audits Ltd. Currently we employ about forty research staff; the research group – the working unit – is composed of a senior research executive, with several years' experience, and two or three junior research executives. Each research group handes *all* the research projects of a number of clients, and research groups are responsible to associate directors. Some degree of specialization occurs at this level, with consultancy service being available from associate directors to *any* group in the areas of, for example, attitude and motivation research techniques, advertising research techniques, product testing or media research. In this way we aim to achieve the availability of specialist advice within the context of continuity of client contact and service.

Apart from a limited number of research staff who have equivalent professional qualifications, all are University graduates and six have post graduate qualifications. Most of our research staff have qualifications in the social sciences – economics, sociology, psychology and anthropology, but some have degrees in English Literature, mathematics, statistics, modern languages, geography or general science subjects.

Previous recruitment methods

Before the introduction of the present system, the method of recruitment of research executives was on an *ad hoc* basis. Candidates applied for a job spontaneously and intermittently throughout the year, or were recommended by University Appointment Boards or other bodies. They were then interviewed – usually on the basis of their written letter of application taken in conjunction with qualifications and possible personal introductions – by two or three senior staff, including the managing director, and a decision to engage or not depended on subjective personal evaluation of the applicant in the light of B.M.R.B.'s employment opportunities at that time. This approach had several disadvantages. In the first place the field of candidates was limited; in the second place the criteria of selection were variable; thirdly, good candidates might be passed over because of lack of vacancies at that time – vacancies possibly having been recently filled by less suitable applicants; and fourthly successful applicants, after some time in the job, might find that the job differed considerably from what had been expected – not because it had been wilfully misrepresented to them, but because their perceptions of the job and its relationship to their occupational needs differed from the perception of the job by a more senior research man.

This should not be taken to imply that in the past we did not obtain a fair share of good research men – as the presence of Dr Treasure and Mr de Vos, both distinguished ex-B.M.R.B. men, in this discussion session will testify, as would many other well-known men in the marketing and market research fields.

The Thomson Gold Medal has been won on two occasions, and a special award once, and the Coglan award has been won on four occasions by members – or ex-members – of B.M.R.B. research staff who joined us under the old system. We are confident that the present system is still attracting research men of similar stature – and identifying them and keeping them – while at the same time avoiding most of the less obvious errors which we also made in the past. Nevertheless, with the growth of the firm it gradually became apparent that B.M.R.B. had an unacceptably high turnover rate among its junior executive staff, and that we were recruiting, along with the good, too many indifferent researchers.

Re-appraisal

The previous method of executive selection was therefore subjected to a rigorous and critical re-appraisal by B.M.R.B. management, and a new approach to the problem was formulated, which may be summarized in the following basic principles:

1. *Estimate manpower requirements* for a period of at least one year in advance.

2. Define objectively and operationally the *content of the job* – or specified sub-components of the job – and who will derive most satisfaction from it.

3. *Define the kind of person who is most satisfactory* in the job – or in specified sub-components of the job and who will derive most satisfaction from it.

4. Set out systematically to *attract as many people as possible* who appear to be broadly of this type.

5. Make sure they *understand* what the job is like, in all its aspects.

6. Devise a *selection procedure* which will enable more reliable and valid assessments to be made of persons as in 3 above.

7. *Select the best applicants* having regard to both general job requirements and specialist area needs.

8. Provide occupational conditions – material and psychological – which will *attract and retain in post* those to whom an offer of employment is made.

It will be observed that underlying this approach are two complementary principles:

(a) 'Selection *in*': aiming towards the ultimate employment of the 'best' applicants – 'best' both from the point of view of efficiency in the job and occupational satisfaction.

(b) 'Selection or self-selection *out*': aiming towards elimination of 'unsatisfactory' candidates – 'unsatisfactory' either in terms of probable job-performance or probable dissatisfaction with the job on the candidates' part.

Preliminary Planning

Research into job content

Observation and experience had provided a good over-all appreciation of the content of the job of a research executive, but there was no objective evidence of the time spent on various aspects of the job. Furthermore, specialization in particular work functions could be expected to have introduced considerable variation between the jobs of executives working in different groups. This in turn would have important implication in selection, training and organization of work within the firm. A detailed work study was therefore planned and executed, with the basic aim of showing how research executives spent their working time.

After preliminary pilot work, a job observation sheet was drawn up, designed to be completed by interviewers during observation periods. This was used in a systematic study of research executives over a period of three complete working weeks in 1963. The sample was of 150 half-hour periods of working time, and aimed at equal representation of each research executive with equal probability of selection of each half-hour period for each R.E. throughout the working day.

The results showed that the typical executive spent rather over one third (35 per cent) of his time *writing* – primarily preparing plans and reports, but also in making up tables, preparing analysis instructions and writing questionnaires. (From the limited amount of time spent on this latter function, however, it seemed clear that this was a job element which Senior Research

Executives preferred to keep in their own hands). They spent rather more than a fifth (22 per cent) of their time in meetings, discussions and briefings – mostly in discussing research problems with their immediate group head, and next most frequently with analysis groups and other internal departments: R.E. discussions with clients occupied little of their working time. Finally, 18 per cent of the time was spent in reading and preparing the ground for planning and report writing by checking on the accuracy of prepared written material. The remainder of the time was spent in travelling and other miscellaneous activities.

This limited study therefore provided a first factual framework within which selection planning could proceed and provided a useful supplement to existing observational knowledge of the skills required for the job. It seemed that these could be comprised under four main headings:

1. Creativity and imagination.
2. Analytical skills, both logical and numerical.
3. Verbal and literary skills.
4. Social and personal attributes.

If one accepts the distinction between 'think factories' and 'survey-mongers' to borrow two neat descriptions of market research organizations which have been used, then B.M.R.B. aims to fall into the former category. While competitive in speed, accuracy and cost we would also aim to provide a high level of research ability at the conceptual, planning and analytic stages, and this is borne out by our study of the way in which the B.M.R.B. research executive spends his working time.

'Specification' for research executives

Arising out of this study and a careful consideration of all the ways in which a research executive's time is spent, an evaluation or 'specification' of requirements for the 'ideal' R.E. was evolved. The closer the R.E. could approach to this specification, the more efficient would he be.

In order to carry out the job satisfactorily he should be a good 'problem-solver' in the widest sense: capable of 'seeing through the trees to the wood' in order to isolate the essence of a problem; capable of working at speed with meticulous accuracy; possessing originality and imagination in devising means of solving the problem, possessing insight and understanding in formulating the right hypotheses for testing; being at ease with quantitative data bearing on a problem and capable of understanding the implications of these; and he must be able to express his ideas and conclusions lucidly and concisely in speech and writing. Moreover, not only should he be *capable* of all these, but he should take an active pleasure in exercising these skills, in order to achieve satisfaction in his work.

Apart from these *individual* characteristics, however, important *special* skills enter into the task. The research executive must be able to communicate effectively at all levels: contribute to meetings, discuss his work with seniors and juniors, explain projects to clients, brief interviewers. He will be a member of a working group, and must fit into that group effectively, and into the firm as a whole – not as an 'organization man' but as one who respects others' opinions while still holding his own – and willing to learn while appreciating that he too has something original to contribute.

It was on the basis of this analysis that selection procedures and tests were developed.

Publicity and media

Since the primary target of recruitment information was University undergraduates in their final year, good working relationships had already been established and maintained with University Appointment Boards. However, it was felt that sufficient coverage was not being obtained through this medium on the one hand because of lack of enthusiasm for Market Research as an employment opportunity on the part of some Boards – particularly the older Universities who, it was felt, favoured public service, academic institutions and larger industrial concerns – and on the other hand because a considerable proportion of undergraduates might not make use of the services of the Boards. In particular, it was felt that the outstanding graduate was being introduced and directed elsewhere, leaving Market Research as a comparatively low occupational priority.

Accordingly, as a first step, B.M.R.B. decided to do what any market research firm would usually advise its clients to do – to undertake a survey to establish the facts of the matter. For this purpose we confined ourselves to Oxford and Cambridge Universities, and from the 1st Class or 2nd Class Honours degree passes in the 1965 pass lists, published in the national press, selected a sample of 1082 names. A mail survey was carried out among these graduates, designed to find out their:

(a) Occupational aims and motivations.
(b) Sources of employment information and attitudes towards these.
(c) Timing, frequency and method of applications.
(d) Details of job accepted.
(e) Attitudes towards Market Research and related fields as a career.

A 31 per cent response rate was achieved, and the following interesting results emerged from the survey.

About the same proportions of graduates stressed the need for interest, intellectual stimulus and variety of job-content (42 per cent) as good material conditions, rewards and prospects (38 per cent). In negative terms, they were more anxious to *avoid* boredom in the job (24 per cent) than less satisfactory material prospects (13 per cent).

University Appointment Boards had been consulted as a primary source of employment information by two out of every three graduates, and had been found very useful by 41 per cent. Press advertising was used only half as frequently, while 30 per cent had mainly used personal contacts.

On average, a student had made four applications before accepting his first job: 13 per cent had made seven or more applications – and 13 per cent had not made any. On average, each student had received two offers of employment; 30 per cent one offer, and 15 per cent three or more offers.

Only 6 per cent had started actively seeking employment before their final year, while only 8 per cent had left it as late as their final term.

About one student in three in the sample had remained at the University and continued in post graduate studies and teaching – and this proportion rose to one in two of first-class honours students.

Only 11 per cent had considered Market Research as a possible career, although 10 per cent had considered 'Commercial Research', 'Economic Research' and 'Marketing', 14 per cent had considered management consultancy and 17 per cent operational research. 58 per cent had considered *none* of a list of nine management services and techniques including those mentioned and all of which were related to market research, in the broadest sense, to greater or lesser extent.

This survey provided useful guides not only to the aspects of the job of research executive which should be stressed in our *publicity* of vacancies, but the *media* through which we should work and the *timing* we should adopt in our recruitment planning.

B.M.R.B. Selection in Practice

The present selection system falls into three phases:

1. Attracting applicants.
2. First filters.
3. Final assessment.

Attracting applicants

The basic aim is to attract as wide a field as possible of suitable applicants and to inform them of the opportunities, satisfactions – and possible disadvantages from some points of view – of a career in market research. To this end good relations have been established, and kept, with Universities and Colleges of Technology; senior staff are encouraged to give talks to individuals, to student societies and meetings; personal contact is encouraged between present research staff and previous University colleagues and teachers. Vacation visits to B.M.R.B. are arranged for any interested candidates.

A four page pamphlet called 'A career in market research' describing market research in general, and the work and prospects of a B.M.R.B. research executive in detail, is widely distributed through Universities and to every interested applicant who writes in. A short reading list of M.R. text books is included.

When the time is near for initiating the active phases of

selection – usually over the Easter university vacation – press advertising may also take place, advertising through appointment circulars of professional bodies, and through the Professional and Executive Register of the Ministry of Labour.

First filters

The basic aim at this stage is to eliminate those applicants who clearly would have a low probability of success or satisfaction in the job, and to identify those whose probability of success is reasonably high. We aim to do this both by *informing* applicants (by the descriptive brochure, by personal interview, etc.) and by *assessing* them.

Both from the point of uniformity, and for purposes of information and assessment, it has been found useful to develop a special application form which all candidates must complete. The questions in this form are not only *factual*, referring to academic achievements, age, part-time and full-time employment experience, interests, health history, etc. but also attitudinal, designed to evaluate the applicants' vocational interests, level of aspiration and insight. Questions are included which are designed to make the applicant think seriously and carefully about the kind of job for which he is applying, since by this means some unsuitable candidates will realise that this is not really the kind of job for which they should be competing. In addition to the above indications, the application form gives evidence of literacy and legibility – important characteristics which are not universal, even among University graduates.

Wherever possible, the application form is used as the basis of a preliminary personal interview, but if a large volume of applications is received, inevitably selection of the final list of candidates takes place on the basis of the form alone.

Final assessment

The aim of this stage of the procedure is to provide a frame of decision, based on observation and testing, so that we may select sufficient numbers of the best candidates to fill the next year's vacancies. Depending on the numbers of applicants and the numbers of vacancies, as many as is practicable will be called forward to this stage of the procedure.

Applicants assemble in groups of six at B.M.R.B.'s London office, and spend a whole morning for the assessment procedure. The aim is not only that *we* can get to know *them*, but that *they* can get to know *us* and our work, and this is made clear to them on arrival. There are four main elements in the final assessment procedure:

(a) Tests.
(b) Group discussion.
(c) Formal and informal interviews.
(d) Informative tour of the firm.

(a) *Tests*

In B.M.R.B.'s experience a University degree, as such, is insufficient evidence of problem-solving aptitude of the type most relevant in market research, and we decided that special tests should be used for this purpose. Two tests were chosen: the first is a logical-numerical test (the 'B.M.R.B. Problems Test') and the second an analogue test of planning ability (the 'B.M.R.B. Research Planning Test').

The B.M.R.B. problems test. The Problems test is, in psychometric terms, a 'speed' test rather than a 'power' test. It is primarily a test of nonverbal general intelligence based on reasoning, but has a numerical component. In non-technical terms, it could be said to be a test of ability to solve a problem through manipulation and selection of verbal and numerical data. This test was originally developed in order to discriminate within the highest intelligence levels – the top 10 per cent on general I.Q. ratings. It is composed of items such as:

'There are four sacks. A, B, C, D, containing unequal numbers of potatoes. B has more potatoes than C and D together, and as many as A and C together. If there are more in D than in C, which bag has least potatoes?'

'If a brick weighs one and a half pounds and half a brick, how much does a brick and a half weigh?'

(These are not actual test items.) The test has already been subjected to rigorous item-analysis and standardization, but has

147

again been re-standardized for market research purposes on B.M.R.B. applicants and staff in post.

In order to estimate the validity of this test as a selection tool, all B.M.R.B. research staff have been confidentially graded by senior research men (who knew them but did *not* know their test scores). In these gradings, research staff were compared with the 'average' research executive of previous years on 'over-all research competence'. Grading was in three simple categories – 'good or definitely above average', 'average', 'poor or definitely below average'. The test scores range from three to twenty-three with a mean of 12·9 and s.d. of 4·4 (there are twenty-seven items in the test), and the relationship of scores to gradings is as shown in Table 1.

Table 1
Problems Test Scores and Overall Gradings

Grading: Test score:	'Good'	'Average'	'Poor'
—8	—	4	3
9—16	12	7	4
17+	8	8	—
Average score:	15·6	14·2	10·3

An analysis of variance shows that the between-grade average score differs significantly ($P < 0·05$) and allows an operational interpretation of the test score to be made in the following terms: 'do not accept an applicant who scores eight or less unless there is some exceptional reason to the contrary; accept an applicant who scores seventeen or more, unless there is some exceptional reason to the contrary. Decide about those who score between nine and sixteen on grounds other than their Problems test score.'

Indeed, on the basis of all 118 test results to date we know the percentile rank on the total distribution of all applicants and staff in post, which is a very useful aid to decision taking.

The B.M.R.B. research planning test. This is a test of planning ability, designed to test insight, ingenuity and inventiveness: it also gives a good indication of clarity of exposition and reasoning. It is a 'power' test, rather than a 'speed' test, and no objective scoring is applied to it. Rather it is used as a means of subjectively assessing the extent to which an applicant can appreciate the nature of the problem with which he is confronted, devise a solution and present his plan in a lucid and convincing manner.

Table 2
Problems Test Score Percentile Ranks

	25%	50%	75%	90%	95%
Score:	9	12	16	18	20

Candidates are given a selection of several problems, from which they must choose *one* and, in half an hour, write a brief outline of how they would approach it. The problems are analogues of market research problems, such as: 'A manufacturer says his sales are falling and he needs some market research. What questions would you put *to him* at a preliminary discussion?'

(b) *Group Discussion*

The objectives of the group discussion are two-fold: *firstly* to assess, by observation, social interaction, leadership in a group context, acceptability to other group members, etc. and *secondly* to test insight, imagination and inventiveness in interpretation of unstructured interview material.

Candidates assemble under the 'non-directive leadership' of two senior B.M.R.B. research men. They listen to a ten minute tape recording of part of a depth interview, and they then interpret and discuss this. After about fifteen minutes' discussion a transcript of the interview is provided, and discussion continues on the basis of these more detailed data.

(c) *Formal and informal interviews*

Each applicant attends a formal interview with a board of three members of B.M.R.B.'s management group. The interview is based on details in the application form, but an attempt is made to go beyond this and form an opinion on the candidates' maturity, breadth of interests and outlook, and motivation for the job. At the end of the morning all candidates are invited to remain for a buffet lunch, and the remaining members of the management have an opportunity of meeting them in an informal setting. This is regarded not only as an assessment procedure, but also as an opportunity for candidates to learn about B.M.R.B. and its policy, and to ask any questions or raise any topics they wish.

We recognize the unreliability of interviewing procedures as a basis of personnel assessment, but feel that, both from the point of view of the candidate and ourselves, an interview is desirable. It gives the applicant an opportunity to raise any issue he wishes, it gives us an opportunity to follow up any points or leads suggested at previous stages, and it allows a first assessment to be made of whether or not he is likely on personal grounds to fit into the existing structure of the firm.

(d) *Informative tour of the firm*

The aim of this part of the procedure is to give applicants a clear understanding firstly of the way in which the firm operates, and secondly of how the Research Executive fits into the structure. In addition, we wish applicants to hear the attitudes and opinions of other junior research staff to their jobs. In our view, this is an important element of selection – to allow candidates to form *their own* views of the desirability, or undesirability, of the total working environment in which they will find themselves. We therefore arrange for applicants to be shown round all departments of B.M.R.B., in groups of three by a research executive who has joined the firm in the previous year. They have the opportunity, at all stages, of asking any questions they wish or following-up any special lines of interest, and this part of the selection procedure is quite informal, with all questions and answers (on both sides) entirely off the record.

Decision Taking

The selection procedure as described is not intended to provide a definite and pre-determined decision on each applicant, but to give a framework within which management can take better decisions. To this end, minor administrative details are worth bearing in mind: it is not easy to remember each of a large number of candidates over an extended period of final selection boards, but photographs attached to the candidates' papers are a useful recall aid. It is useful for candidates to wear lapel badges with their names clearly written on them: and it also helps if staff do the same – but on a different background colour, to avoid doubt and possible *faux pas* for candidates.

At the end of each selection board certain applicants can usually be eliminated as definitely not up to the standard required: sometimes an exceptional candidate is seen to whom one can decide to make an offer without waiting to see the remaining boards. Usually, however, it is a question of relegation until the end of the procedure, and choosing perhaps four from a possible sixteen.

In coming to this final crucial decision two balancing factors will provide the basis of choice: the needs of the firm and the qualities of available candidates. There is also the question of the sex ratio to be borne in mind: while men and women are equally acceptable as executives, and while there is no evidence that either sex is better as research staff, there may be difficulties involved in persuading junior male executives, recently joined, to work under senior women research executives. In so far as we aim to take on the best people, we would hope that many would progress to senior positions, and therefore some degree of sex balance must be maintained if only to avoid constraints on this account at a later date.

We must consider current anticipated demand for particular kinds of work – creative and qualitative, psychological, economic forecasting, statistical, experimental, industrial, etc. – and our present capabilities or weakness in these areas – and try to match the firm's demand to available supply of research skills.

But the final decision, inevitably, will be a subjective choice, based on personal weighting of all the information available to decide 'who, of all those available, and on all the evidence, is most likely to make a successful member of a research team, and a future senior researcher?' We make no apology that the final decision is subjective: we are undertaking judgements about complex human beings in complex working relationships, and tests and procedures can only help to make our judgements better – they can never themselves supply the answers.

Since introducing the present system, over four hundred first applications have been considered; over one hundred applicants have been through our final selection procedures; twenty have been appointed; eight have been offered posts but did not accept. We are constantly improving both our methods, and our judgements. That we are achieving some measure of success is shown by the following Table comparing confidential gradings of staff in post before the present system was introduced and staff introduced under the present system.

Table 3
Gradings of Research Staff Selected by Previous and Present Methods

Grading: Selected by:	'Good'	'Average'	'Poor'
Previous system	8	13	5
Present system	12	6	2

Although the probability level associated with this contingency table is only 0·15, it should be borne in mind that the previous system of selection was by no means entirely invalid or unreliable, and had served our purposes adequately from 1933 until three years ago. It has been said that in selection one should seek to validate not the *system* but the *selectors*. If that is so, B.M.R.B. management can feel some degree of satisfaction – without becoming complacent, and still hoping to improve our selection skills in the future.

References

ADKINS, D. C. (1956), 'Selecting public employees', *Public Personnel Review*, vol. 17, pp. 259–67.

BARRETT, R. S. (1963), 'Guide to using psychological tests', *Harvard Business Review*, vol. 41, pp. 138–46.

FRASER, J. M. (1962), *Industrial Psychology*, Pergamon.

HANDYSIDE, J. D. (1960), 'Some issues in the selection of market research executives', *Commentary*, vol. 4, no. 1, pp. 10–20.

VERNON, P. E., and PARRY, J. B. (1949), *Personnel Selection in the British Forces*, University of London Press.

8 K. Rogers

The Identity Crisis of the Market Researcher

K. Rogers, 'The identity crisis of the market researcher', *Commentary* (now *Journal of the Market Research Society*), vol. 8, 1966, pp. 3–15.

The Issue

Disquieting feelings about market research and its application to marketing decisions are increasingly in evidence. Marketing itself, in its mechanics and even more so in its hierarchical position in the organization has been undergoing important changes for some time. This has resulted in the growth of two roles, that of the Marketing Manager and of the Market Researcher. The purpose of this paper is to report on a pilot study designed to examine the researcher's role and its relationships with the marketer and with others, both within the same, and in separate organizational structures. Many of the concepts used in this examination are socio-psychological, some are psychoanalytical, all are directed to the economics of the market.

The causes for the growth of marketing can be found in the economic and social developments that have occurred throughout the world, at least since the end of the Second World War: technological improvements in the production and distribution of goods and services; the tendency towards professionalization of work; the gains effected by organized labour; the commitments of government to provide social welfare services; education extending over longer periods; greater life expectancy; earlier marriages; more leisure time; the shift from an 'inner-directed' (Riesman *et al.*, 1950) Puritan to an 'other-directed' (ibid.) hedonistic life style; and, possibly most important, the widely held belief that such trends are irreversible. As a consequence an important change came about in the distribution of disposable income, and a corresponding spur in industrial capital spending. Combined with increasing competition, these factors, among others, make marketing possibly the most important and certainly the most glamorous business function today. It has assumed the role of providing, and is expected to deliver, the planned corporate profit.

Although its techniques derived from the various disciplines have also developed rapidly, when compared to the corporate demands made on marketing, they are not yet adequate to replace hunches with scientifically derived data, so that marketing decisions can be seen primarily as results of technological competence. As yet, there is still much in marketing that is unknown or hazy.

The growing concern among market researchers, their marketing managers, and clients, about the factors that determine the results of market research studies and their use in the process of making marketing decisions, finds several different and on the surface seemingly disconnected expressions. Some assert that it is management's responsibility to use research sophisticatedly; others claim that the quality of the research results is shaped by the ability of both marketer and researcher to realistically perceive the marketing problem; the resources in time and money made available by the marketer; and the methodology chosen by the researcher. Still others believe that marketing decisions are successful to the degree that the researcher has done his work properly. According to Carlson (1962) the marketer-researcher interaction is an important determinant in marketing. Many marketers believe that the social sciences, especially, do not provide the degree of insight they think necessary and desirable for the execution of their work.

These anxieties seem to be more noticeable in industrial market, than in consumer or public opinion research. One reason may well be the industrial market researcher's lack of intimate knowledge of technologies related to the production or use of the product. Even should he have this knowledge it will likely be less complete than that of his marketing manager or client. The team approach, employing engineers, economists, and social scientists, only occasionally provides the integration necessary to allay the client's anxiety. Another possible reason is the absence of a generally accepted research methodology; sampling based on statistical probability is frequently impossible, at times not even desirable. The use of 'confidential information' often not verifiable and the source of which it is not ethical to identify represents another factor. Aggravating though these special conditions might be, the anxieties related to market research in general seem to cover common or at least largely overlapping ground.

The Research Sample and Methodology

The pilot study, extending over a five-year period, was conducted to investigate the work of eighty-five market researchers in nine countries, including the U.S., U.K., Germany, Austria, Switzerland, Kenya and Tanzania. The industries involved were textiles, consumer durables, foods of convenience, household supplies, business services, heavy engineering and public entertainment, thereby relating to industrial users and consumers, and providing them with products and services. All researchers involved were nationals of the country in which they worked; all but one were male; about 40 per cent had baccalaureate or post-graduate degrees in the Social Sciences, about 35 per cent in Economics or Statistics, and the remaining 25 per cent had what one researcher proudly termed 'graduated by practical experience'.

Sixty-eight researchers were interviewed about their work, each during one or two extended meetings. In twenty-four instances, there was also an opportunity to follow up the information provided, with the researchers' managers, the marketers. There was also an opportunity to observe sixteen researchers in their work, for time periods of between two and ten months. In these cases the author was a consultant to their firms.

In addition to these interviews the relevant marketing literature was scrutinized.

The Findings

The findings of the study are summarized under ten main headings:

1. *Market research findings* in each instance, played an important part in the formulation of the marketing plan of these

organizations. Frequently, however, marketers considered the validity of these findings as debatable. Initially, their anxieties were focused on the data and their interpretations, but subsequently included the role and competence of the researcher and his employer.

2. *Mutual judgements of marketers' and researchers' competence* generally indicated that the marketer's judgement of the researcher's work depended on the information provided, the form in which it was presented, and the working compatibility between the marketer and the researcher. The marketer's performance was judged not only by the relevance of his planning decisions, but also by how he decided to implement his marketing plan.

Frequently, marked anxiety prevailed between marketer and researcher. It seemed to be engendered by the perception of each towards the other's technical competence and performance. Particularly in instances of marketing inefficiencies, whether consciously perceived or unconsciously felt, by either or both, mutual blame and attempts at scape-goating were in evidence.

Researchers claimed that marketers neither understand nor appreciate research; do not permit researchers to acquaint themselves with all the relevant aspects of the problem; do not provide adequate resources in expenditure or time for 'good research'; are disinclined to permit 'general research' essential for long-range planning; and frequently misuse research for purposes other than information gathering related to marketing. Often, they felt, they were expected to furnish convincing reasons for what they thought were 'wrong decisions'. When they were unable to do so, they were subjected to their marketers' outbursts of banalities and even invectives. They were often accused of not understanding the complexities of practical marketing problems and of being over-ambitious empire-builders.

An analysis of several of these situations indicated that the complaints had some validity. There were occasions when researchers, especially those with independent agencies, were not permitted to know the whole of the marketing problem. At times, there was a strong implication that research was commissioned to prove someone in the organization right or wrong, as a justification for firing him, as a substitute for, even to delay marketing implementations. Some marketers, who perceived market research reports as critical of their intuitive methods, seemed to consider them as *quasi* acts of subversion. In hampering the researcher, marketing managers produced self-fulfilling prophecies. Expecting research to be inadequate, even to fail, they enforced decisions that induced failure. This provided the rationale for 'returning to the old though not always proven method' of intuitive hunches, that had so often produced favourable results.

3. *An examination of the American, English and German marketing literature* revealed a paucity of published and unpublished material related to the problem of identifying the researcher's role, and its relationships with other roles, in the course of the marketing process. In itself this gives cause for considering the significance of this condition.

4. By contrast there was *a wealth of papers dealing with methodology*. Though we are cognizant of the scientific importance of methodology, it was impossible to not notice some researchers' infatuation with their chosen instrument. At times, methodology described as useful for the solution of one problem was uncritically applied to others, even though the results did not meet the researcher's expectations.

There seemed to be a relation between the researcher's motives and his newly acquired technique: the technique was considered not only as a tool by which to gain knowledge about a marketing problem; but, it also seemed to offer the promise for successfully manipulating the marketing manager or client. This impression was reinforced by observing that considerable differences among researchers regarding the validity of some methodologies were given relatively little attention in professional meetings or in shop talk. Yet these differences were discussed quite freely during presentation to potential clients, and in public statements.

5. *Jargon* was over-stressed by researchers in their conversations and even more so in their reports. In some instances, marketers seemed to be equally addicted to this practice. The tendency to use terms, often newly coined and seldom well defined, seemed to serve less the illumination of relations important to the market-

ing process, than a substitute for the understanding that could be gained by rigorously tested observations (Rogers, 1965).

6. *Confused perceptions of the researchers' role* by both researchers and marketers was noticed almost throughout this study. When the researchers' own descriptions of their roles were compared with those of their managers, the marketers or with the official company job specifications, substantial differences were evident. In two instances where this was not so, the researchers had written their own job specifications at the time of their promotions.

It is curious that this should exist so pronouncedly among specialists whose chosen field is the observation and description of relationships among people and objects. Particularly striking, at least in some instances, was the rapidity of changes in the perceptions of the same researchers' roles, by both researchers and marketers. This shifting was noted in several interviews held within periods of a few weeks. The changes sometimes coincided with the preliminary discussions about a research project, the time of the interim report, the final report, and the use of the findings in the marketing process. Each time, the descriptions of the scope, and even more so the discretion allowed in the work, changed considerably. In one interview it occurred almost kaleidoscopically, three times.

During one firm's preliminary discussions of a market research study to be conducted, the researcher's role seemed to be focused on helping the marketer define the marketing problem and, then, to present his suggested research design for the marketer's approval. When the interim report was presented, the marketer asserted that he 'was only informed about the methodologies to be used. The decision to use them was the researcher's responsibility'. While discussing the final report, the marketer insisted that 'it is the researcher's job to formulate the problem, and, being the expert, not to be influenced by anyone else.' On both occasions, the researcher argued unsuccessfully against the marketer's assertions. The final marketing plan bore little resemblance to either the problem as it originally was posed in the research study, or to the evalutions of the study's findings.

7. *Researchers' reporting to the chief executive directly* was

frequently suggested by researchers as important to the company and, therefore, organizationally appropriate. Independent researchers, contracting for specific jobs, repeatedly spoke of the benefits to be derived from continuous and direct relationships with the heads of their client companies; those employed within industrial organizations, expressed their convictions of corporate needs for them to advise the chief executive at first hand.

The researcher's desire to report directly to the chief executive represented, at one level, his complaints about the marketer's lack of professional competence. Correctly perceived or not, there would be no improvement because of a change in the researcher's position. Such a change could only place the researcher on a par with or possibly on a higher organizational level than the marketer. Because the chief executive is responsible for the conduct of the entire organization and for evaluating, at least, his immediate subordinates, including the marketing manager, the researcher's complaint is not only about the marketer's lack of competence, but also against the chief executive who permitted such lacklustre performance, especially in his immediate span of control.

The researcher's request also expresses his need to be decisively effective in the company operation, and at the highest level of authority, which is, of course, the chief executive's role. By asking to be only his 'persuasive advisor', the researcher is in fact aspiring to highest organizational authority while being unwilling to accept its full responsibility. This may manifest an awareness of the lack of competence to handle the chief executive's tasks.

In terms of organizational reality, it represents a lack of clarity in the perception of the researcher's own role. In fact, these researchers are repeating the clamour made in the past by other specialists, e.g. public relations men, advertising men, image makers, and accountants, who argued that they possessed the ultimate insight necessary for the corporate good.

8. *Marketers' formal training for their work* was often found to be non-existent. Of the total sample, consisting of forty men, only twelve had formal marketing training. Ten were Americans, two British, both American-trained by their parent-companies.

Of the forty marketers fifteen had some college-level education, but not all had graduated.

9. *Marketers verbalizing their marketing philosophies* can be placed into two groups. One, consisting of fourteen college and three non-college educated men, expressed adherence to the 'integrated marketing concept' (Cordiner, 1952), although in varying degrees of acceptance and understanding. A member of this group referred to this marketing concept as 'castor oil that keeps the organization well-purged and functioning'.

The other group, all marketers who had learned their business techniques by practical experience only, stressed a marketing concept in which reliance on economic strength and tightly controlled organizational structure seemed all-important. Members of this group expressed resistance to market research to which they often sarcastically referred as 'the scientific methods and their results'. Market research reports implying, or recommending, reviews of company marketing policies were termed 'sweeping', 'irregular', 'disruptive', 'unorganic', and even 'destructive'.

10. *Researchers' personal background.* In reply to questions related to their personal background and, in particular their childhood, twenty-six researchers of the forty provided data that seemed to fit a consistent pattern; father, frequently a professional man, apparently ambivalently loved by the son, often described as disciplinarian or authoritarian, but considered worthy of emulation; mother, over-protective, frequently quarreling with the son and refusing to let him grow up; the family usually well-to-do, having reached or aspiring to a higher middle-class status.

The researchers' academic background revealed a main interest in Literature, the Social Sciences, or sometimes Chemistry. Almost without exceptions was there mention of some health problem, often of apparently psycho-somatic nature. The other fourteen researchers interviewed did not fit this pattern nor indeed did any other pattern clearly emerge.

The researchers were put into two categories, according to their attitudes towards their marketing managers. One group consisted of those who clearly pictured the relationship one of dominance-submission accompanied by aggressive and hostile verbalization. The other consisted of those who thought the relationship unsatisfactory, moderately good or even good, but who nevertheless accepted it without hostility. From this division the following grouping emerged:

Table 1

	Dominance submission relationship with aggressive and hostile verbalization	Relationship not always satisfactory but acceptable without hostile verbalization	Total
Personal background pattern described before	17	5	22
not adhering to this pattern	9	9	18
Total	26	14	40

$$x^2 + 3.2387 \qquad p > 0.05$$

The statistical analysis shows that the two groups do not differ from each other significantly. The probability is close to, but does not quite reach the 5 per cent significance level which in this instance represents a x^2 value of 3.481.

But even if the data were significant, three *caveats* must be entered here. One, the sample is small and not randomly drawn. Second, the data reported here are derived from interviews only and not supported by any other evidence; they may well have some impressionistic quality. Third, the explanation suggested in the following is in part based on psychoanalytic theory. Although a close working contact had been maintained with many researchers of this sub-group, no prolonged psychoanalytic study of any of them was carried out. Consequently, the psychoanalytic concepts integrated into the following psychological explanation cannot be considered as proved in terms of this study but rather tending to throw light on facts that otherwise might remain, at least in part, obscure.

Analysis

There are two questions at this juncture:

1. What are the dynamics of the organizational friction causing anxiety and potential inefficiency of personnel otherwise well-qualified in marketing?

2. What are the dynamics causing confusion about the identity of the individual researcher's role and the principles that govern the acceptable conduct in this role?

The former may well have its matrix in the working environment, particularly in its social and technical conditions. The latter's may be found in the personality structure, and possibly also in the individual's physical condition. It is important to note, however, that these three assumptions are likely to be interrelated, thereby presenting different aspects of a common core problem.

Some Socio-Technical Aspects of the Problem

To examine the underlying dynamics of the organizational friction described in this paper, it is useful to view a business organization as a socio-technical system (Rice, 1960; Trist and Bamfort, 1951). This implies that an organization carries out its technical or operational tasks through people working together in an organized way. Consequently, the structure and policies of the organization need to be clearly and consistently related to its overall objectives, or what Selznick (1958) calls its mission: all the tasks that are essential for the organization's survival, regardless of the number or priority of these tasks.

To carry out these essential 'primary tasks' (Rice, 1963), the organization employs strategies (Argyris, 1960). One is its marketing plan: its determined method of dealing with the external world – the market. Another is its organizational structure: the way it arranges itself internally to effect the marketing plan (Rogers, 1963a). These strategies, by the way in which they have been conceived and are carried out, will affect the organization's development, its flexibility, its effectiveness and its commitment towards its mission. They will also affect the opportunities it affords its members to satisfy their own personal

163

needs and thereby further the growth of their own personalities.

It can, therefore, be assumed that to the degree to which the organization's mission and the members' personal needs coincide, we may find efficiency in the use of technologies designed to carry out the primary tasks. Conversely, to the degree that this congruence is lacking, there will be a loss of both organizational effectiveness and personal satisfaction.

A marketing organization can be seen as a sub-system with its mission to create and implement the company's marketing plan. To carry out its primary task of creating the marketing plan it requires information to be supplied by the market researchers. This information is derived from judgements about the dynamics of the market, the organization's own work force, its suppliers, the government, public opinion, and other forces too numerous to mention here, each in varying degrees of importance. It is essential to bear in mind that the determinants of the weight of these forces, dynamic in character, are neither finite in number, nor are they stable. Those who might contend that the market researcher's work is related to the market only, and not to the other areas mentioned before, may well ponder a little about what happens to research findings that prove useless because of forces in those areas. It will highlight the fate of simple answers to simple questions dealing with complex marketing situations.

It is, therefore, the work of the market researcher to advise and assist the marketer in the specified formulation of the marketing problem, and then, to provide that kind of relevant and meaningful information that will facilitate the marketer's work to plan creatively for the approximate satisfaction of the market. This marketing plan affects all activities of the organization. Starting from the needs or the prospects for the product or service, expressed into specifications for production of the products and services, inevitably importantly touching all work of the organization, it culminates in the delivery of these products and services to customers and consumers in a manner satisfactory to them and profitable to the company. The marketing plan ultimately approved by the chief executive can thus be seen as a complex of the market's needs and desires, from which the marketer then selects those he deems most profitable to his company.

The inadequacy of the techniques available for this primary task, especially considering its complexity and importance, may well engender the dynamics of the organizational friction described before. However, since certainly not all but only some researcher-marketer relationships show this organizational friction, it cannot be fully explained in terms of economic, social or technological determinants exclusively. Without denying their importance, there is a need for a psychological analysis of the individual's behaviour, involving, if necessary, unconscious components of their motivations.

In his book *Managers: Personality and Performance* (Rogers, 1963a) and in other articles (1963b; 1963c) the author has shown that organizational behaviour which on the face of it or in the light of economic and social factors appears contradictory or at least difficult to explain, is quite likely to become comprehensible in terms of the psychology of the individual who is engaged in it. In this sense, no assumption is made that people are 'stupid', but rather that their ability to use more fully their capacity for decision making related to their work, may be affected by an excessive use of psychological defense mechanisms.

Some Possible Psychological Aspects of the Problem

The marketers and researchers who were troubled, when relating to one another and to their own work, seemed to have relied on defence mechanisms to a degree greater than warranted by the nature of their roles. The marketers were frequently inadequately trained for their tasks and their past experiences did not seem to suffice for solving complex marketing problems of the present day. They seemed to compensate for their inability to operate creatively in their markets by acting negatively towards market research. Rather than utilizing the functioning but imperfect tools of market research, they experienced them as additional threats, and defended against their mounting anxieties by projecting the feelings of their own inadequacies on to the researchers and their scientific methods.

The researchers felt frustrated in their desire to utilize their professional skills in the production of 'good research'. Wishing to stay on their jobs, or to retain their clients, they felt it essential to develop research findings approximating the marketers' expectations. They assumed that exercising their professional skills and thereby 'proving themselves' may have entailed the loss of their roles. Considering the lack of perfection of their own tools and the lack of adequate competence of their marketing managers, they accepted methodological innovations, at times indiscriminately, and felt that it would be appropriate if they were placed closest to the hierarchical top. Yet, they also experienced the value of their own work doubted, their organizational position unchanged, being misunderstood and often made scapegoats for their marketing managers' shortcomings. They felt that they were responsible for the implementation of their marketing managers' operational plans; they also felt an obligation to be decisively effective in decision making processes of the hierarchical top, all functions which in reality were never theirs.

They appeared deeply involved in the task of understanding their marketing problems and ascertaining information about them. They were, however, less involved in analysing the effects of their work on the marketers as individuals. While pointing to inefficiencies in the marketer's work and suggesting remedies through altering their own social position in the organizational structures, they often seemed to be aware of the improbability that such changes would occur. In short, there was a critical confusion about the identity of their roles and the principles that govern the acceptable conduct in these roles. Erikson (1956) defined such an identity crisis as a stage in which the individual endeavours to detect some meaningful resemblance between what he has come to see in himself and what his sharpened awareness tells him others judge and expect him to be.

At a surface level, the troubled marketer-researcher relationship can be seen to result from two factors. One is social – the expectations each has of the other's performance. The other is technical – the expertise that each has in his work. These factors must affect the tolerance the people in those two roles will have about the other's and their own 'shortcomings'.

In reality not all marketers are insecure autocrats. Those who might be, do in fact need the help of the researchers quite badly, albeit in an understanding and palatable manner. Moreover, modern economics, particularly in the countries in which this study was conducted, almost constantly has job opportunities in marketing and market research. As a result, the hated dependence on dominating managers cannot be adequately explained in terms of external reality. At a deeper level, this relationship can be seen to be affected by personality traits, certainly those of the researchers.

Psychoanalytic theory would suggest that the personality syndrome of some researchers described before can be seen as a description of a personality essentially having received too little love in childhood, and having never felt entirely accepted by the parents. As a result, there is inadequate security within the individual, a great need to prove himself worthy, thus becoming accepted by others and eventually being superior to them. This personality type is envious of other people's success and security, capable of great hostility, and frequently subject to psychosomatic illnesses. Unconsciously, such individuals are likely to perceive managers as symbolic representations of the unloving parents whom they wish to tame, punish or degrade, and thereby to eventually prove themselves superior.

It is in this sense, that the desire to report directly to the chief executive can be understood. The first step – egalitarianism with the marketing managers – seems to represent at a deeper level an unconscious denial that there are differences between children and parents. The subsequent desire for further elevation can then be seen as a wish to lord over the parents, who then should feel as the child had felt when he experienced them to lord over him. It may also represent an expression of the fantasy of the family romance, in which the child believes himself to be a changeling reared by parents of a lower station and character than those to whom he was born and with whom he should rightfully be. All this is fantasied to come about by magic, which enables the child to be more powerful than the parent.

This, then, might provide an explanation for the blind faith in methodology that had proven successful for others. This analysis could be carried out in greater detail, but its basic approach and function may well have become clear by now. If there is validity about the kind of infantile aspects which appear in the market researcher's identity crisis, then it may well be that there is a tendency for market research to attract, among others, people who, in the psychoanalytic sense of the term, want to 'act out' in their daily work, unresolved problems in their personality structure. If this is predominantly the case, these researchers may be vociferous about the need to clear up this role confusion, while simultaneously tending to perpetuate it because it satisfies other co-existing needs. On the other hand, market researchers predominantly motivated by a genuine curiosity about the market, are likely to go about their work in a manner designed to clarify their roles. Should further research verify these assumptions, thereby indicating a differential capacity among researchers to cope with stress in their work situations, this would have an important bearing on the selection policy for researchers and also on remedial steps for those whom a company may wish to help further in developing their personalities and thereby free more of their work capacity from being encumbered by defence mechanisms.

Recommendations

No claim is made as a result of this pilot study of a precise or complete analysis of the identity crisis of the market researcher, nor, indeed, of a remedy for this problem. Yet there is an unmistakable aspiration to move towards both. In this sense, three recommendations are put forward, hopefully conceived to provide a measure of remedy.

1. *Detailed role specification* for marketers and researchers when both are members of the same firm, or a mutually agreed proposal describing the marketing problem, the scope and depth of the required information, the methodology to be used, the resources in time and monies allocated and an approximate time schedule for the various phases of this work, when the researcher-marketer relationship is that of an independent organization and its client. In either instance it is important that the content of these documents is re-examined periodically or whenever the business situation requires it. Re-examination, which at times may result in revisions, will tend to enhance a closer awareness of the business reality and its dynamic changes.

2. *Sensitivity training* for both marketers and researchers,

making for greater awareness and enhancing conceptual skills: creative thinking, seeing new relationships, manipulating variables, recognizing unconscious processes, and thereby reducing their effect on organizational efficiency (Argyris, 1962; Katz, 1955; Rice, 1965).

3. *An educational function specified in the role of the researcher and directed towards the marketer.* In this context, education is seen strictly in terms of its Latin base *educere*, that is – bringing out, developing from latent and potential existence – thus helping the marketer to bring out his potential to understand marketing research problems and thereby facilitate his work. The concept excludes training, instructing or inculcating. It is based on the teaching principle of discovery free from any advocacy. In this, the researcher's work should be aided by his close acquaintance with social sciences. It will require an essential further ability to sympathise with the marketer. That does not imply agreement with his views or attitudes, but rather their acceptance as being important and meaningful to the marketer. Nor does it imply that the researcher has to like the marketer any more than he did before. It should, however, enable him to see his relationship with the marketer in a different light, conductive to greater organizational efficiency.

The problem area dealt with in this paper is, in the opinion of the author, acute enough to warrant further study. As it frequently happens in research, this study produced more data than could be accounted for in the hypothesis. Following these and other leads, the author hopes that his continued investigations may reveal additional findings potentially leading to recommendations and to further questions.

References
ARGYRIS, C. (1960), *Understanding Organizational Behaviour*, Dorsey Press.
ARGYRIS, C. (1962), *Interpersonal Competence and Organizational Effectiveness*, Dorsey Press.
CARLSON, O. (1962), 'High noon in the market', *Public Opinion Quarterly*, vol. 25.
CORDINER, R. J. (1952), 'Report to the stockholders of General Electric'.

ERIKSON, E. H. (1956), 'The problem of ego identity', *Journal of the American Psychoanalytic Association*, vol. 4, pp. 56–121.

KATZ, R. L. (1955), 'Skills of an executive administrator', *Harvard Business Review*, vol. 33, no. 1.

RICE, A. K. (1960), *Productivity and Social Organization*, Tavistock Publications.

RICE, A. K. (1963), *The Enterprise and its Environment*, Tavistock Publications.

RICE, A. K. (1965), *Learning for Leadership*, Tavistock Publications.

RIESMAN, D., GLAZER, N., and DENNEY, R. (1950), *The Lonely Crowd: A Study in the Changing American Character*, Yale University Press.

ROGERS, K. (1963a), *Managers: Personality and Performance*, Tavistock Publications.

ROGERS, K. (1963b), 'Psychology and the Manager', *New Society*.

ROGERS, K. (1963c), 'Where the marketing concept is missing', *Engineering*, vol. 96.

ROGERS, K. (1965), 'Marketing's sacred cow – what is it?', *New York Chapter Newsletter*, vol. 20, no. 9, American Marketing Association.

SELZNICK, P. (1958), *Leadership in Administration*, Row, Peterson.

TRIST, E. L., and BAMFORT, K. W. (1951), 'Some social and psychological consequences of the Longwall method of coal getting', *Human Relations*, vol. 4, no. 1.

Part Two Marketing Research Methods

The development of sampling procedures is the major foundation of modern marketing research. Two specific but often ignored facets are explored by Blunden (Reading 9) and Emmett (Reading 10), sampling frames and sample design. Model building procedures are of growing significance in many areas of marketing, and Kotler (Reading 11) examines their full gamut.

Data collection is normally accomplished by some form of questionnaire, and an extract from Payne's classic book *The Art of Asking Questions* is included (Reading 12). Rothman (Reading 13) explores the relative merits of various scaling methods as indicators of propensities to purchase, and Goldman (Reading 14) evaluates the strengths and pitfalls of group depth interviews. Two further major forms of data collection, the consumer panel and the retail audit, are reviewed by Sudman and Fothergill. Adler analyses the use of telephone interviewing and Levine and Gordon the Postal Survey Method.

Although many of the data collection methods described will be used in association with one another, or indeed simultaneously, they are generally treated here in isolation and in depth emphasizing for each the major advantages and disadvantages.

9 R. M. Blunden

Sampling Frames

R. M. Blunden, 'Sampling frames', *Commentary* (now *Journal of the Marketing Research Society*), vol. 8. 1966, pp. 101–12.

In undertaking surveys we must at the onset ask ourselves what population the study is to cover – is it households, adult individuals, some special age-groups, schoolchildren, shops, offices, farms, undergraduates, caravan-dwellers or some other specialized group such as members of the various professional bodies? In its role as the Government's social, economic and operational research unit, the Social Survey has covered all of these and more besides. Whatever the subject of the survey, and assuming that random sampling methods are to be employed, the method and planning is to a considerable extent determined by the availability of, or the possibility of the construction of, a suitable frame for the population under consideration. Having defined the population which our study should relate to, we have to ask ourselves – is there a suitable frame or can I obtain the data to construct a suitable frame fairly readily? This then brings a further question to our minds – what qualities should we look for in our frame? As the frame is going to play such an important part in our survey it is advisable that we should bear the criteria in mind, and see to what extent any frame we are considering matches up to these criteria. It could well be, and in fact it has happened, that a survey could not be undertaken because of the lack of a suitable frame or the inability to construct a suitable one without considerable expense.

Whenever we are considering a frame therefore we have to ask ourselves these questions:

1. Does it adequately cover the population to be surveyed? Does it cover the whole of the population with which we are concerned or only part of it? (For example, a list of persons draw-

ing retirement pensions would not be an adequate frame from which to draw a sample of people of pensionable age). Does it give us sufficient information about each unit of our population?

2. Having determined its adequacy, how complete is it? Is every unit that should be included in fact included? Is everyone who should be, say, on the electoral register, in fact on it?

3. Is it accurate? Is the information about each individual unit correct? Does the frame as a whole contain units which no longer exist? Does it include the dead, or the demolished dwelling? If so, then it is not accurate.

4. And with some frames it is vitally important to ask this question – is there any duplication? If there is, then the probability of selection is disturbed and a unit can enter the sample more than once. As an example, although there is no duplication in the primary frame itself, this problem can arise when using a frame such as, say, exchange telephone numbers to select a sample of businesses. One may select the same firm through several numbers and this necessitates acquiring additional data to allow for re-weighting in the processing stages. There is of course straightforward duplication in frames such as the Electoral Register where one can register in more than one place.

5. We must ask ourselves is our frame up-to-date? It could have met all the criteria when compiled but could well be deficient when it came to be used. This could well be true of all frames involving the human population as change is taking place continuously.

6. How convenient is it to use? Is it readily accessible? Is it arranged in a way suitable for sampling? Can it easily be re-arranged in a way to enable us to introduce stratification, to undertake multi-stage sampling, etc.?

These are quite demanding criteria and it is most unlikely that any frame would meet them all. Nevertheless, they are factors to be borne in mind whenever we undertake random sampling. Frequently, it means carrying out a considerable amount of research; for what might on the surface seem ideal, can show a number of defects on investigation. We need to know how and when our frame is constructed, what is included and excluded, what, if anything, might possibly have been left off, how and when it is brought up-to-date. When we know the answers to these questions, then at least we are in a fairly strong position to be able to define the population we are in fact covering in our survey.

Before considering the types of frames suitable for use when sampling human populations, let us mention the three broad categories into which surveys fall:

1. *Census type* – the full census type in which a limited amount of information is obtained about every member of the population. The design is a single stage one and there is some natural stratification. The major problem is an administrative one. Sample censuses can be a very different problem.

2. *Local surveys* – covering a town or some small area. The sampling may be a single or possibly two-stage design; these are frequently quite detailed studies.

3. *National surveys* – sample surveys covering the whole population from which fairly accurate estimates for the whole population or certain large cross-sections of the population can be made. Such surveys allow scope for increased efficiency through efficient sample design. They invariably call for multi-stage sampling, the use of stratification and possibly on occasion the use of varying sampling fractions.

Types of sampling frame

What types of frames are suitable for sampling populations? Broadly, they may be classified as follows:

(a) Lists of individuals, either of the whole population or of some special groups within, used for administrative purposes.
(b) Census returns from a complete census.
(c) Returns from an earlier survey.
(d) Lists of dwellings within specified areas.
(e) Large scale maps.

Frames from lists of individuals

In this category we can include the electoral register – of which we will say more later. There are others such as lists of members of professional bodies, the blind, etc., most of which are produced for some administrative purpose. Their suitability as frames depends on the administrative machinery, not only centrally but frequently locally, and therefore their accuracy may vary for different areas. Such lists often have defects which could make them unsuitable as frames and careful investigation is needed. In most cases, lists of individuals are not suitable as frames for sampling households, although in the case of the electoral register where the individuals are grouped, there are suitable methods of obtaining samples of households.

Frames from a complete population census

If the data were readily available, the returns from a complete census would be ideal as a frame; there would be information about every member of the population, it would be arranged geographically, and would permit a multi-stage, stratified random sample design. Unfortunately, the manner in which the data are collected and analysed tends to preclude its use. As a full census in this country is conducted only every ten years, unless a sample were drawn immediately the data were collected, the information would be badly out of date for the greater part of the existence of a frame based on this. A complete census can, of course, be a very convenient frame for data to be obtained simultaneously from a sample of the population as in the case of the 10 per cent sample at the time of the 1961 census. For various reasons such an undertaking presents a number of problems. Nevertheless, the 1961 census is being used as a frame for the 1966 sample census supplemented by a sample of dwellings coming into existence since then.

A previous survey as a frame

A survey which has been undertaken can be used as a frame to provide a sample of perhaps some special section of the population or as the basis of a later survey on the same subject where some measure of change over time is required, e.g., a housing survey.

Experience has shown that where such a survey is undertaken the initial sample needs to be designed with this in mind and the data should be brought up to date continuously during the intervening period. As in the case of the 1966 sample census the sample has to be added to, to take account of new building.

Lists of dwellings as a frame

As we shall see later lists such as the valuation or rating lists can be very useful as a frame for obtaining a sample of dwellings. Although produced periodically they are revised in the interim and such lists will include dwellings which were not necessarily occupied at the time of compilation but may be at the time of the survey.

Using large scale maps as a frame

The grid system on the ordnance survey maps enables one to break down an area into suitably sized blocks to which other data, such as perhaps noise contours can be related. If large scale maps – such as six inch – are used, the location of buildings are shown and a sample of dwellings can be obtained. Such a method of sampling demands a considerable amount of preliminary work, the amount depending to a large extent on what estimates are being made and the accuracy required. Apart from anything else, one major problem is the availability of up-to-date large scale maps.

The two most generally available frames

Even today it is, I suppose, true to say that those of us who are concerned with samples of individuals or households have to resort to the use of the valuation lists or the electoral register as a sampling frame. Often we are interested in one sex only or some specific age-group and we have to use one of these two frames to obtain our particular population because there is nothing else available to us. This being so, let us look at these two frames in the light of our experience over the years and see how they match up to our criteria, and what are their advantages and disadvantages in use.

The Valuation Lists

Under the Local Government Act, 1948, the Valuation Department of the Board of Inland Revenue is responsible for the preparation of the listing and valuation of all hereditaments. The valuation lists are divided into three parts.

Part 1: *Hereditaments other than industrial and freight transport hereditaments*
This section contains dwelling units, shops, offices, cinemas, theatres etc., and other forms of property not included in Parts II and III.

Part II: *Industrial hereditaments*
Including mines and factories.

Part III: *Freight – transport hereditaments*

These include railways, road transport depots, docks and canals.

The lists are prepared by the board for each local authority administrative area in the country so we have data available for each. A new valuation list should be prepared every five years, but for various reasons there have been postponements.

However, not only do the local inland revenue valuation officers have these lists, but copies are given to each local authority, and from these the authority prepares its own rating lists and levies its rates on the valuations laid down by the inland revenue. During the life of the list it becomes amended. The local authority advises the local valuation office of changes, demolitions and new buildings, and the valuation office in turn issues directives to the local authority. Of the local authority's own rating lists, which are used as its working documents, let me just say that they take various forms throughout the country; sometimes in the form of ledgers, sometimes card index, and the current trend is to put the data on computers.

When wanting to use these records as a frame therefore it is usually the authority's copy of the valuation list which one has access to. The data available for each separately rated unit can be:

(a) Name of occupier or of owner.
(b) The situation (i.e. address) of the unit.
(c) Brief description of the unit, e.g. 'house', 'flat', 'shop', 'shop and rooms', 'house and garage' etc.
(d) The gross and rateable values.

Experience over the last few years has shown that (a) is rarely included and even where reference has been made to the local rating list the names given there have not been up-to-date.

As a frame then, what advantages and disadvantages are there in using the valuation lists?

In the first place it must be remembered that permission of the authority must be sought before use can be made of the list and there is the risk of refusal.

We are fortunate in that there is available a publication called 'Rates and rateable values' which gives us not only data on the total number of hereditaments and total rateable value for each local authority in England and Wales, but gives us a breakdown of these into various categories, e.g. domestic, industrial, shops, offices, other commercial, crown, etc. and further breaks down domestic into three strata of rateable value. Thus we are able to introduce various forms of stratification, e.g. geographical as well as some economic factor based on rateable value, before selecting our primary sampling units.

Within each p.s.u. we have for each hereditament a certain amount of useful information such as its description and rateable value although the description can leave doubts in one's mind. Does 'shop and rooms' mean there is living accommodation included? This is not always clear and can be determined only when the interviewer is at the address.

The address, in urban areas, is usually adequate if interviewers are being used, but not if one is conducting a postal enquiry. In rural areas the situation of the unit may give nothing more than the name of a village and a certain amount of research is necessary to identify the particular unit. As has already been stated, an up-to-date name for the occupier is not necessarily readily obtainable from the records.

So much for the individual units; what of the list itself for sampling from? At the beginning of its life it is fairly straightforward, normally arranged in alphabetical order of street – it is not usual nowadays to find the lists broken down into smaller units within an authority – and frequently with 'council' property kept separately. The frequency with which alterations and additions are incorporated in the lists varies so that one cannot say that at any one time they are necessarily correct and up-to-date in any one area. As time progresses, more and more items are deleted either as they are demolished, or directions are issued due to alterations or revaluations, and these get added later on in direction sheets. The process of drawing a systematic sample of dwelling units therefore can be quite a demanding operation, especially when it is remembered that Part 1 of the list also contains non-dwellings. Unfortunately also, there is not always an equal number of entries per page.

One can draw such a sample, again making use of 'Rates and rateable values' to determine our sampling interval. Having determined this, taking a random start, one counts through *every* item on the list recording every 'i th' item, whether or not it is deleted, or a non-dwelling unit, and recording precisely as it it given. In other words, if one lands on a unit and it is crossed through, you record it and cross it through in the same manner. Where it is an alteration and has been crossed through, that item will appear again in its altered form, in the alteration sheets; in fact one may find the same item entered and crossed through several times. Although this is a laborious process and some editing is required later, it is the most satisfactory way of drawing a sample. The alternative of counting only those items not deleted and only those which are dwellings can lead to a considerable amount of error which is virtually impossible to put right.

Experience with the valuation lists has shown it can be expected that there will be included in one's sample, dwellings which have been demolished, units which have not yet been constructed and those with which the description does not tally.

The valuation lists do not match up to all our criteria but for some studies, e.g. housing surveys, they form the most suitable frame, especially if it is remembered that it is sometimes possible to obtain some supplementary information about the selected units.

So much for the valuation lists and some of the problems with which one is faced when making use of the same. Now what of the electoral register?

Electoral Register

It is the responsibility of the Electoral Registration Officers to compile a new register each year. The 'qualifying date' is 10 October, and it comes into force the following 16 February. It remains in force, without any alteration, until the next register comes into force on the same date in the next year. Thus the register is four months old when it comes into force and is sixteen months old at the end of its life.

The same register is used to record electors for both parliamentary and local government elections, and is therefore arranged so that electors can be defined by ward or parish, by local government administrative district, by parliamentary constituency and by county. The smallest unit into which any constituency is divided is a polling district.

Four categories of electors are recorded:

1. Civilian parliamentary electors.
2. Civilian local government electors.
3. Service voters.
4. Persons who will become twenty-one (now eighteen) after the qualifying date (10 October) and before the following 16 June. These latter are entitled to vote at elections held after the 1 October following the qualifying date. Their names are prefixed with the letter 'Y'.

Service voters are also distinguishable, their names being prefixed with the letter 'S' and likewise electors entitled to vote *only* at local government elections are prefixed with the letter 'L'.

The general qualifications necessary for registration as a civilian parliamentary elector are:

(a) To be a British subject or a citizen of Northern Ireland.

(b) To have reached the age of twenty-one years (now eighteen on the qualifying date, except for 'Y' voters who will be entitled to vote at elections held after the following 1 October.

(c) To be resident on the qualifying date in the area in respect of which the register is prepared.

Arrangement of the Register

In urban areas the register is usually arranged in alphabetical order of street within a polling district. Within each street the addresses are generally arranged in number order, where there are numbers, up one side of the street and then down the other. Where dwellings are named only, these usually appear in adjacent order in the street.

The order in which the registered electors appear at each address varies; frequently it is alphabetical order, but not always necessarily so. Why the order is altered from that in which names appear on the forms which are returned, one would not know, but it would be most useful to those conducting surveys if they could be given showing the householder first.

In most rural areas electors are usually arranged in alphabetical order of surnames, and where surnames are the same, in alphabetical order of forename. Names therefore do not appear in address order; someone with a surname beginning with the letter 'A' can appear at the top of the list, and someone residing at the same address whose surname begins with the letter 'W' appears right at the end. This presents problems when drawing a sample of addresses.

Each elector is given an elector's number which usually starts at 1 at the beginning of a polling district, and runs consecutively throughout the polling district. 'S' voters' names may be included with other electors at an address or may be added at the end of the polling district with no address being given.

It might be appropriate here to say that in an analysis of a sample of addresses in the electoral register approximately 87 per cent were numbered, about 11·5 per cent were named only and the remainder were neither numbered nor named.

From what has been said so far, the electoral register should present us with a frame which has a number of advantages. We have a list of persons aged approximately twenty years and five months and over at the qualifying date, together with their addresses. The registers are arranged in such a way that they permit a wide choice of primary, secondary and so on, sampling units in multi-stage designs. They are fairly readily accessible, locally or centrally, and in many cases copies of the entire or part of the register can be purchased. For a long while it has presented us with an index – the J index – for units of all sizes from polling districts upwards. Because of the high proportion of the electorate (about 22 per cent) now shown as being liable for jury service, as against 1·5 million (about 4·8 per cent) in 1955, a current J index can no longer be looked upon as a satisfactory indicator.

In practice how does it match up to the criteria we laid down for our frames? As a frame for sampling individuals, how satisfactory is it?

Not everyone aged twenty-one years and over is entitled to be registered as a parliamentary elector, but it is estimated that approximately 98 per cent of the resident civilian population are. Various estimates of the deficiency of the register in this respect have been made, so let us look at some figures:

	England and Wales
	millions
Estimated number of civilians aged twenty-one years and over	32·28
Estimated number of civilians ineligible to be registered	0·65
Estimated number of civilians eligible for registration	31·53
Civilians aged twenty-one years and over recorded as parliamentary electors on the 1965 register	31·33

This figure will include dead and duplicated names, and therefore cannot be taken as a true figure for the number of persons registered, but it suggests that there are at least some 200–250,000 eligible adults not registered.

But how about the 'Y' voters? Unfortunately, these entries appear to be far from complete. On the 1965 register there were 302,600 civilian voters prefixed with the letter 'Y' – and a further 6100 service voters so prefixed. Estimates of this population which is eligible to be registered as 'Y' voters suggest that only about two-thirds of them are in fact registered. As a frame for this younger age-group the register as such would not be altogether satisfactory. Fortunately, in many cases we are not concerned with 'Y' voters as a group on their own, but as part of a younger age-group of perhaps sixteen to twenty year-olds.

As we have already stated, the register is out-of-date when it comes into force and becomes more so during its life. Thus it will contain those who have died, and there will be those who have moved from their given address. Figures suggest that there is a cumulative removal rate of about $\frac{3}{4}$ per cent per month, so that by the end of its life some 12 per cent of electors will no longer be living at their registered address. This increase in the removal rate has been noticeable over the past few years, but it is also estimated that about 70 per cent are still to be found living near their registered address, so that the loss due to removal can be cut quite considerably if some trouble is taken to try and trace our named individual. It is hoped that some further and perhaps more accurate information might become available as a result of some work being carried out in connection with the forthcoming sample census.

With the defects we have mentioned, and provided some trouble is taken to follow up 'movers' and possibly to compensate for those who cannot be followed up, the electoral register is still a satisfactory frame for a sample of adult individuals or of adults of one sex, as the sex is generally readily identifiable from the data given, i.e., the forename.

What of the register as a frame for households or given classes of the population, such as the elderly or younger people?

There is no completely straightforward way of obtaining samples of households from the electoral register since only addresses are distinguished. Various methods are used – a sample of electors can be drawn and the interviewer be instructed to interview the household containing the named person. This would necessitate reweighting by the reciprocal of the number of registered electors in the selected elector's household. Apart from this, there is the problem of what to do in those cases where a new household is living at the address.

A second method is to draw a correctly weighted sample of addresses, and interview all the households at the address. This in turn gives a correctly weighted sample of households. Drawing such a sample in rural areas becomes something of a problem and particularly in areas where the only address given is that of the district. Under some circumstances one could be expected to interview all other households whose only address is that of the district. The possibility of interviewing a large number of households could also arise in other normal areas where multi-occupation of addresses occurs. One practice has been to limit the number of households to be interviewed at an address. This is not a correct thing to do, but is acceptable when it affects only a very small proportion of addresses.

A possible method of overcoming this weakness is to treat the larger multi-household addresses in a different manner. A sample of electors is drawn and where the number of different surnames at the chosen elector's address is say five or more, only the household which contains the selected elector, or the one which has replaced it where that person has moved, is interviewed. It entails determining how many persons in the household are eligible to be included on the register, and carrying out a rejection process afterwards, accepting all those with one eligible person, half of those with two, two-thirds of those with three, and so on. This method obviously is acceptable only when the number of rejections is likely to be small: the wastage in areas of heavy multi-occupation would be too great, and in such areas recourse to the valuation lists as a sampling frame would be more expedient.

Let us consider the register as a frame for obtaining samples of special sections of the population.

To select a sample of persons of pensionable age one can find from census data the proportion in the population, calculate the average number per household and draw the appropriate number of addresses from the register. It entails calling at addresses to ascertain those containing our population, and interviewing all those in the age-group at the address where they are living. Whether a sample of addresses is drawn from the register or of rateable units from the valuation list, this has proved satisfactory.

What of the younger population? It frequently happens one wishes to extend a sample of individuals down to the age of sixteen years, including the 'under twenty-one's' with their correct probability. A sample of adult individuals can be drawn from the register in the normal way and the younger persons be included where the selected elector is the head-of-household. Each household will have had a chance of coming into the sample proportional to the number of registered electors it contains, and if all younger persons were included reweighting would have to take place. By assuming each household has only one head, and taking the 'under twenty-one's' in those households only, they appear in the sample with their right probability. Experience so far is showing that a sample of sixteen to twenty year olds obtained in this way is deficient.

Occasionally a sample of 'sixteen to twenty's' only is required and the same procedure can be adopted as that used to obtain a sample of 'elderly' i.e., calculate the number of addresses to give the required sample size and interview all those at the addresses containing them.

At present it would appear that samples obtained in either of these ways can be deficient by as much as 18 per cent. This is an alarming figure, and satisfactory ways of obtaining a sample of this population is the subject of some research. Some use has been made of the valuation lists and a preliminary glance at the results tends to show deficiencies exist which cannot be accounted for by the numbers in 'institutional type' addresses, etc. It would be interesting to know of other people's experience with this age group.

I have spent a great deal of time talking about the valuation lists and electoral register as frames for sampling the population, as these are, to a large extent, the only frames available to many of us for this purpose.

Sample Census 1966

As you are aware, a sample census was undertaken in April 1966. This is an instance where the 1961 census data are providing the frame. A systematic sample of one in ten of the units will be taken and a sample of new units obtained from the valuation list will be added to it. Without going into it in any great detail – for I am sure that the method, procedure and problems are going to be written up very fully – may I just use it to illustrate that using as a frame, data obtained at an earlier time is not necessarily as straightforward as it might seem.

Assuming that the facts as obtained earlier are correct, changes will have been taking place continuously since then. Some changes will be quite straightforward – dwellings will have been demolished – these are no longer a part of the population. New dwellings will have come into being; what does one do about sampling these? In England and Wales a sample of one in ten dwelling hereditaments which have come into rating for the first time since the 1961 census will be added to the sample drawn from the enumeration records. In this there is a danger of overlap. Delays in units being added to the valuation lists means that they can have been included in the census and will appear again through having been given an 'N number' after the date of the census. Also, units designated as 'new' may be reconstructions of old buildings or extensions to existing buildings.

How does one identify the unit to be called at? An address which may have seemed perfectly adequate at the time of enumeration may be insufficient to identify the unit now. A unit could have been identified as 44A High Street at the time of the census and may have been one of three separate units in that building at the time. Now, what was previously three units has been rearranged as two units, one of which is still numbered 44A but in fact includes part of what was formerly 44B or C. And how about identifying units where the street numbering has changed – and this is quite a frequent occurrence. Having identified a unit by the number of rooms would not necessarily be adequate as rooms can be put to different use and may not have qualified as rooms at the time of the census.

This and a number of other problems are ones which are having to be faced and decisions made, not only as to what procedure to adopt in the field but how to process the data afterwards. These same problems were met with when recalls were made on an earlier housing survey for the Milner-Holland Committee on Housing in Greater London.

In the case of the sample census, one feels that there is much to be said for drawing the sample from the valuation lists. These would be brought up to date at the end of the financial year and could possibly cut out some of the problems of using two separate frames. In Scotland, where new valuation records are drawn up each year, the sample census is in fact being drawn from the Valuation Rolls.

A post-enumeration study is being carried out by the social survey in a sample of areas and this may well produce data which will be of value when considering future censuses, whether complete censuses or sample ones.

Each survey presents its own particular sampling problems; nevertheless it is hoped that what has been said about sampling frames generally, and the electoral register and valuation list in particular, may be of some value in helping to design efficient samples.

10 B. P. Emmett

Cost Factors in Sample Design

B. P. Emmett, 'Cost factors in sample design', *Commentary* (now *Journal of the Market Research Society*), vol. 8, 1966, pp. 116–22.

The ultimate question to be decided when designing a sample – after settling matters such as the number of stages, the choice of primary units, the stratification at each stage and so on – is to determine the allocation of the sample to the various stages in such a way as either to minimize the variances of the estimates for a fixed cost, or alternatively to minimize the cost of making estimates with specified variances. To do this involves making as good a guess as possible at the appropriate values to be given to quite a number of different functions. The theory has been fully explored and will be found in all worthwhile text books on sampling. Unfortunately the different authors use their own nomenclatures and have their own ways of formulating the problems. I shall follow the approach of Hansen, Hurwitz and Madow (1953).

The cost function these authors explore for a three-stage sample with m primary units, a mean of $\bar{n}$ secondary units per primary unit and a mean of $\bar{q}$ ultimate units per secondary unit is

$C(\text{total cost}) = c_0\sqrt{m} + c_1 m + c_2 m\bar{n} + c_3 m\sqrt{\bar{n}} + c_4 mn\bar{q}$

For a two-stage design the function reduces, of course, to

$$C = c_0\sqrt{m} + c_1 m + c_2 m\bar{n}.$$

This formulation proposes that the costs of a survey can be approximated by a function which has elements implying increases at fixed rates for each addition to the number of units at the three stages, namely an extra cost of c_1 for each new primary unit, c_2 for each new secondary unit and c_4 for each new final unit. In addition, the formula says, costs increase in proportion to the square roots of the number of primary units and the number of secondary units, the reasoning behind this being that travel between units may be proportional to the distances between them and the mean distance between points chosen at random in a fixed plane area falls in proportion to the number of such units.

The adequacy of this cost function may be questioned. In the first place it contains no term in $\sqrt{\bar{q}}$ and hence does not make allowance for the travel time between final units. This may have arisen because in American practice the final units are commonly adjacent addresses, but even so the travel element in making recalls on non-contacts cannot be allowed for directly. It may also be doubted whether the 'square root rule' for travel costs holds in practice. I suspect it may be a gross over-simplification of the true situation. Furthermore, it is also doubtful if the other, non-travel, costs of adding primary units to the sample are of the simple linear form $c_1 m$. A much more complex discontinuous relationship has been proposed, as illustrated below, but the theory has not been worked out yet.

Though it is easy to see possible flaws in the cost function considered above, and whilst it would no doubt be possible to construct more realistic cost functions for any given survey operation, it may prove rather unrewarding to do so, as the equations giving the optimal distribution of interviews between the various stages would almost certainly be difficult to solve. The simple form being considered will probably serve reasonably well under most practical circumstances and has the inestimable virtue of leading to straightforward solutions for optimal values of m, $\bar{n}$ and $\bar{\bar{q}}$.

The constants c_0 to c_4 are the first things that need to be estimated. For sample design problems, no great precision is needed in making the estimates, but a clear idea of their relative magnitude must be obtained if optimum design characteristics are to be calculated. The following list gives ten ingredients of the cost of a survey, suggesting which coefficients each of them contributes to:

(a) Planning and direction. Contributes to fixed overheads only.
(b) Selecting primary and secondary units. Proportional to number of such units. Contributes to c_1 and c_2.

(c) Listing the final units. Mainly proportional to number of final units. Contributes to c_4.

(d) Interviewer training and briefing. (?)Proportional to number of primary units. Contributes to c_1.

(e) Interviewer travel between units. Proportional to numbers of primary and secondary units. Contributes to c_0 and c_3.

(f) Printing schedules etc. Partly fixed overheads and partly proportional to number of final units. Contributes to c_4.

(g) Interviewing. Mainly proportional to number of final units, but may depend also on number of secondary units. Contributes to c_2 and c_4.

(h) Field supervision. (?)Proportional to interviewing costs. Contributes to c_2 and c_4.

(i) Editing, coding and tabulating. Mainly proportional to number of final units. Contributes to c_4.

(j) Report writing. Fixed overheads.

We first estimated values of the coefficients in our own survey operations only four or five years ago, but when we did they turned out to be rather surprising. The important revelation was that for a two-stage sample the ratio of c_1 to c_2 was much lower than had been expected, whilst c_0 was negligible. Different organizations will no doubt discover different values for the coefficients but it is unlikely that the relationship between them will differ greatly.

In practice, it seems that c_0 and c_3 can be ignored. As has been said, these expressions involving square roots are intended to represent the 'travel components' of cost and would be substantial only if, for example, the whole sample enquiry was being undertaken by a few investigators who travelled around all the units. Even then, however, there may be no great loss in omitting these two coefficients, alloting their contributions of cost to the terms involving coefficients c_1 and c_2. As Hansen, Hurwitz and Madow say: 'Although total travel increases with increasing numbers of primary sampling units within the sample, it increases at a rate considerably slower than the increase in the size of the sample. Consequently the relative contribution to the total cost or to the average cost per primary sampling unit becomes less with increasing numbers of primary sampling units within the sample.' The advantage of eliminating the two terms involving square roots is that approximate solutions for optimum values of m, $\bar{n}$ and $\bar{\bar{q}}$ can readily be obtained. The optimum value of q, i.e. the size of the ultimate cluster, is

$$\bar{\bar{q}} \, (opt) = \sqrt{\left(\frac{1 - \delta_2}{\delta_2} \times \frac{c_2}{c_4} \right)}$$

From this, the values of m and n are obtained from the formulae

$$\bar{n} = \frac{1}{\bar{q}} \sqrt{\left(\frac{1 - \delta_2}{\delta_1} \times \frac{c_1}{c_4} \right)} \text{ and } m = \frac{C}{c_1 + c_2\bar{n} + c_4\bar{n} \, \bar{\bar{q}}}$$

If the travel components are retained, the optimal solutions involve a tiresome iterative process, but often will not change the optimal solutions a great deal.

The above formulae introduce two new unknowns, δ_1 and δ_2, functions which measure the relative variances between and within the different stages. For instance δ_1 is large if the variation between the primary units is considerable in relation to that within them, i.e. between secondary units. δ_2 similarly reflects the relative variance between and within the secondary units. When considering optimal designing in practice one can only guess at the likely values of these two variables, basing one's guesses on previous experience, or estimate them from pilot studies, a slow and expensive operation. In the two-stage case, of course, there is only one δ to be estimated, given by

$$\delta = \frac{\sigma_b - \sigma^2/N}{(N-1) \, \sigma_2/N}$$

Clearly if all elements in a cluster are identical, $\sigma_b^2 = \sigma^2$ and $\delta = 1$, whilst if there is no difference between the clusters $\sigma = 0$

$$\text{and } \delta = \frac{-1}{N-1}$$

Hansen, Hurwitz and Madow quote a few values for two-stage samples drawn from the U.S. Census results, using various sizes of clusters of adjacent homes. The largest value of δ found was 0·43, for the variable 'Rent \$40–49', with tiny clusters of only hree adjacent households. The value fell to 0·112 for clusters of sixty-two adjacent households. For most of the other variables they quote, the values of δ start below 0·2, even with small clusters, and fall to below 0·05 with larger clusters. There seems little reason to believe that the values we would obtain (with the less close clustering normally used in this country) would equal, or even approach, these values, except very occasionally.

The following table reproduces extracts from one of the tables in Hansen, Hurwitz and Madow for the two-stage case, showing the optimal values for the ultimate cluster size for different values of δ and with different relationships between the cost coefficients. I have added further entries for a lower value of δ (0·01) than any they give.

Optimal values of ultimate cluster size in two-stage samples:

$\dfrac{c_0}{cc_2}$	$\dfrac{c_1}{c_2}$	δ			
		0·01	0·02	0·1	0·25
0	0·1	3	2	1	1
	1·0	10	7	3	2
	4·0	20	14	6	3
	16·0	40	28	12	7
0·2	0·1	9	6	2	1
	1·0	13	9	4	2
	4·0	23	16	7	4
	16·0	42	29	12	7
1·0	0·1	14	10	3	2
	1·0	19	13	5	3
	4·0	26	18	7	4
	16·0	44	31	13	8
8·0	0·1	30	21	8	4
	1·0	32	22	8	5
	4·0	37	26	10	6
	16·0	53	37	15	9

As we have seen, c_0, the travel component, is rarely likely to be substantial and therefore c_0^2/cc_2, the first column in the table, will probably be very small. In our own work I find that c_1/c_2, the second column, has a value of less than four, so that for most variables, clusters of about ten would probably work pretty

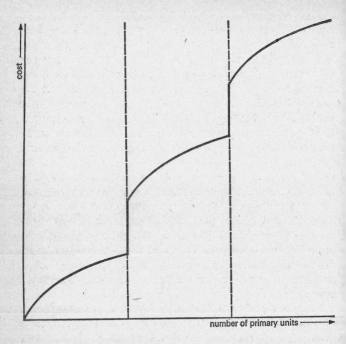

close to the optimum. The only published result relating c_1 to c_2 that I have been able to find is in Gray and Corlett's paper (1950), from which it can be deduced that their ratio of c_1 to c_2 must have been as high as 7·5 to 1, and hence their optimal cluster size was comparatively large. Turning to the three-stage case, small clusters of not more than ten again seem most likely to be optimal under almost any reasonable assumptions about δ_1 and δ_2. A practical example which I gave in an earlier paper produced the following optimal design.

For an expenditure, excluding fixed overheads, of £1000

$$\bar{\bar{q}} = 7, \ \bar{n} = 4\tfrac{1}{2} \text{ and } m = 40,$$

the total sample size, of course, being $7 \times 4\tfrac{1}{2} \times 40 = 1260$.

The unmistakable conclusion from all this is that, with cost components of the kind we experience, very small clusters are almost always to be preferred to large ones.

It is instructive to examine the conditions under which larger clusters would be preferred. Neglecting the travel components, c_0 and c_3, the ultimate cluster size is large only if $c_2 \gg c_4$ and δ_2 is tiny, i.e. if the cost of including a new unit is great compared with the cost of the interview and if the means of secondary units do not differ much. In other words, a short interview and (assuming the clusters are from different strata of second stage units) poor stratification at this stage. A recent paper by Sedransk (1965) points to another situation in which large clusters may be preferred, namely when the survey is concerned with measuring differences between values for two sub-groups rather than the population values themselves. He points out that such differences could be the same whichever primary unit the sub-group observations come from; for example the differences between values for men and for women might be similar in all clusters, whether the *proportions* of men and women in the cluster were the same or not. In the Hansen, Hurwitz and Madow nomenclature this would at least imply a tiny value for δ, and hence a larger optimal cluster size than if the population values were being estimated.

Zarkovitch and Krane (1965) have followed up the lead given in most text-books to show that, given the possibility of making ratio estimates based on supplementary information, a close cluster sample can even be as efficient as a simple random sample. A number of conditions are necessary for this to occur, notably a high correlation between cluster totals and the supplementary information, this correlation to *increase* with the cluster size. I have summarized some of their findings below, the variable being measured being 'personal expenditure on health'.

Size of cluster	Correlation of cluster means with supplementary information	Variance compared with simple random sampling	Variances of ratio estimate compared with S.R.S.	Relative cost for fixed variance
2	0·51	1·13	1·11	1·14
4	0·57	1·43	1·22	1·12
16	0·61	2·39	1·87	0·81
64	0·81	3·81	1·44	1·10

Column 2 shows that the correlation coefficient between the cluster means obtained in two surveys, one made a year after the other, increased from 0·51 with clusters of only two households to 0·81 with clusters of sixty-four. Comparing the variances of the cluster sample with the variances of a simple random sample of the same size shows the great reduction in efficiency due to clustering. If, however, a *ratio estimate* is used, i.e. taking into account the correlation between the two surveys to increase the precision of the estimate, the difference in efficiency becomes much smaller – though simple random sampling still wins (see column 4). When the costs are brought into the argument, the reduction in cost due to clustering shows the 'cost efficiency' to be similar to that of simple random sampling. (This 'efficiency', shown in the final column, is measured in terms of cost for a given standard error of the estimate compared with the cost of achieving the same standard error with simple random sampling.) As will be seen the cluster samples are about as efficient as simple random sampling whatever the size of the cluster.

Neither of the two situations described, in which large clusters would be optimal, is likely to be encountered very often in normal market research work though it is not impossible that shop audits, for instance, in which the overall cluster values for shops in a district may correlate highly with prior information, might parallel the Zarkovitch and Krane position. Apart from this it seems that the superficial attractions of large close clusters are likely to be largely illusory.

References

EMMETT, B. P. (1965), 'Reflections on the state of population sampling in the United Kingdom', *Applied Statistics*, vol. 13, p. 148.

GRAY, P. G., and CORLETT, T. (1950), 'Sampling for the government social survey', *J.Roy. Statist. Soc.*, vol. 113, p. 150.

HANSEN, M. H., HURWITZ, W. N., and MADOW, W. G. (1953), *Sample Survey Methods and Theory*, Wiley.

SEDRANSK, J. (1965), 'Analytical surveys with cluster sampling', *J.Roy. Statist. Soc. B*, vol. 27, p. 264.

ZARKOVITCH, S. S., and KRANE, J. (1965), 'Some efficient uses of compact cluster sampling', *Bulletin of the International Statistical Institute*, vol. 41. bk. 2, p. 875.

11 P. Kotler

Models of Buyer Behaviour

P. Kotler, 'Mathematical models of individual buyer behavior',
Behavioral Science, vol. 13, 1968, no. 4, pp. 274–87.

Buyer behavior has been studied from a variety of theoretical perspectives, resulting in a number of interesting and occasionally incompatible explanations. Depending upon one's scientific predilection, there is the Marshallian buyer, Pavlovian buyer, Freudian buyer, Veblenian buyer, and Hobbesian buyer (Kotler, 1965a). Less grandiose but equally interesting new breeds of buyers can be formulated, such as the Festinger buyer (Festinger, 1957), Riesman buyer (Riesman, Glazer and Denney, 1956), and Rogerian buyer (Rogers, 1951).

It should be recognized that all these models of buyer behavior are true to some extent, and yet each is incomplete. Buyer behavior, as an aspect of human behavior, is so complex that theory develops in connexion with particular aspects of the phenomena. The contemporary effort of behavioral scientists in marketing is to analyze well specific aspects of behavior in the hope that someday someone will put them all together.

The complexity of buyer behavior requires the language of prose to convey all the intricate nuances. Virtually all the classical models of behavior are formulated in prose terms and continue to derive their power through the flexibility and delicious ambiguity of prose. At the same time, the polar viewpoints in behavioral theory are the direct consequence of this ambiguity. This has led an increasing number of scholars to express their behavioral explanations in mathematical terms. Though this involves a high degree of simplification, it promotes increased rigor in the communication and comparison of theories. The development of mathematical behavioral models is a welcome complement to the abundant verbal formulations of individual buyer behavior dynamics.

This is not the place to present a detailed history of mathematical formulations of human behavior, but it would be desirable to highlight a few major works. Some of this work stretches back into the 19th century, when economists such as Edgeworth (1881) and Jevons (1871) first formulated their utility maximization equations of buyer behavior. Early experimental psychologists described many of their findings on learning memory and motivation in terms of mathematical relationships between two or more variables. However, it is only recently that whole systems of equations have been developed to describe more comprehensive aspects of human behavior. A significant step in this direction occurred with the mathematical formulation by Herbert Simon (1954) of George Homan's verbal propositions on human interaction. Simon's model related the strength of positive sentiments, the amount of interaction and the number of common activities of individuals through a series of simultaneous differential equations, each equation showing the change in one of the variables as a function of the others.

Another milestone is represented in the set of papers delivered at a conference on computer simulation and personality theory held at the Educational Testing Service, Princeton University in June 1962 (Tomkins and Messick, 1963). These papers contain impressive speculations and suggestions as to the programming of a computer to duplicate some of the perceptual, cognitive, affective, motivational, and behavioral aspects of homo sapiens. As for representing mathematically the more social interactions of human beings, the recent book by James S. Coleman (1964a) presents an impressive collection of mathematical tools, studies, and possibilities in this area.

With regard to consumer behavior, the literature on mathematical models or individual behavior is scant. A pioneering article by Carman and Nicosia (1965) offers a formulation of buyer decision processes in terms of five simultaneous differential equations. This work is an extension of the Simon approach mentioned earlier (1954). Most of the Markov process articles on consumer brand choice deal with aggregate brand loyalty and switching tendencies rather than with individual consumer behavior. The exceptions are found in the work of Amstutz (1966), Duhamel (1966), Frank (1962), Lipstein (1965), Massy

(1965), Montgomery (1966) and Morrison (1966). Germane research of still a different character is found in Guy Orcutt's work (1961) and that of the Simulmatics Corporation (1962). Orcutt has modeled individual persons who are born, age, marry, divorce, save, spend, and die. The Simulmatics Corporation has modeled the media habits of a hypothetical population of 2944 persons who choose their programs and reading material probabilistically in a way related to their varying social-economic characteristics. As for business and marketing games, hardly any of them have incorporated individual buyers as the *modus operandi* for determining market response, but instead utilize total market or market segment response functions directly.

This brief review of the existing literature is intended to show that the mathematical formulation of human behavior and particularly consumer behavior is in its infancy. Some would say that it ought to stay there because the concept of mathematizing human behavior is either repugnant, simple-minded, or useless. The hostility aroused by this work justifies some discussion of the possible benefits which might emerge from these mathematical investigations. Among the scientific contributions which might be forthcoming from the development of mathematical models of individual buyer behavior are the following.

1. These models will force a more rigorous statement of the variables operating in buying situations and the nature of their relationships.

2. These models will facilitate the comparison of different theories of buyer behavior. The similarities will show up more clearly and the differences can be subjected to sharper empirical tests. The models will highlight the degree to which the differences are structural, functional, or only parametric.

3. These models will help pinpoint more accurately the data needs of marketing decision makers who seek to understand and to some degree influence consumer behavior.

4. These models will stimulate inferences not ordinarily obvious from verbal formulations, much in the way a set of postulates about points and lines stimulates a large number of theorems about spatial relations.

5. These models will facilitate the construction of microconsumer market simulators. The use of microconsuming units in a simulation permits the study of some important properties overlooked in gross market response models, such as the distribution of preferences, the distribution of delays in response to marketing stimuli, and so forth.

These various contributions will be achieved in different degrees depending upon the buying situation which is being modeled and the resources and imagination of the model builder. Each buying situation makes salient a different set of consumer mechanisms and marketing factors. For example the problem of brand choice of frequently purchased consumer nondurables (say coffee, bread, and so on) does not involve the consumer's affective or motivational mechanisms (emotions and drives) as much as his perception and learning mechanisms. Thus a model of buyer behavior in this situation is likely to be most explicit on the perception and learning questions. On the other hand, modeling the buying process for a new automobile does require the imputation of strong and conflicting drives, affective feelings and information seeking.

In short, at the beginning we will have to tolerate a variety of models tailored to specific buying situations. Eventually, they may be forced into higher order abstractions, serving to explain a broader range of buying situations. The beginnings of such a fusion may be found in John Howard's recent verbal model (1963) of the elements describing buying behavior and their interrelationships. By modifying the model in different degrees, one has a flexible framework for examining buying situations ranging from the simple purchase of a staple grocery item (which he classifies as Autonomous Response Behavior), to the purchase of a fountain pen (Limited Problem Solving), to the purchase of a whole computer installation (Extensive Problem Solving). This type of fusion is the ultimate goal of buyer behavior theory. But at the beginning, the most useful mathematical models may be developed for highly specific buying situations.

The Brand Choice Problem for Frequently Purchased Consumer Staples

This paper takes a highly specific buying situation – the weekly shopping for branded staple grocery items – and seeks to describe mathematically the nature of the individual's buying process. This buying situation has been selected for two reasons. First, it is one of the most important and familiar types of buying situations. Second, the type of buying situation has the virtue of being relatively simpler than others in the number and type of psychological processes and marketing factors. It is a good strategy to start with the modeling of simple buying situations and move gradually to more complex ones.

For ease of reference, the brand choice behavior will be thought of as taking place with respect to coffee, a product which has the advantages of familarity, a wide availability of factual information (see Kotler, 1965b, footnote 15), and several sophisticated analyses of consumer panel data designed to appraise the influence of price and price deals (Massy and Frank, 1965; Duhamel, 1966).

The specific problem will be to formulate a mechanism which will cause a hypothetical consumer to make a weekly selection of a coffee brand from three available brands called A, B, and C. The brands can be thought of as having some differences between them in product and merchandising characteristics which partly contribute to variations in buyer response. The task is one of describing how outside stimuli and internal psychological mechanisms interact to produce individual buyer choice behavior over time.

The problem can be made concrete by viewing consumer brand choice behavior in the larger context of the competitive marketing process. The view which will be taken is illustrated in Figure 1. Assume that each week (Box 1) individual consumers go to the supermarket and buy, among other things, a one-pound can of coffee. Three brands are available: A, B and C. They differ slightly in quality, price, sale promotion features, shelf space and position, and other marketing characteristics. In fact, each week may produce some changes in the marketing characteristics of one or more brands (Box 2). The first buyer enters the store with certain brand predispositions (Box 3) and makes a brand choice (Box 4). Buyers continue to enter the store during the week and make coffee brand choices. After the last buyer has made a purchase (Box 5), brand shares are computed for week *t* (Box 6) and they influence through a feedback process the *marketing strategies* of the three competitors in the following week. This process continues week after week until the simulation is over (Box 7), at which point the computer program prints out the brand selection history for each individual buyer and also the brand shares in each period (Box 8). These data can be analyzed for various purposes, such as evaluating different competitive marketing strategies (Kotler, 1965b), examining the validity of different statistical techniques now used to develop demand estimates, and other purposes.

The objective of this paper is to review and extend current models that implement the individual buyer brand choice process in Boxes 3 and 4. These models produce simulated individual brand choice histories that hopefully resemble actual consumer panel histories. To the extent that the simulated histories resemble actual histories, they help sharpen the underlying theory.

It is in fact very difficult to proceed the other way, moving from actual consumer brand histories to inferences about the underlying brand decision processes. Some analysts have sought to interpret buyer decision processes on the basis of their individual brand purchase histories. Consider the following ten-week purchase history: AAABAACAA. The most plausible interpretation is that the buyer has a strong preference for Brand A and occasionally tries other brands for sundry reasons but always returns to A. Yet this same purchase history is subject to a variety of interpretations:

1. *Brand loyalty hypothesis.* The consumer consciously prefers Brand A, feels loyal to it, and buys it at every opportunity. She may occasionally buy another brand for variety but always returns to her favorite brand.

2. *Habit persistence hypothesis.* The consumer buys Brand A out of habit rather than conscious preference. She gives little thought to brand choice and simply tends to reach for the familiar. Her

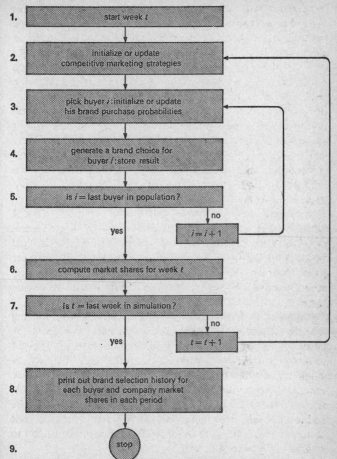

Figure 1 Simulation of the competitive marketing process

behavior may be characterized as autonomous response behavior.

3. *Maximization of quality-to-price hypothesis.* The consumer has no loyalty to any brand and makes her choice strictly on the basis of which current brand gives her the most for her money. She feels that Brand A currently offers the most quality for the price and only buys another brand when A is not on sale.

If another brand is upgraded in quality or if its price is permanently reduced to a sufficient extent, she will buy the other brand more often.

4. *Shifts in brand availability hypothesis*. The consumer patronizes a store which is well stocked only in Brand A and this accounts for her choosing A most of the time.

Other hypotheses may also offer a plausible explanation of the observed purchase history. The point is that an actual purchase history gives rise to a multiplicity of hypotheses about the buyer's brand decision processes.

Yet the nature of the brand decision process is the crucial issue. The theory that a firm holds of buyer behavior in its markets will influence and determine its marketing strategy. For example, a view of the consumer as 'stimulus prone and highly persuasible' leads to a great reliance on advertising, price deals, and point-of-purchase displays. A view of the consumer as 'a creature of habit' leads to some complacency with respect to holding present customers and some despair in attracting new customers. A view of the consumer as 'an economic calculating machine' leads to a policy of improving real values (a better ratio of quality or quantity to price) rather than emphasizing brand or company image advertising. A view of the consumer as 'fantasy prone' leads to a great reliance on imaginative advertising and packaging.

Given the importance to marketing planning of developing correct interpretations of buyer behavior, we shall now examine a succession of mathematical models describing how the buyer chooses a brand. They are, ranging from the simple to the complex: brand loyalty model; constant brand probability model; last brand purchased model; learning model; variable Markov model; competitive marketing mix model; and total behavior model.

The Brand Loyalty Model

The first model is hardly a model at all, but it offers a good point of departure. The brand loyalty model says that the buyer develops a strong preference or habit for a particular brand and purchases it repeatedly, giving little or no thought to the other brands. This explanation of buyer behavior can be described mathematically in the following way. Let there be three brands on the market, A, B, and C, and let the respective probabilities of their purchase by buyer i be represented by the vector (P_A, P_B, P_C). The latter will be called the *brand purchase probability vector* $(BPPV)$. If buyer i has developed a strong and unyielding preference for Brand A, then the brand probability purchase vector for buyer i at time t $(BPPV_{it})$ is:

$$BPPV_{it} = (1 \cdot 00, 0 \cdot 0, 0 \cdot 0) \quad \text{for all } t.$$

Rationale

That some people display this behavior is incontrovertible, especially in the buying of frequently purchased grocery staples. In the buying of coffee, many consumer panel members report the same brand choice in the last ten or more purchases. It may be hypothesized that these consumers spend very little time thinking about brand choice or seeking brand information. As long as their brand provides the anticipated satisfactions, they are insensitive to cues from other brands and are unlikely to try them.

An important problem not answered by this model is how consumers develop a strong brand preference in the first place. Do they try several brands and then settle on one? Or do they stick with the first one they try? To what extent are they influenced by friends, mass media, and in other ways?

In other words, this model describes the process of being brand loyal rather than becoming brand loyal. A market made up entirely of brand loyal buyers would be highly uninteresting. There would be no shifts in brand share, and merchandising variables such as price deals, advertising, and point-of-purchase displays would be largely wasted. Price deals would only subsidize present customers, and advertising and point-of-purchase displays would mainly sustain present customer loyalties rather than attract away competitors' customers.

In a simulation using a population of hypothetical consumers, programming some fraction of them to behave according to the brand loyalty model may well be warranted. But the behavior of many buyers is not described by this model. The model's main contribution is to describe some buyers and to provide a starting point for further model building.

The Constant Brand Probability Model

The brand purchase histories of many members of consumer panels show brand switching behavior which is inconsistent with the brand loyalty model. The task is to formulate an explanation of brand switching behavior.

Brand switching can be explained as the result of response uncertainty, response change, or some mixture of the two (Coleman, 1964b).

Response uncertainty means that a buyer's behavior is probabilistic rather than certain, and that probabilities are fairly stable. It would be illustrated by the housewife who buys Brand A approximately three out of four times, Brand B one out of four times, and never Brand C. Her next brand choice cannot be perfectly predicted but the average frequency of each brand choice can be predicted quite well.

Response change means that a buyer's behavior is probabilistic and that probabilities undergo systematic change. It would be illustrated by the housewife who grows to like Brand A more and more through time, with the result that Brand A's repurchase probability increases through time.

Now the problem is that observed individual brand switching histories do not immediately suggest whether response uncertainty or response change is at work. Both tend to be confounded in the observed data. Coleman (1964b) has developed interesting techniques for trying to unravel the two. Here, for the sake of systematic theory construction, we shall treat the case of pure response uncertainty first, under the rubric of the constant brand probability model.

This model says that it is not possible to predict exactly the next choice, but that one could predict the average proportion of times each brand will be purchased by the buyer. For example,

$$BPPV_{it} = (0.50, 0.30, 0.20) \text{ for all } t$$

says that buyer i will purchase Brand A 50 per cent of the time,

Brand B 30 per cent of the time, and Brand C 20 per cent of the time.

Through the adoption of more extreme probabilities, one would almost be describing the brand loyalty model subject to a small amount of response uncertainty. This is accomplished, for example, in

$$BPPV_{tt} = (0{\cdot}90,\, 0{\cdot}08,\, 0{\cdot}02) \quad \text{for all } t.$$

The buyer is highly loyal to Brand A but for sundry reasons occasionally buys B and less frequently C.

While it is easy to state this mechanism, it is not easy to provide a plausible psychological explanation of it. Clearly the housewife does not have a random chance device in her head which she spins prior to selecting a brand. About the closest behavioral explanation is that she has some stable pattern of brand preference such as $A > B > C$ and when she goes to the store, she is subject to a large number of random influences affecting her actual choice: the presence of a point-of-purchase display, an out-of-stock condition, a price deal on an off brand, an advertisement in the morning newspaper, and so forth. In general, behavior may be described as having a random component when a great many small factors operate in a situation and may affect the normal predisposition of the actor.

Can observed brand switching in the coffee market be explained by a model which postulates constant household brand probabilities? Ronald E. Frank (1962) found that this hypothesis provided a statistically satisfactory explanation of brand choice behavior in the coffee market. It was not necessary to evoke the hypothesis of learning to explain observed brand histories.

If this model is used to describe a hypothetical population of consumers, each having a different but stable brand probability purchase vector, it is possible to derive analytically the long-run implied average market shares. At the same time, the constant brand probability model has a number of shortcomings. First, it does little to promote the development of psychologically rich theory in the area of buyer behavior. At the most, it may stimulate the development of better techniques for mapping brand preference rankings or ratings into brand probability vectors and for relating them to individual social-economic-personality characteristics.

Second, it denies the possibility of finding systematic relationships between changing marketing stimuli and consumer response. It treats marketing stimuli on too implicit and random a level to permit a study of their effects on buyers.

Third, it denies learning, the tendency for a person's predispositions to change with experience. There is much psychological evidence that favorable experiences increase the probability that an individual will respond in a similar way to the next occasion.

Finally, this model is unable to reproduce the serial correlation that is observed in many actual brand histories. Specifically, the data often show various length runs of the same brand purchases, and such runs cannot be explained on the basis of pure random drawings.

For all these reasons, we must formulate a more sophisticated model of the brand choice process, although we may have occasion to revert to this model as a bench mark for judging the more elaborate ones.

The Last Brand Purchased Model

In the previous model, the buyer's brand purchase probability vector remains constant throughout the simulation, a direct denial of learning theory. Learning theory holds that a person's responses to stimuli are determined through experience. If a stimulus leads a person to try something, and if that experience is rewarding, it strengthens the habit connexion between stimulus and response so that on the next trial there is a greater probability to respond in the same way. Conversely, if a person is dissatisfied, this reduces the probability that he will respond in the same way to similar cues. In either case, the brand probabilities are likely to change after the purchase.

There are a number of mathematical devices for incorporating or representing the effects of learning. The general problem is to formulate a model which makes

$$BPPV_{i,t+1} = f(BPPV_{i,t}, B_{i,t}),$$

where $B_{i,t}$ is the last brand purchased by buyer i.

A simple Markov formulation

As a start, consider the first-order Markov probability transition matrix in Figure 2. The original marketing use of this matrix is to represent the aggregate switching and staying tendencies

		A_{t+1}	B_{t+1}	C_{t+1}
	A_t	0·70	0·20	0·10
From	B_t	0·50	0·40	0·10
	C_t	0·60	0·20	0·20

Figure 2 A first-order Markov matrix

of the market as a whole rather than of the individual buyer. Thus, it may be observed that of those consumers who buy Brand A this period, 70 per cent buy A again, 20 per cent switch to B, and 10 per cent switch to C. The other two rows are similarly interpreted. If these percentages hold from period to period for the market as a whole and if other assumptions are satisfied (Ehrenberg, 1965), then the matrix can be used to derive a number of interesting propositions about the market, including the ultimate level of brand shares and speed of convergence to this level (Maffei, 1960).

The same matrix can be reinterpreted to describe the effect of the last brand choice of an individual buyer on her current brand purchase probabilities. Suppose a housewife purchased Brand A in the last period. Then there is a 0·70 probability that she will buy A again and some chance that she will buy B and C. Suppose she buys B next time (the chance is 0·20). Then we would expect the probability of her repurchasing B to go up (assuming satisfaction with B) and the probability of her repurchasing A to decline. Both effects are captured in this matrix. The probability of her buying A (having just bought B) has fallen from 0·70 to 0·50, and the probability of her buying B has risen from 0·20 to 0·40. (The probability of her buying C has been unaffected in this example. If, however, she buys C in the future, the probability of her repurchasing C will rise from 0·10 to 0·20.)

There are however at least two unsatisfactory features in

using a first-order Markov matrix to interpret the effects of the last brand purchased on the buyer's future brand probabilities. The first problem is that while the matrix provides for probability modifications when a switch occurs, it does not provide for probability modifications when the same brand is repurchased. Thus, if A was purchased last time with a purchase probability of 0·70 and is then purchased again, we would expect A's repurchase probability to increase from 0·70. It doesn't, and therefore this model produces learning only when switching occurs rather than when staying occurs.

A second fault is that the model is static: it builds in only one-period learning. It implies that the buyer is influenced only by the last purchase and not the last n purchases. It is static in postulating the same row vector every time the buyer returns to a particular last brand.

A frequent suggestion is to use a two- or more-period Markov matrix to generate period-to-period brand choices (Harary and Lipstein, 1962). But it soon becomes apparent that this is a cumbersome device for expressing the impact of cumulative learning, and that some better mechanism must be found.

The Learning Model

A different way to express the reinforcement effects of past brand choices uses a learning model developed by Bush and Mosteller (1955), and later applied to consumer behavior by Kuehn (1961). This model postulates the existence of a pair of 'learning operators' which explicitly alter current brand probabilities on the basis of the last brand choice.

The basic device is illustrated in Figure 3. The horizontal axis represents the probability of choosing brand j in period t, and the vertical axis represents the probability of choosing brand j in period $t + 1$. The figure contains a positively sloped 45° line as a norm. The figure also contains two positively sloped lines called the purchase and rejection operators. These operators show how the probability of purchasing brand j is modified from period t to period $t + 1$, depending on whether or not brand j was just purchased.

For example, suppose the probability that a housewife will

purchase brand *j* this period is 0·60. Suppose this is actually what she buys. What is the probability that she will buy brand *j* again? This is found by running a dotted line up from the horizontal axis at 0·60 to the purchase operator line (because brand *j* was purchased) and going across to the vertical axis and reading the new probability. In this illustration, the new probability is

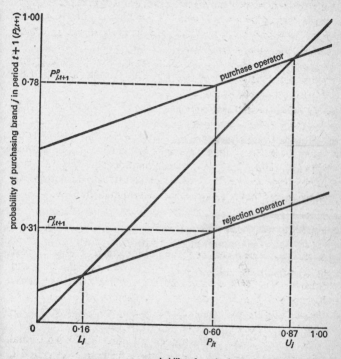

Figure 3 The cumulative learning model

0·78. Thus as a result of buying A, the housewife's predisposition toward A has increased from 0·60 to 0·78. If she had not purchased A, the dotted line from 0·60 would have been run up only to the rejection operator and read on the vertical axis. Her probability of buying A next time would have fallen from 0·60 to 0·31.

Thus, the prevailing probability of buying brand j is incremented or diminished according to whether brand j is bought. And the amount of increase or decrease depends on the probability of buying brand j in period t. If brand j is purchased three times in a row, starting with a probability of 0·60, the probability increases each time according to the following values: 0·60, 0·78, 0·83, 0·86 (not shown).

If the consumer continues to buy brand j for a long number of trials, the probability of buying brand j approaches 0·87 in the limit. This upper limit is given by the intersection of the purchase operator and the 45° line and represents a phenomenon known as incomplete learning. No matter how much brand j is bought, there is still some probability left that the consumer may buy another brand. On the other hand, if the consumer does not buy brand j for a long time, the probability of buying this brand falls continuously but never to zero. This is the phenomenon of incomplete extinction. There is always some positive probability that a consumer may buy a previously neglected brand.

The particular rates of brand learning or extinction, as well as their upper and lower limits respectively, depend upon the slopes, intercepts, and curvatures of the two operators. In Figure 3, the operators are assumed to be parallel and linear. The parallel condition is required when there are more than two brands in order that the probabilities sum to one. The linearity condition greatly simplifies the estimation problem (Carman, 1966). Yet it is conceivable that the actual learning process for a household is subject to more flexible operators.

Although this model represents an improvement over the last brand purchased model as a way of handling the effects of learning, it presents a number of difficulties. In the first place, the model is couched not in terms of the buyer's brand purchase probability vector but in terms of her probability of buying brand j. When her probability of buying brand j increases, the total probability of her buying the other two brands must decrease by the same amount. The problem is how to distribute the decrease between B and C. There is no *a priori* reason that the total decline should be distributed in a proportional way.

Another difficulty is that this model implies that the purchase of a particular brand always increases the probability of repurchasing it. This implies that there are no significant product quality differences and that the only psychological process operating is that of habit formation and habit extinction. This may be a fairly safe assumption for relatively homogeneous products such as coffee, bread, frozen orange juice, cigarettes, and so forth. In other cases, however, product differences are above the just noticeable level. In these cases, it is not the choice of the brand which increases its probability of repurchase but rather the buyer's degree of satisfaction or dissatisfaction. The purchase operator is too rigid in implying inevitable satisfaction with use.

Third, this model, like the previous ones, ignores the effect on brand choice of variations in the marketing mix. It describes the buyers' brand purchase probabilities as being modified solely through past brand choices. This might be remedied through making the slopes and intercepts of the two operators a function of relative brand marketing effort. However, other methods of bringing marketing variables explicitly into the brand choice process will now be considered.

The Variable Markov Model

One of the earliest suggestions was made by Alfred Kuehn and involves a novel interpretation of the probabilities in the Markov matrix (1961). Each cell probability is considered to be made up of the more basic elements shown in Figure 4.

This model was formulated by Kuehn to explain aggregate switching and staying behavior, but it can be reinterpreted in terms of the individual consumer. In this case, r_j represents the unadjusted probability that the buyer will choose brand j again. It reflects essentially the buyer's degree of preference for brand j after having used it; a_j represents the relative merchandising attractiveness of brand j. Then the cell probability that a buyer will switch from B to A is given by

$$(1 - r_A)a_B,$$

that is, the product of the degree to which she is not committed to brand B and the relative merchandising attractiveness of brand A. Similarly, the cell probability that a buyer will repeat her purchase of B is given by

$$r_B + (1 - r_B)a_B,$$

that is, the degree of the buyer's loyalty to brand B (r_B), plus the extent to which her nonloyalty to B is overcome by brand Bs relative merchandising attractiveness.

With this formulation, we need the parameters a_A, a_B, a_C, r_A, r_B, r_C to generate an individual buyer's behavior over time.

$$
\begin{array}{c}
 & A_{t+1} & B_{t+1} & C_{t+1} \\
\begin{array}{c} A_t \\ B_t \\ C_t \end{array}
\left[
\begin{array}{ccc}
r_A + (1 - r_A)a_A & (1 - r_A)a_B & (1 - r_A)a_C \\
(1 - r_B)a_A & r_B + (1 - r_B)a_B & (1 - r_B)a_C \\
(1 - r_C)a_A & (1 - r_C)a_B & r_C + (1 - r_C)a_C
\end{array}
\right]
\end{array}
$$

where r_j = the unadjusted repurchase probability

$$0 \leq r_j \leq 1.$$

a_j = the relative merchandising attractiveness of brand j.

$$\sum a_j = 1.$$

Figure 4 The variable Markov model

(Actually one of the a_j terms is redundant since $\sum a_j = 1$.)

The a_j terms reflect the current differential attractiveness of competitive marketing policies. For example, $a_A = 0 \cdot 5$, $a_B = 0 \cdot 3$, $a_C = 0 \cdot 2$ would indicate that brand A is the most appealing brand at the time to the average customer, brand B is the next most appealing brand, and brand C is the least appealing brand. Relative brand attractiveness can change from week to week as competitors change their merchandising strategy.

Relative brand attractiveness is not measured directly, but rather represents the result of averaging several dimensions of brand competition. The averaging can be accomplished in a number of ways, one of which is suggested in a later model.

The r_j terms are generally treated as constants in the original model describing aggregate behavior. However, in the application of this model to individual buyer behavior, the r_j terms can be treated as changing each period as a result of the reinforcement effect of last period brand choice. Specifically the probability of repurchasing brand j through habit should be increased if j

was bought last time and reduced if it was not. This can be accomplished readily through linear learning operators.

Thus, it is possible to modify the Markov model in a way which brings in two desirable effects: firstly, the effect of brand learning, and secondly, the effect of company merchandising variables. This approach might prove to be quite fruitful as a framework for developing specific consumer behavior hypotheses and marketing measurement techniques. At the same time, the model over-simplifies the learning phenomenon and also the dimensions of brand competition. It is with this in mind that the writer developed two further models.

The Competitive Marketing Mix Model

The variable Markov model described in the previous section used the device of a_j terms to describe the net effect of competitive merchandising strategies on brand switching behavior. From a marketing point of view, it is desirable to make more explicit the specific effect of each marketing element on the buyer.

Assume that the current marketing characteristics of the different brands can be represented in a matrix called the *competitive marketing mix matrix* at time t (M_t). An illustrative competitive marketing mix matrix for three brands and eight marketing variables is shown below:

| | | Brand | | |
		A	B	C
List price	P	0·31	0·33	0·36
Price deal	D	0·33⅓	0·33⅓	0·33⅓
Premium	G	0·33⅓	0·33⅓	0·33⅓
Packaging	C	0·35	0·33	0·32
Quality	Q	0·40	0·33	0·27
Shelf space	S	0·20	0·50	0·30
Advertising	A	0·25	0·42	0·33
Point of purchase	L	0·33⅓	0·33⅓	0·33⅓

Each row represents the relative attractiveness of the three brands on a particular marketing dimension. The higher the number in a row, the more attractive the brand is on the dimension relative to the other brands. The numbers in each row add to one.

Consider price. Brand C stands at 0·36, making it the most attractive brand pricewise on the market. This implies that it has the lowest list price. As for price deal, all three brands stand at 0·33⅓, indicating either that there are no price deals or that all the brands have the same deal. Moving to packaging, note that brand A is rated as having the most attractive package, followed by B and C; at the same time, the ratings are quite close. In the case of quality, the ratings are further apart, indicating that A is perceived to be of substantially higher quality than B and C. The brands also differ in shelf space exposure, brand B being the best exposed. Ratings are also available for advertising and point-of-purchase display differences among the three brands.

The competitive marketing mix matrix is used to summarize the average market perception of the three brands along the different dimensions of competition. A sample of consumers is surveyed and asked to rate the three brands on each dimension, in such a way that the ratings add up to one in each case. The ratings of all the consumers on each dimension are averaged and normalized to add to one. It is in this sense that the matrix represents the average market perception of competitive marketing mix differences.

The competitors have the capability of influencing the average market perception through specific marketing actions. A competitor can increase his relative rating on price deals by offering one; he can improve his relative rating on advertising by finding a better message. The efforts of competitors to increase market favor will be reflected in the competitive marketing mix matrix.

In principle, each buyer has his own perception of the marketing mix differences among the brands. But for our purpose, it is more useful to work with the concept of an average perception of the market. Individual variations are assumed to enter in a different manner, specifically in the fact that households vary in the importance they attach to different marketing elements. Their individual differences in response can be expressed through a second construct known as buyer *is marketing response vector* (W_i):

$$W_i = (P, D, G, C, Q, S, A, L).$$

It represents the relative weights placed by buyer i on the eight marketing variables. The weights in the vector are scaled to add to 1·00. An illustrative marketing response vector for buyer i is:

$$Wi = (0·08, 0·05, 0·06, 0·18, 0·20, 0·08, 0·20, 0·15).$$

This vector shows that buyer i places the most value on quality (0·20), advertising (0·20), packaging (0·18), and point-of-purchase (0·15). A possible inference is that this is a middle-class housewife interested mainly in quality and brand image, and uninterested in small price differences.

In a simulation involving a population of buyers, each buyer would face the same competitive marketing mix matrix but would respond differentially according to her individual marketing response vector. Each week the marketing mix matrix would change to reflect the latest competitive marketing actions. But the individual buyer's marketing response vectors would remain constant from week to week. In this way, brand share changes would be due entirely to marketing competition, not to individual buyer changes. In a more elaborate model, the individual buyer's response vector would also change through time as a result of brand usage, learning social influences, and other factors.

The model is set up to yield a brand probability purchase vector for each household in each week ($BPPV_{it}$). For example, the brand probability purchase vector for buyer i at time t is derived by multiplying buyer is response vector and the marketing mix matrix at time t:

$$W_i M_t = (0·08, 0·05, 0·06, 0·18, 0·20, 0·08, 0·20, 0·15) \begin{pmatrix} 0·31 & 0·33 & 0·36 \\ 0·33\tfrac{1}{3} & 0·33\tfrac{1}{3} & 0·33\tfrac{1}{3} \\ 0·33\tfrac{1}{3} & 0·33\tfrac{1}{3} & 0·33\tfrac{1}{3} \\ 0·35 & 0·33 & 0·32 \\ 0·40 & 0·33 & 0·27 \\ 0·20 & 0·50 & 0·30 \\ 0·25 & 0·42 & 0·33 \\ 0·33\tfrac{1}{3} & 0·33\tfrac{1}{3} & 0·33\tfrac{1}{3} \end{pmatrix}$$

$$= (0·32, 0·36, 0·32)$$
$$= BPPV_{it}.$$

The resulting brand purchase probability vector will necessarily be a unit vector, because it is the product of a unit vector and a matrix composed of unit row vectors. In effect, the buyer's brand purchase probabilities depend on: (a) how attractive the relative brand characteristics are; and (b) how much weight the buyer attaches to the different characteristics. In the example, the combination of the relative brand characteristics and buyer *i*s weights put brand B ahead of the other two brands. Buyer *i*s brand purchase probabilities would change from week to week as the competitive marketing mix matrix changes.

The simulation task is to derive the brand purchase probability vector for each buyer in the particular week, and use Monte Carlo methods to generate the brand choices. The brand choices of all buyers are totaled each week to derive weekly brand shares.

This conceptual approach requires several refinements before it can satisfy theoretical and operational requirements for a good model. One problem is that the method does not allow for interaction effects among marketing mix variables. Because the model is linear, the effects of different changes in merchandising are treated additively. A second problem is that the brand purchase probabilities cannot fall outside the range of the lowest and highest numbers within each column of the marketing mix matrix. This is because the multiplication operation essentially amounts to taking a weighted average of the columns, which means that the results cannot fall outside the limits. Thus it would take extreme differences in relative marketing ratings to produce extremely low or high brand purchase probabilities. A third problem is that the model as it now stands does not provide for learning. As mentioned earlier, this could be remedied by updating the buyers' response vectors for the effect of recent purchases and experiences. A fourth problem is to develop a meaningful way to scale the different dimensions of competition and to talk about the average perception of the market. One of the benefits of this conceptual approach is the stimulus it gives to finding better ways to scale relative awareness and attitudes toward brand differences.

The Total Behavior Model

All the previous models dealt with one or more effects that belong in a total model for generating consumer choice behavior. At this stage, it would be worthwhile to restate all the effects that ideally should be designed into a model. Five effects can be distinguished:

1. The effect of current attitudes on brand choice (predisposition effect).

2. The effect of interim experiences on brand choice (interim experience effect).

3. The effect of out-of-stock conditions on brand choice (availability effect).

4. The effect of in-store stimuli on brand choice (in-store experience effect).

5. The effect of using a brand on brand choice (usage effect).

The relationships between these effects are illustrated in the flow diagram in Figure 5 and explained below.

At periodic intervals, the housewife buys coffee. The first box poses the question of whether it is time for her to buy coffee. In the simplest case, it will be assumed that the answer is yes after a week passes, although a more complex model can be developed which makes interpurchase time a stochastic function of several variables, including the family consumption rate, current inventory level, social occasions, and other variables.

It is then postulated that the housewife goes to the supermarket with a particular predisposition toward the available brands, represented by a brand purchase probability vector.

When she enters the store, her predisposition vector may be altered by in-store experiences, such as price deals, premiums, and point-of-purchase displays. This is accomplished by pre-multiplying her brand probability purchase vector by an in-store experience matrix.

A further adjustment is made for the chance that particular brands may be out of stock. It is assumed that each competitor spends a specific amount of money on making sure that its brand is in stock – a table is used to indicate the cost of achieving

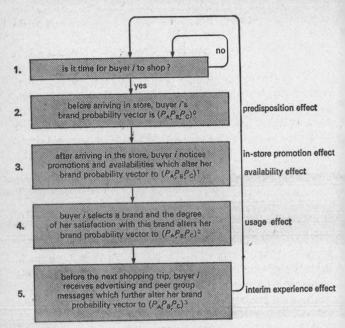

Figure 5 The total behavior process model

different probabilities that the brand will be in stock. The appropriate probabilities are used in the simulation. A random number is drawn to indicate whether each brand is in stock. If a brand is not in stock, the brand purchase probability vector is rescaled so that the remaining brand probabilities add to one.

The housewife takes home the brand and her experience has some effect on her predisposition vector. If the brand is satisfying, her probability of buying it again increases and of buying the other brands decreases. If the brand is dissatisfying, the reverse consequences take place. The effect of using the brand on future brand purchase probabilities is accomplished by multiplying the latest brand probability purchase vector by a usage effect matrix.

During the week, various events may happen to alter the housewife's brand probability purchase vector. The two main categories of events are impersonal communications such as advertising and personal communications from friends and neighbors.

The simplest way to handle advertising is by assuming that every advertising exposure has a positive effect on the housewife. Her predispositions toward the brands will be altered in proportion to the relative number of brand messages she receives. Later, this can be modified to allow for more subtle effects, such as: (1) the fact of selective perception – that is, she is more likely to notice advertisements of brands she uses than of others; and (2) the effect of differences in advertising quality and scheduling.

The effect of personal communications can be handled by assuming that her brand purchase probabilities are altered according to the number of competing brand messages she hears and whether they are negative or positive. In a simulation of coffee buying behavior, word-of-mouth messages are probably not an important factor in brand choice and can be neglected in the modeling process. In simulations of product markets where word-of-mouth influence is critical, care must be taken to formulate this process. Some progress has been made in modeling word-of-mouth influence in at least two marketing simulations (Amstutz 1966; Stanfield, Clark, Lin, and Rogers, 1965).

This type of model takes a more comprehensive view of the factors operating in brand choice behavior than the previous models. It is represented today in its most developed form in the work of Arnold Amstutz (1966). He designs operational models in which markets are represented by a representative cross-section of highly specific consumers. Each person is specified in terms of economic-demographic characteristics, present brand ownership status, retailer preferences, attitudes toward different brand characteristics, recall of specific communications regarding product characteristics, advertising media habits, and personal relations with other consumers. Each week each consumer receives new communications, forgets some previous communications, may have some experience with the product, may decide to shop, and if she does, has a specific set of in-store experiences with salesmen and the product that may or may not lead to purchase. All of these events are determined by Monte Carlo draws based on situation-related probabilities. By summing the brand purchases of his sample population over time, Amstutz is able to develop a time series of brand shares and compare them to historical time series in an attempt to validate the model.

In spite of the many points at which this type of comprehensive model is still conjectural, it highlights major challenges facing the theorist and methodologist in this area, along with desirable directions of future work. It reminds us of the main limitations of the previous models in representing the complexity of the brand choice process.

Conclusion

The issue of statistically estimating the data has not been specifically dealt with. This involves a separate and detailed discussion of underlying assumptions, data availability and alternative estimating procedures. The estimation problems that arise, even in fitting the simple models, are often so tricky that many researchers have shown a bias against more elaborate model construction. Simple models have the virtue that data can be found and predictions can be tested. Complex models, on the other hand, meet the desire for a richer understanding of the phenomenon. The development of both types of models has its place, and the utility of each is to be judged by the purpose it is intended to serve.

References

AMSTUTZ, A. E. (1966), 'Management use of computerized micro-analytic behavioral simulations', Working Paper no. 169–66, Alfred P. Sloan School of Management, M.I.T.

BUSH, R. R., and MOSTELLER, F. (1955), *Stochastic Models of Learning*, Wiley.

CARMAN, J. M. (1966), 'Brand switching and linear learning models', *J. Advertising Res.*, vol. 6, no. 2, pp. 23–31.

CARMAN, J. M., and NICOSIA, F. M. (1965), 'Analog experiments with a model of consumer attitude change', in L. G. Smith (ed.), *Reflections on Progress in Marketing*, American Marketing Association, pp. 246–57.

COLEMAN, J. S. (1964a), *Introduction to Mathematical Sociology*, Macmillan.

COLEMAN, J. S. (1964b), *Models of Change and Response Uncertainty*, Prentice-Hall.

DUHAMEL, W. F. (1966), 'The use of variable Markov processes as a partial basis for the determination and analysis of market segments', unpublished Ph.D. dissertation, Stanford University.

EDGEWORTH, F. Y. (1881), *Mathematical Physics*, C. K. Paul.

EHRENBERG, A. S. C. (1965), 'An appraisal of Markov brand-switching models', *J. Marketing Res.*, vol. 2, pp. 347–63.

FESTINGER, L. (1957), *A Theory of Cognitive Dissonance*, Stanford University Press.

FRANK, R. E. (1962), 'Brand choice as a probability process', *J. Business*, vol. 35, pp. 43–56.

HARARY, F., and LIPSTEIN, B. (1962), 'The dynamics of brand loyalty: a Markovian approach', *Op. Res.*, vol. 10, pp. 19–40.

HOWARD, J. A. (1963), *Marketing Management: Analysis and Planning*, rev. edn, Irwin.

JEVONS, W. S. (1871), *The Theory of Political Economy*, Macmillan.

KOTLER, P. (1965a), 'Behavioral models for analysing buyers', *J. Marketing*, vol. 29, no. 4, pp. 37–45.

KOTLER, P. (1965b), 'The competitive marketing simulator – a new management tool'. *California Mgmt Rev.*, vol. 7, no. 3, pp. 49–60.

KUEHN, A. A. (1961), 'A model for budegting advertising', in F. M. Bass *et al.* (eds.), *Mathematical Models and Methods in Marketing*, Irwin, pp. 302–56.

LIPSTEIN, B. (1965), 'A mathematical model of consumer behavior', *J. Marketing Res.*, vol. 2, pp. 259–65.

MAFFEI, R. B. (1960), 'Brand preferences and simple Markov processes', *Op. Res.*, vol. 8, pp. 201–18.

MASSY, W. F. (1965), 'A dynamic model for monitoring new product adoption', Working Paper no. 95, Graduate School of Business, Stanford University.

MASSY, W. F., and FRANK, R. E. (1965), 'Short term price and dealing effects in selected market segments', *J. Marketing Res.*, vol. 2, pp. 171–85.

MONTGOMERY, D. B. (1966), 'A probability diffusion model of dynamic market behavior', Working Paper no. 205–66, Alfred P. Sloan School of Management, M.I.T.

MORRISON, D. G. (1966), 'New models of consumer behavior: aids in setting and evaluating marketing plans', in P. D. Bennett (ed.), *Marketing and Economic Development*, American Marketing Association, pp. 323–37.

ORCUTT, G. H., GREENBERGER, M., KORBEL, J., and RIVLIN, A. (1961), *Microanalysis of Socioeconomic Systems: A Simulation Study*, Harper.

RIESMAN, D., GLAZER, N., and DENNEY, R. (1956), *The Lonely Crowd*, abridged edn, Doubleday.

ROGERS, C. (1951), *Client-Centered Therapy*, Houghton Mifflin.

SIMON, H. A. (1954), 'The constructions of social science models', in P. F. Lazarsfeld (ed.), *Mathematical Thinking in the Social Sciences*, Free Press, pp. 430–40.

Simulmatics Corporation (1962), *Simulations Media-Mix: Technical Description*, The Simulmatics Corporation.

STANFIELD, J. D., CLARK, J. A., LIN, N., and ROGERS, E. M. (1965), 'Computer simulation of innovation diffusion: an illustration from a Latin American village', Paper presented at a joint session of the American Sociological Society.

TOMKINS, S. S., and MESSICK, S. (eds.) (1963), *Computer Simulation of Personality*, Wiley.

12 S. Payne

Asking Questions

Excerpt from S. Payne, *The Art of Asking Questions*, Princeton University Press, 1957, pp. 214–37.

Now for an attempt at wording a question from the first statement of the issue to the point where it is ready for pretesting. Let us not make fools of ourselves, however. Just so that neither you nor I need feel self-conscious about the stupidities that may come to light, I suggest that we induce a third party to carry out the experiment for us. And I have a man in mind for the job, too. But I don't want to embarrass him either, so I'll conceal his identity by using only his initials, S. P.

We ought to confront him with an issue that is not too easy to put into shape for general public consumption but which is not entirely impossible for laymen to answer either. In other words, let him try one that is typical of the tough problems we question worders are up against most of the time. As good for this purpose as any issue we are likely to find is a horrible example of a general public question.

(1) Which do you prefer - dichotomous or open questions?

We must admit one virtue in the issue as it is stated here: it is short and to the point. It is a safe bet that our friend, S. P., won't succeed in holding it down to anything like its present eight words. What we realize and he may not understand, is that one precise term used by the technician often does the work of many more common words. That's the conflict between precision and brevity on the one side and familiarity and wide usage on the other. A single word like 'dichotomous' has to be replaced by several more general words to define it, or make it intelligible, for the layman.

Let's ask S. P. to take this problem step-by-step, even though he might be tempted to essay it in one big jump. If at the same time he happens to make a few false starts, it won't be the first time such mistakes have been made. Besides, he can probably learn more fundamentals through a plodding trial-and-error approach than by a brilliant or intuitive leap to the conclusion.

And don't let him start rephrasing this as a question for respondents until we are reasonably sure that all of us are in agreement about the issue ourselves. In his recent treatise on sampling Dr Deming lists seventeen errors common to both complete counts and samples of which, the first is 'failure to state the problem carefully and to decide just what statistical information is needed'. If we can agree about what we want to get out of this issue and can be sure that its meaning is unmistakably clear to us, then it will be time enough to let S. P. try to make it meaningful to respondents.

Is this issue at all meaningful to us? Well, it certainly ought to be. We have spent a lot of time discussing the advantages and disadvantages of the various types of questions. And even though I once tried to dismiss the issue as a bootless argument, I'm sure that other people will not soon stop discussing it. In that case, the preferences of respondents should have some bearing on the matter. At least, it would be helpful to know how they feel about it, if they are able to tell us.

The issue is not as meaningful as it might be if it were complete, however. It presents only two of the three major varieties of questions. We could conceivably leave the multiple-choice type out of consideration, but if you and S. P. have no objections, I'd like to put that third candidate on the ballot. In a sense, the multiple-choice question is the compromise candidate since it fits between the other two types, but I don't expect that many respondents will realize that it is the middle-ground alternative.

(2) Which do you prefer – dichotomous, *multiple choice* or open questions?

Notice that we have now changed the question itself from a dichotomous to a multiple-choice question.

S. P. may be satisfied that the statement now is a complete and adequate expression of the issue, but let's see whether it stands up under the Who?-Why?-When?-Where?-How? appraisal. It's clear enough that the Who is the respondent. The Why doesn't apply here. The answer to the When and Where is 'In a survey'. Maybe we ought to make this last idea clear.

(3) Which do you prefer *in surveys* – dichotomous, multiple-choice or open questions?

S. P., beginning to catch on, interjects here that we ought to explain the kind of survey. After all, some people might prefer categorical questions in census surveys and free-answer questions in opinion surveys. Perhaps he has a possible point, so:

(4) Which do you prefer in *opinion* surveys – dichotomous, multiple-choice or open questions?

That leaves only the How to be answered, and apparently the only thing that isn't stated so far is whether we mean preference as a questioner or as a respondent. That's easy enough to take care of:

(5) Which do you prefer *to be asked* in opinion surveys – dichotomous, multiple-choice or open questions?

There, that does it. The issue is defined completely and precisely. All that remains to be done is to let S. P. convert it into understandable form for the man on the street. We'll have to make sure that in converting it he doesn't stray away from the issue as it is now defined. Let's remember this version, number five, as the one his final wording has to paraphrase.

Now that we know what the issue is, we can judge whether it is meaningful to the public. I think you will agree that the concept of three types of questions is not, whether we are talking about the present wording or any other wording. The public cannot be expected to have thought about this matter before. This is not the kind of issue that provokes debate in the press or on the radio. It's practically a nonentity to everyone except public opinion pollers.

S. P. is at first inclined to argue that we have no corner on asking questions. He says that everybody does it. The experience is universal. Not only that, he says, but people are familiar with all these kinds of questions – they use them all the time. He is stopped, though, when we explain that questions just come naturally to most people, but that we make work out of ours. Other people don't give a thought to the type of question they are asking. We are the strange ones who are concerned about the characteristics of form. He finally admits that maybe people don't give much consideration to question types, but strongly affirms that he thinks they ought to.

What we have is an uncommon query about a very common thing – something like asking which variety of wood you like best in a pencil. I first used this issue on question types to illustrate the problem of taking things for granted. We are going to have to be very careful about that in this case. A colorless subject that people have never thought about presents a more difficult wording problem than an issue on which we know that respondents have strong feelings. Even when respondents finally understand what we are driving at, I'm afraid that the idea will at best be vaguely unfamiliar to them. Our biggest problem will be to make this issue come alive for them.

S. P. has an inspiration: 'Why not ask it this way?' he suggests 'Put it at the end of a questionnaire and explain that we are referring to surveys like the one they have just been interviewed on. Then we'll be sure that respondents have just had experience with each of the three types.'

Now, that sounds like a good idea! It's the kind of approach that can change an ethereal abstraction into meat and potatoes that people can sink their teeth into. If we can get respondents to realize that we are talking about something no farther away than the questions they just answered, we will have some chance of making the issue meaningful to them.

(6) Which do you prefer to be asked in opinion surveys *like this* – dichotomous, multiple-choice or open questions?

'Opinion' is redundant when we are speaking of 'surveys like this', so let's suggest to S. P. that he drop it.

(7) Which do you prefer to be asked in surveys like this – dichotomous, multiple-choice or open questions?

That still sounds more hypothetical than it need be. To carry S. P.'s idea a little farther, let's suggest that he put it in the past tense and stick to this particular survey.

(8) Which *did* you prefer to be asked in *this survey* – dichotomous, multiple-choice or open question?

Now the 'to be asked' is practically unnecessary, since the respondent is definitely on the receiving end when we speak of 'this survey':

(9) Which did you prefer in this survey – dichotomous, multiple-choice or open questions?

S. P. thinks that he would like to try another slightly different angle and get away from the stilted 'prefer' at the same time.

(10) *Which type of question did you like best* in this survey – dichotomous, multiple-choice, or open?

Since we end up the question with the three *types* of questions, the 'type of' may not be needed. Furthermore, the distinction between 'questions' and 'type of question' looks like a distinction without a difference as far as most people will notice.

(11) Which *questions* did you like best in this survey – dichotomous, multiple-choice or open?

S. P. is really beginning to identify himself with the whole idea. Now he would like to substitute 'my' for 'in this survey'.

(12) Which *of my* questions did you like best – dichotomous, multiple-choice or open?

This makes me wonder whether the past tense doesn't enable us to get along without either phrase, thus:

(13) Which questions did you like best – dichotomous, multiple-choice or open?

We've gone a long way around to get the preamble into this shape and it may still present some problems. Perhaps the antecedent isn't clear, so that we will have to reinstate the 'in this survey' phrase. Maybe the 'type of question' distinction would make a difference. Those are two problems which we can earmark for the pretest. S. P. wants to get on with the alternatives, so let's see what he can do with 'dichotomous':

(14) ... *Two way* ...

Would you want to bet that our unimaginative respondent will know what is meant by a 'two-way question'? It is a translation of 'dichotomous' all right, but it still would require explanation. The meaning of the phrase in this context is very specialized, even if it is logical. Our respondent could figure it out eventually, but let's ask S. P. to try again.

(15) ... Two way *questions like yes-no* ...

Oh, oh! He had better back away from the example idea fast. In the first place, some respondents will think strictly of the Yes-No example rather than the general two-way type it is supposed to illustrate. In the second place, an example for one of the three types demands an example for each of the others, which would be just too much and too difficult.

What if he spells out the two-way idea, like this:

(16) ... *those that gave you only one choice* ...

Technically, that's right for a two-way question. It affords *one* choice – the one choice of this or that. Still, there would be those who would not understand it clearly unless we called it 'two choices'. Consequently, because it is important to get the correct idea over and because there is a question of whether it should read one choice or two, let's ask S. P. to try again without that unfortunate word.

(17) ... those that gave you only *two answers to choose between* ...

Do you suppose that S. P. is prejudiced against the two-way question? In both his last two trys he has used 'only' in a way that might be taken as disparaging. He says that he didn't mean to belittle but was simply trying for contrast and is willing to drop it.

(18) ... those that gave you two answers to choose between ...

This statement may not be sufficiently limited because the respondent may think of a free-answer question that also comes down to only two possible answers as far as he can see. The idea to make clear is that the two-way question *itself* *mentions* the two possibilities. So try again.

(19) ... those that *stated* two answers to choose between ...

Notice that S. P. also dropped the 'you', which is very clearly implied anyway.

As long as we are worshippers of the fetish of brevity, we might as well take every means of saving words that we can, so how about combining the 'that stated' into 'stating'?

(20) ... those *stating* two answers to choose between ...

S. P. may think I am being picayune, but there is one little thing about that word 'choose'. It missed being on the list of words in chapter 9 [not included here] because the Lorge magazine count placed it in the second thousand words by order of frequency. I would not say a thing about it except that so far all the rest of the words are on our frequent-familiar list and an adequate substitute for it happens to be there for the taking:

(21) ... those stating two answers to *decide* between ...

Maybe it's a point of honor with me, but I really would like to show you that a thousand words are enough for our needs even on a tough question like this. I think that now we can go on to the multiple-choice or cafeteria question alternative. I hope that S. P. will capitalize on what he has already learned from

(22) ... *those stating four or five answers to decide among* ...

Yes, sir! He is being downright slavish in following precedent. Still, the idea of deciding should carry over from the first alternative, so that he should be able to drop the last three words leaving:

(23) ... those stating four or five answers ...

No one has ever restricted the meaning of 'multiple-choice' to 'four or five' answers before, at least not to my knowledge. Perhaps S. P. will accept this suggestion:

(24) ... those stating *three or more* answers ...

Have you been noticing the prime example of 'or' as a problem word in the last three versions? It may make this one alternative sound like two for those people who try to decide whether to take three *or* more answers. Fortunately, there is an easy way out of this problem.

(25) ... those stating *more than two* answers ...

So far, so good. S. P. moves on to the simplest, and therefore the hardest, idea of all to express – the free-answer question.

(26) ... *those not stating any answers but where you made up the answers yourself*?

That seems to be a correct enough statement, but it is awfully long. We should be able to get along without that first clause.

(27) ... those where you made up the answers yourself?

I can anticipate that our unimaginative respondent might bridle at this. I can hear him saying, 'Do you suggest that I would *make up* an answer? I'll have you know that I'm absolutely honest!' How about getting S. P. to make another try?

(28) ... *those that you answered in your own words?*

Prestige rears its ugly head! Of course a person can state his idea better in his own words than in the words of someone else! The same would go for this next version, too.

(29) ... those that you answered in your own *way?*

The fault with these wordings is probably in the 'your own' term, which plays up the respondent's individuality. S. P. says that it is easy enough to fix that.

(30) ... *those where you had to think of an answer?*

His loading here is in the other direction, and I for one would say that it is almost justified. People do have to struggle more to answer open questions than to answer the other types where the answers are placed before them. Perhaps they need to be reminded of this difficulty. But, who am I to say that this kind of loading is correct? How about another tack?

(31) ... those where you *provided the* answer?

No, we're sorry, but it won't do. The respondent 'provides' the answer to every question. The same goes for the word 'supply', so don't waste time in that direction.

(32) ... those where you *gave whatever answer you wanted?*

The same trouble! Respondents give whatever answers they want to two-way and multiple-choice questions, too.

(33) ... those where you gave *an original answer?*

Whoops! He has slipped back into prestige again! Who doesn't want to be original? S. P. had better start over again.

(34) ... those where you gave *any answer you thought of?*

That sounds harum-scarum, as though the respondent is expected to say the first thing that comes to mind.

(35) ... those where *there was no limit to the possible answers?*

This wording is technically correct, but it is stated from our point of view, not from the respondent's. It will probably not conjure up the idea of a free-answer question in his mind at all. He individually may not see limitless possibilities of answers in a free-answer question, but possibly only the one answer he gives. It is when we take all respondents as a group that we obtain the infinity of replies.

(36) ... *those that left the matter entirely up to you?*

Maybe S. P. is getting a little closer, but the 'matter' is most indefinite. How about a more precise version of this same approach:

(37) ... those that left the *statement of the answer* entirely up to you?

Rather wordy, but he's on the right track.

(38) ... those that left the *answer open for you to state?*

The 'open' probably contributes little to understanding. We can drop that one word and another by sacrificing the 'that'.

(39) ... those *leaving* the answer for you to state?

Now I am reasonably well satisfied if you are, and I'm sure that S. P. will be glad to get it over with – so let's put it all together. That means the four parts from versions 13, 21, 25, and 39.

(40) Which questions did you like best – those stating two answers to decide between, those stating more than two answers, or those leaving the answer for you to state?

Let's see. We wanted to compare this with our precise version, number 5, did we not?

(5) Which do you prefer to be asked in opinion surveys – dichotomous, multiple-choice or open questions?

It looks to me as though we have managed to stay pretty close to the issue. The only difference, and I consider it a great improvement, is that our version now is based on immediate past experience and not on a hypothetical situation.

Before we try out this wording on respondents, we might well see how it compares with our list of frequent-familiar words in chapter 9 [not included here]. When checked against that list, it looks like this:

(41) ‡ ‡ † * *† * * † ‡
   Which questions did you like best – those stating two
‡ † ‡ ‡ * † * ‡ ‡
answers to decide between, those stating more than two
‡ * * † * ‡ † * † †
answers, or those leaving the answer for you to state?

Remarkable! Every single word is on the list, as indicated by a check mark or other symbol. So, you see, it is possible to get fairly complicated ideas down into familiar words.

The indicated problem words – you, like, best, those, more, or, and the – are not problems in the contexts used here. 'You' clearly means the second person singular, not collective. 'Like' does not introduce an example. 'Best' is not used in the dead giveaway sense. The antecedent of 'those' should be clear. The basis of comparison with 'more' is stated. The 'or' is used only to connect alternatives. 'The' has no special overtones here.

None of the multi-meaning words is likely to be misunderstood in the present context.

The Flesch score would place this question in the readability range of eighth grade or high school students. The Dale-Chall score, on the other hand, would place it at the fifth grade level. The difference in these scores serves to emphasize how hazy the whole subject of readability is. At the same time, the direction the scores take shows us how difficult it is to achieve low-level readability. We have done about everything we can in stating the issue clearly and concisely, but we end up with 28 words as compared with 8 words in the original version.

Our next step is to outline what we want our interviewers to be on the lookout for in the pretesting.

First, have we succeeded in making this issue meaningful to respondents? That is, do they really know what we are talking about when we refer to the differences in the questions they have just been answering, or does it come as a sudden revelation to them that there could be different kinds of questions? If the latter is the case, then it means that we should carry S. P.'s idea a step farther. We could, for example, introduce every one of the preceding questions on our questionnaire in some such fashion as this:

(a) Here is a question that states two answers for you to decide between: Which side of bed do you usually get out of – left or right?

(b) This one states more than two answers: Do you prefer to get up at five a.m., before five, or after five?

(c) On this next one, the answer is left for you to state: What do you like best about your alarm clock?

By the time respondents have answered fifteen or twenty questions with preambles of this sort, they should be conscious of the differences in types of questions, and our issue should by then be meaningful to them. This approach may sound ridiculously involved as a way of getting replies on just a single issue, but it does indicate the great lengths to which we may sometimes have to go to establish a common ground between questioner and respondent. When I tell you that on some subjects special pamphlets have been prepared for respondents to read before certain issues could be posed to them, perhaps this idea will not seem so outlandish to you.

Second, we should try to learn the frames of reference in which people answer this question. Do they think of particular questions instead of types of questions? If so, perhaps we should try a wording in terms of Which *kind of* questions. . . . We are gambling now that the 'kind of' is an unneeded refinement, but we may be wrong. Do respondents tend to answer in terms of specific examples, such as 'that one about my age' or 'the one on my suggestions'? If so, we should try to find some way of steering them toward a more general course.

Third, what about the third alternative in particular? Does it actually bring to the respondent's mind what we intend it to, or does he think that the answers to all of our questions are left for him to state? And do the comments about it bring forth any evidence of the influence of prestige? The statement of this free-answer alternative has provided us an excellent illustration of the ever-present problem of loading. S. P. loaded it first one way and then another. The present version appears to fall somewhere in the middle, but is it loaded realistically? You remember that I almost favored loading it in this form – *questions where you have to think of an answer*? – because I happen to believe that the free-answer question does require more thought than the others do.

The approach we have adopted may enable us to obtain a rough idea of the prestige element here. If we should find in the pretest that a number of people who say they prefer the free-answer alternative have trouble with the actual free-answer questions they had been asked earlier in the questionnaire – if they fumble for words, habitually say they 'don't know' to such questions, or give other evidence of not being at ease with free-answer questions – then we can say that their choice does not agree with their behavior. In such cases, the tester might even use the confrontation technique to ask them why they appear not to like such questions but end up saying they prefer them. This could be a very revealing experiment.

Fourth, is there any tendency for respondents to jump the gun on this question? I would not expect that to be the case, simply because I think that they will require a moment or so to comprehend it. But it does have some pauses indicated, so that our testers might as well be on the alert for anticipated replies.

Finally, if the question does come through the pretest satisfactorily, it would be highly advisable in the full-scale survey to use a split-ballot technique. With such a long question, it is of more than ordinary importance that each version be given an equal break:

Which questions did you like best – those stating two answers to decide between, those stating more than two answers, or those leaving the answer for you to state?
Which questions did you like best – those leaving the answer for you to state, those stating two answers to decide between, or those stating more than two answers?
Which questions did you like best – those stating more than two answers to decide among, those leaving the answer for you to state, or those stating two answers?

If right now or during the pretesting someone should shoot

the question full of holes, that is just our bad luck and let's not hold S. P. responsible for it. It would mean that I would have been wiser to skip this thirteenth chapter just as a hotel builder skips the thirteenth floor.

A Concise Check List of One Hundred Considerations

Nobody wants to read though a book, even a small book, every time he words a question. Yet, any one of the many factors we have considered here may be enough to make the difference between a useful question and one which is misleading.

Here, therefore, I attempt to enumerate at least the most important features of question wording. A quick scanning of the items will help you make certain that every one of the features that applies has been given consideration in your questions. You can figuratively check them off one by one for each question until they become deeply ingrained in your thinking.

Actually you won't need this check list type of stimulus for long because most of these things are only common sense anyway. Having once been pointed out, they should stay with you pretty well with perhaps only an occasional reading for a refresher.

A. The issue

1. Make sure that you have a *clear understanding* of the issue *yourself*. This is of first importance if you are to make it meaningful to others.

2. See that the issue is *fully defined*. Check it for the Who? Why? When? Where? and How?

3. State the issue as *precisely* as you can at first. If in later versions you elect to sacrifice some precision, then at least the sacrifice will be recognized.

4. Attempt to evaluate whether the issue is *meaningful* to your *public*. If in your judgment it is not likely to be meaningful to them, see whether you can find some way of increasing its penetrating power.

5. If you have reason to suspect that the issue still is not *sufficiently well known* to all parts of your public, give consideration to ways of segregating or eliminating the uninformed.

6. Try to assess the *stage of development* of the issue. It may be a mistake to ask a categorical question if opinion is still unformed and hazy on the subject. Conversely, if opinion is well crystallized or falls into definite patterns, the open question may be a waste of time.

7. Decide which *type of question* best fits the issue – free-answer, two-way, or multiple-choice – according to the preceding considerations.

8. Keep asking yourself, '*What am I taking for granted?*'

B. The free-answer question

9. Is it *necessary to ask this free-answer question* in the full-scale survey? Perhaps enough answers to it can be obtained in the pretest or in a subsample to serve the needs of the research. Remember that the coding of thousands of verbatim replies adds up to a lot of work!

10. Consider whether it is *convertible* to a categorical type of question. If the different points of view on the issue are generally well-known, then you may wish to present them as alternatives (multiple-choice) rather than leave them to the respondents to articulate in their various ways.

11. Make it *sufficiently directive*. A free-answer question can be too broad and leave respondents as free as the birds to give answers from every direction and in every dimension. By carefully establishing the course, however, you can confine the answers to a particular frame of reference.

12. Indicate the *number of ideas* you expect from each respondent. If you accept one idea from this person and five ideas from that person, you don't know whether you are weighting respondents according to their articulateness or their weakness of conviction.

13. If you wish to extract all the thoughts you can on the subject, it may be advisable to add a *probe*.

14. Even though the question is in free-answer form, you may be able to provide *precoded* check boxes for the answers. This is especially likely if you are asking for amounts or figures.

C. Two-way questions

15. Avoid *implied alternatives*. No fault can be found with stating the alternative while some harm may result from leaving it to be carried by implication.

16. State the *negative in detail* where necessary. The 'or not' may not be enough to give the negative side a fair shake.

17. In the *argument type* of two-way question it may be better to state both sides of the argument so that the respondent knows both the pro and the con.

18. '*Don't know*' or '*No opinion*' answers have to be provided for except in rare instances.

19. Consider whether there is a reasonable *middle-ground* position which some respondents might take. If so, you must then decide whether to state it for all respondents or not.

20. Ordinarily the choices should be *mutually exclusive*. If they cannot be made so, then you should add an answer box for the 'Both' category and perhaps include the combination idea in the question itself.

21. The problem with *qualified answers* is a little different. Your decision lies between providing a separate answer box for the qualified answers or not providing a separate box, thus forcing respondents into other categories.

22. If you anticipate a *variety of qualified answers*, it may be advisable to set up separate answer boxes for each variety.

23. The alternatives should be *complementary*. In some cases, however, it is wise to take account of the realities of the situation rather than use the literal opposites as complementary.

24. *All the alternatives* should be included.

25. Give consideration to the *mildness* or *harshness* of the alternatives. The stronger the feeling implied by the alternatives, the fewer the choices that will be made.

26. Try to avoid the *unintended double-choice* type of question. Remember the 'better-worse; now-then' example.

27. Many two-way questions are easily converted to the *fold-over* type in which you obtain both the expression of opinion and its intensity, in case you are interested in both.

D. Multiple-choice questions

28. The choices need to be *mutually exclusive* in the multiple-choice question even more than in the two-way question.

29. *None of the alternatives* should be *overlooked* if a true expression of choices is desired. If combinations of the alternatives are possible, as in the royalties example, those combinations should be included.

30. It is all right to *restrict the choices*, however, if you keep this restriction in mind when interpreting the results or actually state the restriction in the question. For example, in terms of 'Aside from price, what . . . ?'

31. The *number of alternatives* need not always be limited to only five or six as some people think.

32. The choices should be *well balanced* within a realistic framework. The number of alternatives presented on one side or another does affect the distribution of replies.

33. The issue should be *clear within each choice* in the degree-type question. That is, if war is mentioned in one alternative, it should not be left to implication in another.

34. Decide whether you want respondents to express *one choice* or *more than one* and then indicate your decision clearly for them.

35. You should give respondents a *card list* if the question has more than three alternatives.

36. Provide for '*Don't know*' or '*No opinion*' answers on the questionnaire, although you need not show them on the card list.

37. *Idea* alternatives may be stated in *varied orders* on different cards without affecting the order of the check boxes on the questionnaire.

38. *Numbers* should be listed in logical order out of courtesy.

39. Placing the *correct numbers* in a knowledge question at the *extremes* of the list is a wise move because respondents tend to guess the middle or average ones.

E. Other types of questions

40. The *sleeper* question is useful in giving some clue to the

amount of guesswork and irresponsible testimony in respondents' answers, but it has to be carefully constructed.

41. The *cheater* question is a means of catching the unwary interviewer who fabricates his interviews, but it is not highly recommended.

42. *Single-purpose intensity* questions may be used after free-answer, two-way, or multiple-choice questions. They have wider application, therefore, than the fold-over type mentioned.

43. *Double-barreled* questions deserve to be split into separate questions for each of the two issues except in special cases where two issues necessarily have to be asked about together.

44. *Symbolized numbers* may help people to grasp box-car figures which otherwise might be outside their comprehension.

45. The '*or what?*' tag end is useful in some circumstances, but it does not give the same results as would either a free-answer or multiple-choice question.

46. *Successive eliminations* are treacherous unless applied equally to each side of the original issue.

47. *Serialized* questions save time and irritation in cases where the same introduction and same alternatives apply to a number of questions.

48. Answers to a *which-is-the-whatest* question can best be evaluated in terms of the relative importance of the competing companies, products, or brands.

49. The *quintamensional design* reminds us of five elements in an opinion – awareness, general opinion, specific opinion, reasons, and intensity.

F. Treatment of respondents

50. Avoid the appearance of *talking down* or otherwise insulting the intelligence of your respondents.

51. Word your question according to principles of *good grammar* but don't make it sound stilted.

52. Don't sling *slang*.

53. And don't try to be *folksy*.

54. Beware the *double entendre* and shun the triple. 'Please check your sex', for example, has three meanings – mark, restrain, and verify.

55. Skip the *salesmanship* – unless you are doing research on a sales approach.

56. Do what you can to help your respondents, not to *confuse* them.

57. When it comes to seemingly inconsistent replies, however, you may discover something by *confronting* respondents with their apparent inconsistencies.

58. *Double negatives* should not be inflicted on anyone.

59. *Tricky* questions can be tricky indeed. Don't be tricked by them yourself.

60. If there can be any possible question about the *antecedent*, restate it.

61. Keep away from wordings that beg for *ambiguous answers*. A 'Yes' that means 'No' is worse than a 'Don't know'.

62. A difficult problem is to make your question *specific* enough without making it over-elaborate.

63. Remember that your *fine distinctions* will often not be understood by the respondents.

64. To avoid unnecessary quibbling on the part of some respondents, it may be necessary to provide a *peg* on which they can hang their ideas.

G. The words themselves

65. Use as *few words as necessary*. You can ask most questions in twenty words or less.

66. Use *simple words* if you can find any that adequately express the idea.

67. When you use a *polysyllabic* word, put a ring around it so the tester will know that it is especially suspect.

68. *Trade jargon* may be all right to use in the trade, if *all* the trade uses it, but it will not do for the general public.

69. Check in the dictionary to see if the word actually does have the *meaning* you intend.

70. While there, see what *other meanings* it may have which could confuse the issue.

71. Make sure the word has only one *pronunciation*.

72. Look into the possibility of *homonyms*, as in the case of the boy with the stomachache who told the hospital attendant his address was 'eight-one-two Greene'.

73. If you use a *synonym*, make sure that it actually is synonymous with the idea at hand.

74. Avoid *concept* words. In fact, you may be wise not to attempt to explore concept issues.

75. Words that are *frequently used* are to be preferred, other things being equal, of course.

76. *Familiar words* are the most useful if they don't have too many meanings in context.

77. The *problem words* may or may not be problems, depending on the context.

H. Loading

78. It is on *marginal issues*, which the public knows little about and cares little about, that loading can most easily distort the picture of public opinion.

79. Citing the *status quo* introduces a powerful influence beyond the merits of the issue.

80. Among the possible *prestige* influences to be eliminated or counter-balanced are appeals to one's wisdom, knowledge, fairness, affluence, physical attributes, morals, and devotion to duty.

81. Expressions of *wishful thinking* need to be exposed for what they are rather than taken as predictions of future action.

82. Unless a *stereotype* is itself an important part of the issue, you will want to avoid using it when obtaining evaluations of the issue.

83. The *dead giveaway* is always bad.

84. Be alert to the difference between *means and ends*.

85. Surrounding *circumstances* may affect the answers unless you find means of counteracting them.

86. The *well-known* may have an advantage over the little-known so that it may be necessary for you to make a complete introduction of both.

87. A *personalized* question may produce different answers from an impersonalized one.

88. Answers to *hypothetical* questions may not be so valid in predictions of future behavior as answers in terms of past experiences may be.

89. You may find it necessary to establish some kind of *standards of comparison* for respondents to use.

90. *Extensive* questions should not attempt to cover more territory than the respondents can readily comprehend.

91. Introduction of *examples* may divert attention from the issue to the examples.

I. Readability

92. *Misplaced emphasis* can be minimized by underscoring the words which should be emphasized.

93. *Gun jumping* on the part of respondents can be reduced by holding back the alternatives until the conditions have been stated.

94. Eliminate *unnecessary punctuation* because a pause may be taken as the end of the question.

95. Indicate *correct pronunciation* of difficult words.

96. Be wary of using *homographs* such as 'lead' and 'lead'.

97. *Tongue twisters* have no place in survey questions.

98. Spell out all *abbreviations* as you want interviewers to say them.

99. Instead of the indefinite '*how much*?' approach, you can save work for yourself by indicating the system in which you want the answers to come – percentages, dollars, miles, pints, or whatever.

100. For possible *trend* purposes, try to imagine how the question will sound five years hence and adjust it to fit that possibility.

One last recommendation that I have already stated many times but which deserves the prominence of these final words is this: controlled experiment is the surest way of making progress in our understanding of question wording. Never overlook an opportunity to employ the *split-ballot* technique.

13 L. J. Rothman

An Index of Propensity to Buy

L. J. Rothman, 'Formulation of an index of propensity to buy', *Journal of Marketing Research*, vol. 1, 1964, pp. 21–5.

We frequently wish to summarize in a single index the various attitudinal elements that exist towards a brand. Such an index should be chosen to suit the purpose for which it is required, most frequently that of measuring an individual's propensity to buy the brand. (To clarify a possible point of confusion it should be emphasized that an index of propensity to buy is not necessarily the same as an index of buying intention.) Such indices of propensity to buy can find application in many fields, such as the continuous measurement of attitudes towards brands, the determination of the characteristics of potential buyers of a product, and the copy testing of advertisements. However, although these indices are so useful and many alternative forms have been proposed and justified on *a priori* grounds, practically no research seems to have been done to assess by empirical techniques the relative effectiveness of different forms of a propensity to buy index. Consequently, pilot research was undertaken to compare the effectiveness of four main alternative methods of measuring propensity to buy.

Criteria Employed

The main criterion employed to assess the relative effectiveness of the different indices was to compare the results suggested by the indices with a behavioral response which could generally be agreed upon to be indicative of a high propensity to buy. One hundred and seventy-two housewives in the Greater London area, in sixteen different sampling points, were interviewed, using an age and class quota control. During the course of the interview, scales which, on *a priori* grounds might be supposed to measure propensity to buy, were administered for two brands in each of two product groups.[1]

After completion of the interviews, the respondents were divided into four matched groups. Each respondent received two letters. Each letter offered to send the respondent a postal order for a sum slightly less than the retail price of the product if the respondent returned a wrapper or box top from it. The letters were allocated to respondents in such a way that each received a letter for one brand only in each of the two product groups. By plotting the proportion of respondents who accepted the offers against their propensity to buy them, as shown by each of the alternative indices, it was possible to see whether those who indicated a high propensity to buy the product on a given scale accepted the offer to a greater extent than those who showed a low propensity to buy on that scale.

We hypothesized that the steeper the regression line of proportions accepting the offer against propensity to buy, the better was the performance of that index as an indicator of propensity to buy.

Scales Tested

Four alternative scales were tested. These are described below:

1. Self-rating scale.
2. Gift method.
3. Guttman scale.
4. Distance method.

Self-rating scale

This, the simplest of all scales, was selected because its use in market research questionnaires has frequently been reported. In this method, respondents are shown a card containing the following statements and are asked which one applies to them for each brand:

1. The brands and product groups selected were Lux and Camay toilet soap, and two breakfast cereals, Welgar Shredded Wheat and Kelloggs Rice Krispies. These brands are well known in the United Kingdom. The manufacturers of these products were, however, not in any way responsible for this study.

1. I *definitely will* buy it
2. I *probably will* buy it
3. I *might* buy it.
4. I *probably won't* buy it.
5. I *definitely won't* buy it.

Gift method

The second method is again one whose use has frequently been reported in market research. In this case, however, it was converted from the straight question (which is the normal form) into a scale question. This is the so-called 'gift' question, where respondents are told that a draw will be held for a year's supply of the product and are asked to select the brand they would prefer to receive. To convert this into a scale question, we obtained from respondents not only the brand they would most like to have, but also a division of the remainder into brands they would not like to have at all, brands they would prefer not to have, brands they would prefer to have, and brands they would particularly like to have. In this way we were able once again to obtain a rating for each product on a five-point scale.

Guttman scale

The third method involved the use of a Guttman scale (Stouffer *et al.*, 1950; Harman, 1960), one in which items can be ranked so that a positive response to one item will predict a positive response to any lower item. A Guttman scale of propensity to buy for Welgar Shredded Wheat was constructed, using seven of an original set of eleven statements. This scale had a coefficient of reproduceability of 0·95, and the same scale was used for all the other brands. The eight positions on the scale were combined into five divisions prior to analysis.

Distance method

The final method was chosen with some reservations. Though logically appealing, measurement errors could be so great as to overcome its discriminant value. However, it was felt that this decision should be made on the basis of experimental evidence, and so the method was included. The method itself can be called the 'distance' method and requires more detailed explanation. Suppose we have a series of products which, in everybody's view, only differ from each other along a single dimension, say, relative sweetness. For each individual we can visualize the existence both of an ideal level of sweetness and an assessment for her of the level of sweetness of each product in the range. It is reasonable to suppose that for a given individual her propensity to buy the different brands will vary with the distance along the sweetness dimension that exists between each product and her ideal brand. This is demonstrated in Figure 1 below:

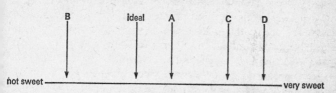

Figure 1

Brand A is the product closest to her ideal on the sweetness dimension, and is therefore the one that she would be most likely to buy, assuming that all prices were equal. Product B is farther away, and therefore her propensity to buy this product ought to be less than that for product A, but should still be relatively high compared with, for example, product D, which is a long way from her ideal. Consequently, we could use these distances as a measure of the individual's propensity to buy.

The same argument holds true for two dimensions, as is illustrated in Figure 2, which could be held to apply to a series

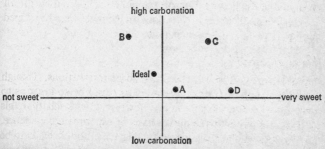

Figure 2

of soft drinks which differed only in sweetness and in carbonation.

Here however we are faced with a further difficulty. While it is feasible to produce an equal increment scale along the dimension of sweetness, and another equal increment scale along the dimension of carbonation, it is not possible to know whether a unit step along the sweetness scale is equivalent in distance to a unit step along the carbonation scale. To overcome this, experiments can be made employing different sets of weights, respondents can be asked to indicate the relative importance of each scale to them either directly or by means of pared comparisons. Alternately, as was done in this case, it can be assumed that the average distance between the brand usually bought and the ideal brand along each dimension should be the same. Hence, weights inversely proportional to the average score differences between the ideal and the usual brand can be used.

The true situation, of course, is that for any given product there are not just two dimensions along which they differ from each other, but a multitude of dimensions. One way of measuring the attitudes of people towards products on dimensions such as these is by the use of semantic differential scales, using dimensions which previous research and depth interviews, etc., have shown to be important. Attitudes shown on these scales are usually correlated with each other. To simplify the analysis, therefore, it is usual to extract from these results a number of mutually uncorrelated factors by the method of principal component analysis. These factors can be considered composite scores derived from the original scales, and serve to simplify the analysis and the presentation of results.

Ten five-point semantic differential scales were therefore administered for the brands under consideration. The items used for these scales varied between the two product groups and were selected from previous experience with the products.

Besides measuring attitudes towards the brands under consideration on these scales, we also asked respondents to rate an ideal brand – one that, as stated in the questionnaire, was perfect, in their opinion, from every point of view – in order to assess the position of the ideal brand in the same set of dimensions. Four orthogonal factors (with means of fifty and standard deviations of ten) accounting for the following proportions of the total variance were produced from these scales, using the method of principal component analysis with varimax rotations (Harman, 1960):

Factors	Toilet soap	Breakfast cereals
1	29%	29%
2	16	11
3	12	11
4	10	11
Total variance explained:	67%	62%

For each respondent, the distances along each dimension between the brands under study and the ideal brand were calculated by the following formula:

$$D_{ik} = \sqrt{\sum_j w_{jk} d^2_{ijk}}$$

where D_{ik} is the overall distance for the ith respondent on the kth brand and d_{ijk} is the calculated distance for her of the kth brand from her ideal brand along the jth dimension. Three sets of weights w_{jk} were used:

(a) Equal weights.

(b) The most important factor was given a weight of one and the rest of zero.

(c) The weights chosen for the brands were inversely proportional to the mean distances along the dimensions for their users.

In practice, the distances given by this last set of weights correlated so closely to the distances calculated by the equal weights method that analysis using this third set of weights was not carried any further.

Results

Each measure of propensity to buy was transformed into five positions. These were given scores ranging from five for the highest position, down to one for the lowest, in each case. The means of these scores for the different brands are summarized in Table 1.

Table 1
Scale Means for Propensity to Buy

Scale	Lux	Camay	Rice Krispies	Shredded Wheat
Self-rating	3·1	2·8	3·2	3·1
Gift	3·0	2·8	3·1	2·8
Guttman	3·0	2·7	3·2	3·3
Distance:				
Equal weights	3·1	2·8	3·0	3·0
Main factor	3·0	2·9	2·9	2·9
Number of interviews	172	172	167	167

Correlations were computed between the ratings of an individual and her tendency to send things by mail or take advantage of special offers. If such correlations had been found it would have been necessary to re-weight by these characteristics before any further analysis could take place. In fact, no such correlation was found, so re-weighting was not carried out.

Table 2 shows the regression coefficients for the different methods in terms of the change in the percentage accepting the offer per unit change in scale position, calculated from the line of best fit (least squares) for the numbers in the different categories. In other words, these coefficients indicate the steepness of the graph of the percentage accepting the offer against propensity to buy. Below each regression coefficient is shown the probability of obtaining a regression coefficient equal to or greater than this value on the assumption of a normal distribution.

It will be seen from these that, of the first three methods (self-rating scale, gift method and Guttman scale), the gift method gave the steepest slope and, on this criterion, is therefore the best.[2]

2. The poor performance of the Guttman scale method is somewhat disappointing. The scales themselves were quite satisfactory in terms of reproduceability, the coefficients being estimated as follows:

Table 2

Regression Coefficients of Per Cent Returning per Scale Position and their Significance Levels

Method	Lux	Camay	Rice Krispies	Shredded Wheat	Toilet soap combined	Breakfast cereals combined
Self-rating	3·7	4·3	4·4	4·6	4·0	4·2
	(0·16)	(0·13)	(0·14)	(0·11)	(0·06)	(0·06)
Gift	5·6	6·8	8·4	10·4	6·2	10·0
	(0·06)	(0·03)	(0·03)	(0·04)	(0·01)	(0·0004)
Guttman	0·3	2·2	4·6	5·6	2·3	3·5
	(0·47)	(0·32)	(0·12)	(0·09)	(0·28)	(0·08)
Distance: Equal weights	5·6	8·7	1·2	−1·1	5·2	−0·4
	(0·07)	(0·02)	(0·38)	(0·61)	(0·03)	(0·56)
Main factor	*	8·5	−0·5	2·2	4·5	0·8
	(0·50)	(0·01)	(0·55)	(0·38)	(0·04)	(0·38)
Base numbers	86	83	84	83	169	167
Mean proportion accepting offer	53%	52%	58%	46%	53%	52%

* Less than 0·005

In view of our earlier reservations, the performance of the distance methods on the toilet soaps, particularly Camay, is very encouraging. With toilet soaps, the use of equal weights for the different dimensions would appear to be the most satisfactory method at present, though further experimentation

Lux	Camay	Rice Krispies	Shredded Wheat
0·92	0·91	0·96	0·96

The coefficient of reproduceability has, however, been criticized as an estimate of the effectiveness of a scale, as, indeed, has the scaling method itself. On this occasion, at any rate, the criticism would seem to be justified and these results emphasize the importance of employing external validity checks in the development of a scale, instead of merely relying on measures of internal consistency.

Table 3

Regression Coefficients and their Significance Levels for those who did not Usually Buy the Brand for which they were Sent the Offer*

Method	Toilet soap combined	Breakfast cereals combined
Self-rating	2·1	−2·3
	(0·27)	(0·71)
Gift	3·5	8·6
	(0·18)	(0·02)
Guttman	−3·2	0·18
	(0·73)	(0·48)
Distance:		
Equal weights	3·8	− 4·8
	(0·18)	(0·90)
Main factor	2·4	−0·3
	(0·24)	(0·53)
Base numbers	113	104
Mean proportion accepting offer	50%	45%

* Since both these markets were ones in which one housewife bought more than one brand, respondents were asked to indicate all the brands they usually bought, and non-usual buyers of a brand were defined as those who did not mention the brand in answer to these questions.

could yield useful results. The failure of the distance methods on breakfast cereals requires explanation. Since the distance methods were most successful for Camay, known to be a toilet soap with a very strong image, it may be that the method only operates satisfactorily on brands with strong images, and that the failure for breakfast cereals is due to the greater fuzziness of their images.

Scales of propensity to buy are also of value in determining the attitude toward the brand of those who claim that they do not usually buy it. The sample sizes were too small to enable the non-usual buyers of a brand who were sent the offer to be studied separately. The bases for the combined figures for the two brands of toilet soap and of breakfast cereals were, however, sufficiently large to warrant analysis; see Table 3. It will be clear from Table 3 that, although the slopes in general are less steep for the non-usual buyers, the same pattern is apparent and the superiority of the Gift method is maintained.

Further Results

Other information on the performance of the scales and their inter-relationships is given in Tables 4 and 5, which show the between scale correlation coefficients, and the within scale between brand correlation coefficients. It will be seen from Table 4 that all the between scale correlation coefficients are positive but that none is sufficiently high to make it a matter of indifference which of two scales is used. Table 5 shows that for the non-distance scales, scale checking patterns were not a significant factor. The equal weights distance method on the other hand appears to have suffered to some extent from this effect.

Follow-Up Survey

Although the postal offer letters sent to the respondent gave no indication of being connected in any way with the earlier interview, it was felt possible that some respondents had decided to accept (reject) the postal offer because they had praised (criticized) it in the earlier interview. In particular, there might have been some confusion in respondents' minds between the gift question and the subsequent postal offer, thus explaining its superior performance. Recall interviews were therefore carried out with half the sample to verify this point, and also to ensure that respondents had not been indulging in any sort of fraud when they accepted the offer. When asked, 'Why do you think you were sent the offer?' only one out of eighty-six respondents mentioned the gift question, and when asked, 'why did you decide to accept/not to accept the offer?' none of the respondents mentioned the gift question. This supports the hypothesis that respondents did not confuse the postal offer with the gift question.

When asked if they had the product in the house at the time of interview, and if they had bought any more after the offer was

Table 4
Between Scale within Brand Correlation Coefficients

	Self-rating	Gift	Guttman	Distance Equal weights	Main factor
Lux					
Self-rating	×	0·70	0·62	0·15	0·49
Gift		×	0·70	0·16	0·46
Guttman			×	0·11	0·49
Distance: equal weights				×	0·47
main factor					×
Camay					
Self-rating	×	0·67	0·58	0·48	0·52
Gift		×	0·61	0·31	0·48
Guttman			×	0·36	0·65
Distance: equal weights				×	0·65
main factor					×
Rice Krispies					
Self-rating	×	0·56	0·62	0·26	0·27
Gift		×	0·63	0·24	0·36
Guttman			×	0·26	0·43
Distance: equal weights				×	0·57
main factor					×
Shredded Wheat					
Self-rating	×	0·61	0·75	0·55	0·60
Gift		×	0·62	0·55	0·51
Guttman			×	0·48	0·46
Distance: equal weights				×	0·68
main factor					×

received, four respondents in the case of cereals, and two in the case of toilct soap, who accepted the offer claimed that they had the product in the house and had not bought any more since. On the other hand, an equal number of respondents in both cases did not take up the offer, although they had the product in the house and *had* bought some more since. It will be seen from this that errors from 'cheating' are slight and tend to be compensated by regular purchasers who did not bother to take up the offer. All the respondents who claimed to have accepted

Table 5
Between Brand within Scale Correlation Coefficients

	Lux/Camay	Rice Krispies/ Shredded Wheat
Self-rating	*	0·07
Gift	−0·15	−0·06
Guttman	*	0·16
Distance: equal weights†	0·45	0·32

* Less than 0·005
† The correlation coefficients for the Distance-Main Factor method were not calculated.

the offer and to have bought subsequently were able to provide as supporting evidence details of the place where they made the purchase.

Conclusion

The conclusion from the comparison would appear to be that the gift scale method has the greatest likelihood of yielding satisfactory results for a variety of brands and products. There would seem, therefore, to be no reason why this method should not be used in the future as an overall index of attitudes toward brands in place of the self-rating method.

We hope, therefore, to make use of this gift scale method in the future, both in *ad hoc* surveys and in continuous consumer surveys, and while doing this to obtain further information on the method's validity for other product groups and under other purchasing stimuli than postal offers. We feel, however, that the self-rating method, because of its high correlation with the gift scale method, can still be applied satisfactorily in circumstances where a question offering the opportunity to win a free gift cannot be employed. In addition, the self-rating method would also seem to be a satisfactory second scale where two different scales are required in order to determine attitude shifts.

The results from the distance method are sufficiently encouraging to warrant further development work, particularly for obtaining information about brands which have strong brand images. It may well be, however, that the importance of the distance method will not be so much as a measure of propensity to buy but as a method for estimating in advance the relative effectiveness of different advertising approaches.

References

HARMAN, H. H. (1960), *Modern Factor Analysis*, University of Chicago Press.

STOUFFER, S. A. *et al*. (1950), 'Measurement and prediction', *Studies in Social Psychology in World War II*, vol. 4, Princeton University Press.

Market Research Society (1960), *Attitude Scaling*, Market Research Society.

14 A. E. Goldman

The Group Depth Interview

A. E. Goldman, 'The group depth interview', *Journal of Marketing*, vol. 26, 1962, pp. 61–8.

Consideration of each of the three elements of the name given to the group-interview technique suggests that, while the label may be as serviceable as any other, under certain conditions it is not wholly accurate. A comprehensive review of group methods is beyond the scope of this article; and the interested reader can refer to the voluminous literature on this technique and its application to marketing, education, and psychotherapy.[1]

Instead, the present article explains what is meant by *group*, *depth*, and *interview* in a group depth interview ... the mechanics of moderating such interviews ... and the five requirements of these interviews.

Group

A group is a number of *interacting individuals having a community of interests*. These two criteria of groups must be satisfied in order to derive the benefits of collecting information in a group setting.

Interaction

In the group situation a person is asked an opinion about something – a product, a distribution system, an advertisement, a television program or, perhaps a candidate for office. In contrast to the individual interview in which the flow of information is unidirectional, from the respondent to the interviewer, the group setting causes the opinions of each person to be considered in group discussion. Each individual is exposed to the ideas of the others and submits his ideas for the consideration of the group.

1. Suggested sources: Lerner and Kelman (1952); Mangold (1954).

This assumes, of course, that social interaction occurs at some overt level. If the group members do not interact with one another, but each member directs his remarks to the moderator, this is not a group. It might better be described as multiple or serial interviewing, since the advantages of the group setting are precluded. It is the interviewer's responsibility to stimulate the group members to interact with each other rather than with him.

Community of interest

The establishment of group cohesiveness is dependent in large part on the second criterion of 'groupness', namely, *sharing a common interest*.

This common interest should, of course, be relevant to the topic under discussion. A number of individuals may be very different in national origin, religious beliefs, political persuasion, and the like; but if they share a common identity relevant to the discussion (shoe buyers, drug manufacturers, purchasers of luxury items), a group can form. This involves some risks that can be minimized by thoughtful selection of group members. For example, in a discussion of a home-decorating product, the inclusion of one or two low-income people in a group of wealthy individuals may serve to inhibit the free expression of the attitudes of all.

How may these two characteristics of a group be exploited in eliciting useful information, and in what way is this information different from that produced by individual interviewing?

1. First, the interaction among group members *stimulates new ideas* regarding the topic under discussion that may never be mentioned in individual interviewing. When a group member does bring up a new idea, however tangential, the group as a whole is given the opportunity to react to it in a variety of ways that indicate its interest to the group.

The idea can be readily and enthusiastically taken up by the group and ultimately accepted or rejected. The idea can be discussed without a decision being reached, with considerable confusion expressed in the process. The idea can be discussed briefly and then dropped not to be mentioned again. Sometimes, and most significant of all, it can be studiously ignored and avoided, despite the moderator's reiteration of the idea. This behavior, when accompanied by indications of anxiety, such as lighting cigarettes, shuffling uneasily in seats, clearing throats, and so on, suggests that a particular idea has provoked sufficient psychic discomfort and threat as to require its rigorous avoidance in open discussion.

2. These possible reactions to a new idea may also demonstrate a second value of group interviewing – *the opportunity to observe directly the group process*. In the individual interview, respondents *tell* how they would or did behave in a particular social situation. In the group interview, respondents react to each other, and their behavior is directly *observed*.

For example, a housewife who hesitantly and timidly describes how she cleans her floors suggests the tenuousness with which she herself regards these procedures. In one group, the timid admission by one housewife that she hated washing floors and did so only when forced to by fear of social rejection brought immediate and firm support from other group members. They then verbally 'turned on' the two group members who washed floors more frequently, and meticulously. Here the attitudes of women toward washing floors was reflected in the way they behaved toward each other *in the group*.

A purchasing decision is frequently a social act in that the items are considered in the context of what others think of the product, and what others will think of *them* for having purchased it. The group creates or recapitulates the marketing situation, depending upon the point at which the decision process is intercepted. Here the process of the decision is exposed in the sharing of experiences, rumors, and anecdotes that go on in a group discussion about a product, service, person, or event. Here we are concerned with the *process* of the purchasing decision, not just in the static end-result of that process. Effective marketing requires understanding of this decision process.

3. A third advantage of group interviewing is that it *provides some idea of the dynamics of attitudes and opinions*. The flexibility or rigidity with which an opinion is held is better exposed in a group setting than in an individual interview. Within the two hours of the typical group session, an opinion that is stated with

finality and apparent deep conviction can be modified a number of times by the social pressures or new information that may be provided by the group. As the discussion proceeds, some group members modify their initial reaction, some defend their positions even more rigorously, some admit confusion. In this way, the group setting offers some idea of the dynamics of opinion – its initiation and modification, and its intensity and resistance to change. This pattern of modification in opinion is often as rewarding with regard to understanding motives as the one initially stated.

4. Discussion in a peer group often *provokes considerably greater spontaneity and candor than can be expected in an individual interview*. This is its fourth advantage. The interviewer is frequently an 'outsider', regardless of how skillful he or she may be. In the group setting it is not unusual for group members, after an initial period of orientation, to ignore completely the presence of the moderator. For example, in a group of small-business managers, several of them admitted blatant acts of petty dishonesty at the expense of their customers. It seems unlikely that this would have been admitted to an individual interviewer.

Because of the demands on their time, physicians are unusually difficult to interview at length. Yet in group discussions with other physicians, two hours does not seem to tax their interest or co-operation. Physicians who appear impatient, constrained, cautious, or curt when interviewed alone, seem considerably more garrulous, frank, and at times argumentative when in a group with other physicians.

Candor is permitted not only because the members of the group understand and feel comfortable with one another, but also because they draw social strength from each other. The group provides support to its members in the expression of anxiety-provoking or socially unpopular ideas.

An example may illustrate this. At the beginning of a two and a half hour session, a group of jobbers individually expressed loyalty to, and appreciation of, their suppliers. After an hour, most of these same group members joined in the expression of a pervasive and deeply felt antagonism toward their manufacturers – attitudes which they had not previously expressed for a variety of reasons, including fears of economic reprisal by the jobber.

In another instance, members of a minority group at first vehemently denied favoritism in buying from members of their own group. Later, following a profound and emotional discussion of racial and religious intolerance, *all* admitted that they preferred to buy from a salesman of their own ethnic group. By virtue of its community of interests, the group permitted exposure of feelings not ordinarily given casual or public expression.

5. A fifth advantage is that the group setting is *emotionally provocative in a way that an individual interview cannot be*. A group composed of housewives ranging in age from twenty-five to forty-five may serve to illustrate how the group can provoke reactions which elicit interesting and useful insights into the motives of its members. This discussion focused on how these women felt about their weight, and what effect this had on their diets. At one point in the discussion, the youngest and most slender woman in the group said, 'Weight isn't a problem for me yet, but I imagine that for older women like yourselves it would be.' Immediately, perceiving the unintended offense to the group members, she explained, 'Well, as you get older, you get fatter.' This attempt at diplomacy fell somewhat short of soothing the injured self-concepts of some of the other women, but it did serve to provoke quite profound feelings toward 'getting old' and how these feelings were expressed in their eating habits. Thus, a member of the group confronted the other group members with anxieties that the moderator could mention only at considerable risk to continued *rapport*.

Thus, by virtue of the interaction and common relevant interests of its members, the group offers more and qualitatively different information than can be obtained from the sum of its individual human parts.

Depth

The use of the word 'depth', in the name given this technique, implies seeking information that is more profound than is usually accessible at the level of interpersonal relationships. While a respondent may be the best authority on *what* he did, he is often an unreliable source of information as to *why* he did it. His response reflects what he wants you to believe, and also what he himself wants to believe. Retroactive distortion helps him to maintain a self-concept of a wise, judicious buyer motivated by reason rather than feeling.

Much of our daily behavior is motivated by subliminal stimuli (sensory impressions of which the individual is only minimally aware). Depth interviewing seeks to bring these motives to light. Technically these motives are *preconscious*, and are distinguished from *unconscious* motives by the more profound depth of repression of the latter.

A study of the factors that determine which of several supermarkets were used by shoppers in a particular neighborhood illustrates the definitive and lasting reaction to subliminal stimuli. Some of the women in each of four group sessions were adamant in their intention not to shop in one of the markets, although they did not appear able to express their reasons in a clear or consistent manner. Some mentioned a vague feeling that the market in question was somehow messy or even dirty. Yet, upon further exploration, these same women agreed that the shelves were neatly stacked, the personnel clean, the floors swept, the counters well dusted. They could not point out anything to support their charges of uncleanliness. Further, they readily agreed that the store they did shop in was more messy than the one in which they refused to shop. A casual reference by one of the women to a peculiar odor evoked immediate recognition from the others. This occurred spontaneously in several of the groups and led to the consensus that it was a 'bloody' or 'meaty' odor. This process of 'consensual validation' suggested that this vague impression of untidiness stemmed not from anything that could be seen, but rather from this faint yet pervasive and offensive odor. Later this information served to bring to the attention of the management an ineffective exhaust-and-drainage system in the supermarket's meat room.

In seeking 'depth' material we do not make the assumption that we can in some way get the respondent to express unconscious motives *directly*. A thing is repressed, that is, remanded to the care of the unconscious, if it is too threatening to the self-concept to allow into consciousness. Generally there is little that a moderator can do, or ethically should do, to provoke the overt expression of such threatening material. What is usually done is to infer the nature of these impulses from who says what, in what sequence, to whom he says it, and how he says it.

However, there are certain conditions under which the moderator may wish to explore some facets on an unconscious motive. By focusing on the motives of one group member, the others are frequently provoked to react to the repressed motive, even if that motive is never made quite explicit. For example, in a discussion of an easy-to-prepare 'instant' food, one woman made the following slip-of-the-tongue: 'Especially when I'm in a hurry, I like foods that are time-*consuming*.' The context of the preceding discussion, which centered upon the role that food preparation plays in the housewife's concept of herself, made it quite clear that the eagerness with which this woman embraced 'instant' foods was not without psychic conflict. In this case, the moderator inquired into the error without interpreting to her the feeling of guilt that this slip may have revealed. It did serve, however, to stimulate other women to discuss this problem more openly.

Probing for unconscious material should be undertaken with extreme caution. The danger, in most cases, is not that any appreciable damage will be done to a reasonably stable personality; the normal protective mechanisms will adequately protect the ego from ill-advised assaults by the moderator. Rather, the danger of unskilled probing is represented by the risk of completely alienating the offended group member, and thereby limiting the co-operation and spontaneity of the whole group. In these situations, the professional psychologist with clinical experience is more likely to avoid such pitfalls.

Interview

The word 'interview' has the least precise meaning of the three elements of the term, group depth interview. An interview implies an interviewer, rather than a moderator. The role of moderator requires using the group as the device for eliciting information. The moderator guides the discussion, keeping it within fruitful bounds, but rarely participates in it himself. When he can lead a group member to ask a question of the group, the moderator will not question them himself.

An interviewer, especially with a structured questionnaire, is frequently restricted to a direct question-and-answer approach, while the moderator has the greatest possible flexibility and freedom in pursuing motivational 'pay-dirt' and may seek to exploit unique characteristics of a particular group in the most effective way by whatever devices are at his disposal.

The Mechanics of Moderating

The best way to describe group depth interviewing is in terms of the specific mechanics of moderating the group. Many of the techniques considered here have been suggested by those used in group psychotherapy. Although psychotherapy has a radically different primary goal, it shares with group interviewing the goal of eliciting information which the group member himself finds difficult, or impossible, to produce.

All sessions are tape recorded, with the recorder placed in full view. For training purposes and client observation a one-way vision mirror is used. All group members are paid, to compensate them for the expense of traveling to where the session is conducted, and to attract people other than the merely curious.

Rapport

The most important factor in producing usable information from the group depth interview is the relationship between the moderator and the panel members, and that among the panel members themselves.

The first job of the moderator is to structure the roles of all of the participants. The purpose of the session, how long it will last, and the manner in which it will be conducted are all explained in as comfortable and friendly a way as possible. Good *rapport* is crucial in establishing the candidness needed; and this is facilitated when the language of the moderator is not too discrepant from that of the majority of the group. For example, when the group is composed of young, poorly educated subjects of marginal socio-economic level, 'they won't dig you if you bug 'em with a lot of high-falutin' jazz.'

Verbal activity

The verbal activity or passivity of the moderator is determined by the nature of the group and its goals. With alert and articulate people the moderator can assume a more passive role – passive, not inert. In an especially talkative group, or at the other extreme, with a very quiet group, a more active role will be required of the moderator, either to inhibit or provoke more discussion.

Relevancy

One of the most important things that the moderator does is to keep the discussion within relevant limits. Here he must be very careful not to rule out that which is apparently unrelated, but may reveal relevant unconscious motives. A general discussion of grandma and grandpa and the 'good old days' may have extensive significance in marketing such things as upholstery fabric or canned foods. Sensitivity to unconscious processes is, of course, important here and a clinical background is helpful, although not essential.

Projective questions

The researcher who pursues those motives of the buying decision of which the consumer is unaware must give particular thought to developing various 'projective' techniques which expose these motives. The answer to a projective question enables the respondent to express needs which he cannot or does not wish to admit. These, of course, must be individually designed to fit the particular marketing problem. For example, in the selection of kinds of housing materials, material design, or fabric pattern, the following question was found to be very effective: 'What kind of family would find this pattern appealing, and why?'

Different reactions to various designs may also be provoked by asking the group what well-known person each pattern suggests to them. In this way, a design that suggests Jayne Mansfield may be qualitatively differentiated from those which suggest Liberace, Eleanor Roosevelt, or Marshall Matt Dillon. Similar material may be provoked by *stereotype photographs and the illustrative cases method.*

Illustrative case method

To explore personal habits, the illustrative case method is valuable. Several people are described who differ from each other according to the intensity or consistency of some behavior. Then the group members are asked to describe the other characteristics of the person. For example, Miss A uses underarm deodorant four times a day; Miss B uses one only in the morning – what kind of people are they? Or Mr A traded his Chevrolet in for a Pontiac; Mr B traded his Cadillac in for a small foreign car – what kind of people are they? Intensive probing follows their responses in order to clarify what motivates Miss A or B, or Mr A or B.

Stereotype photographs

A related type of stimulus is represented by *stereotype photographs*. These are pictures of men and women who typify a particular age, income, or vocational group. Each of these variables, of course, can be independently varied to suit the objectives of the study. The appropriately selected photographs are exposed singly or all together, and a question might be asked, such as: 'Which of these women would be most likely to use instant tea?'

The response is followed up with: 'What is there about the woman you picked that makes you think that?' Such answers as: 'She looks as though she's always in a hurry and can't be bothered with brewing tea', or, 'Not that one! She looks rich enough to afford the best; she would have her maid brew tea', are quite revealing of attitudes toward a particular product.

Serial association

In evaluating the effectiveness of advertising copy, controlled serial association may be used. Prior to exposure of the first ad, the group members are trained in the difficult job of saying words freely one after the other. In this way, they can learn to respond to the test ads with some spontaneity.

For example, to evaluate the impression of the product conveyed to women by a pictorial advertisement in a magazine, group members were shown the advertisement and requested to associate ideas with it. It became readily apparent that this ad suggested licentious intrigue and adventure. While the symbolic meaning of the ad served to attract and hold the attention of the reader admirably well, the dynamic meaning it attached to this particular product apparently was not the most advantageous.

Deprivation questions

Deprivation questions inquire into the relative value of various products or services. A question such as, 'Which of the following canned foods would you miss most if it were no longer available to you?' is somehow more provocative than, 'Which canned food is most important to you?'

Deception

A calculated 'deception' is often effective in testing the limits of the respondent's convictions. A rich source of information and attitudes is tapped by the group's responses to the blatantly incorrect statement that all of ten very different fabrics are made of the same synthetic fiber.

There are times when none of these methods appears to stimulate any but the most mundane and obvious generalities. This, of course, may be significant in itself if it is not a façade behind which reside motives that are not being expressed. Some other procedures that may be useful in these difficult cases are *false termination* and *playing the devil's advocate*.

It is a rule of thumb in group psychotherapy that the most important material may be produced in the last few minutes of the session. In this way the person who would like to contribute something that may be embarrassing or threatening to him has only a few minutes during which he must endure the discomfort. Also, he may deliberately inhibit ideas that he feels are irrelevant to the discussion proper.

Following this lead, especially in group interviews in which emotionally loaded material is involved, the session is 'terminated' early by thanking the group members for being there and inquiring as to whether there are any other comments. Intensive probing into these 'final' comments has been rewarding on a number of occasions.

For example, a group interview devoted to the motives

involved in drinking in taverns as opposed to drinking at home uncovered very little more than mundane and superficial generalities. Following the *false termination*, a group member casually commented laughingly to his neighbor that he is hesitant to drink in a tavern because he holds his liquor poorly and is afraid of making a fool of himself in public. Further probing of this theme with the man who initiated it, as well as others in the group, revealed the specific moral prohibitions against drinking at a bar made by the group member's father. More important, this 'casual' comment led to a quite meaningful discussion about the variety and intensity of impulses and emotions that may be expressed in a tavern but are socially unacceptable elsewhere. Anxiety, provoked by the threat of such emotional expression, may be sufficient to limit drinking to the relative 'safety' of the home.

Playing the devil's advocate requires that the moderator take a very opinionated role. With the goal of provoking a reaction the moderator may himself express an extreme viewpoint on the topic under discussion. This is usually sufficient to move the discussion into more productive channels. The same effect can be achieved without involving the moderator, through the use of an accomplice who takes a pre-established and adamantly stated point of view.

Sophisticated naïveté

In most cases, however, the most effective pose is that of sophisticated naïveté. The group members are assigned the role of educating the unknowledgeable moderator. He thus forces the group members to explain even the obvious – those unverbalized habits of thought and action that are rarely subject to scrutiny.

Here the moderator may make frequent use of such probes as, 'What do you mean?' 'I'm afraid I didn't understand that' ... or, 'Remember now, I'm not a buyer; so, would you explain that to me?' Such probing elicited the realization on the part of one dress buyer that in making selections for her extensive clientele she had primarily four of her regular customers in mind.

Parrying direct questions

There are occasions in which a *direct question* may put the moderator 'on the spot'. Often these questions cannot only be diplomatically dodged, but at the same time they may be used to gain additional information. When group members ask, as they frequently do, about identity of the client, this may be used to open a discussion concerning the relative activity in consumer and scientific research of various companies and the interest of these companies in the needs of the consumer. An effective gambit here in response to, 'What company is paying for this anyway?' is something like, 'I'm curious about why you ask', or 'What's your hunch about who is sponsoring this research?'

Gesture

The use of gestures should not be ignored in conducting the group interview. A raised eyebrow can be an effective probe; leaning forward on the table may encourage more comment by a reluctant or shy person; a shrug of the shoulder can parry many direct questions.

Attention to the gestures of the group members frequently tells more than what is said. Reserve, disgust, disdain, irritation, enthusiasm, and myriad other emotional subtleties are conveyed by gesture. Here is an example. In a discussion of a building material, one woman, while describing her impression of it, continually rubbed her thumb and forefinger together. Here words expressed a mildly favourable opinion, but the gesture revealed a fear of which she was only slightly aware herself. Despite the fact that the material itself was very rigid and hard, probing as to the meaning of her gesture revealed a fear that it would be 'crumbly' and soft.

Non-directive comments

Non-directive comments often help to focus attention on the emotion implicit in a discussion. A non-directive comment such as, 'You seem angry about that', or, 'That memory seems to give you pleasure', recognizes and accepts emotion, and at the same time encourages the group member to reflect further on his feelings in relation to the topic under discussion. Most people need such encouragement to express strong feelings in a group setting, particularly feelings of tenderness and sentimentality.

Five requirements of the group depth interview

Five factors are required of the group depth interview in order to serve its research objectives: *objectivity*, *reliability*, *validity*, *intensive analysis*, and *marketing applicability*. While the first four are required of any scientific research, the last is more relevant to marketing studies. Any endeavor that presumes to be marketing research cannot ignore these guideposts of sound inquiry.

Objectivity

Avoidance of the bias of the interviewer and client indicates *objectivity*. Respondents are unusually sensitive to the attitudes and opinions of the group moderator; and if these are allowed to manifest themselves without the moderator's awareness, it can grossly affect the nature of the data. To further objectivity, it is usually necessary to disguise the identity of the client, and for the moderator to observe rigorous neutrality (except when being the devil's advocate). Objective summary of attitudes sometimes requires the use of some quantitative technique, such as a scaling device, within the context of the group interview.

Reliability

The degree to which the information produced is representative of the population to which it is generalized is called *reliability*. The question of reliability of the sample, or generalization of the results, directs attention to the purpose of the group depth interview. Its basic function is to indicate 'why' rather than 'how many'. That is, it focuses on understanding the motives of behavior rather than cataloging the number of individuals who behave in a particular way.

The group interview is particularly useful in the developmental phases of a research program. It establishes the range of attitudes without, however, asserting the representativeness of these attitudes. Perhaps the major function of the group depth interview is to generate creative and fruitful hypotheses. It does not generally permit broad generalization and thus, in most cases, it should be followed by a probability survey to substantiate these hypotheses.

In certain cases, small-sample group interviews can produce generalizable results. For example, a group panel had represented in its members, jobbers who controlled 50 per cent of all automotive parts distributed in a particular city. The opinions they expressed represented a considerable portion of the automotive parts jobber universe in that city.

In special circumstances which limit a study to a small sample for security reasons, the problem of sample representativeness may be academic. A manufacturer may need to limit a study to a small sample, in order to prevent too many people from knowing about a new product prior to its introduction to the market.

Group interviewing does not preclude quantitatively adequate sampling; but in most cases it makes it very expensive.

Another kind of reliability problem is the representativeness of the time sample. Purchasing decisions for higher-priced items begin as vague, general ideas of the product and become progressively more specific as decision-making proceeds. Intersecting this process at any one point in time may not adequately reflect its dynamic nature. The purchasing decision can be viewed as a learning process that may be altered many times from the initiation of the need to the actual purchase of a product.

One way in which this process may be investigated may be illustrated by a problem involving the assessment of consumer reaction to a radical styling innovation of a major appliance. Six groups of eight members each were shown scale models of the appliances at three different sessions held at weekly intervals. At each session, attitudes were intensively probed. A gradual shift in acceptance of the radical change was observed over the three week period. However, when those who had been exposed to the product three times were combined in the same group with people who had never seen the product, the effect was immediate and dramatic: the quality and intensity of their attitudes reverted to what they had been at the very first exposure. Since this kind of interaction duplicates what happens in the market place, it produced a valuable insight into this social-learning process and permitted a more effective marketing decision to be made.

This study suggested that while there may be increasing

acceptance of the styling innovation with more exposure to it, this preference was not a stable one and could be reversed by contact with someone who was seeing the radically styled appliance for the first time. Here, it was decided that the style was too radical, and a more moderate style was elected.

Validity

A source of continual concern to researchers is the *validity* problem, the assumption that a measure really measures what it purports to measure. The group situation attempts to get as close to the actual purchasing decision as possible.

For example, the task given the group member in a problem which concerned purchase of prepackaged bacon was actual selection from among a number of samples the very bacon that she would serve her family, and not merely enumerating the criteria according to which she usually buys bacon.

Similarly, in a discussion of wine preference, the group members ordered and drank the wine of their choice.

When the topic was that of selecting a garment for themselves, women were asked to act out in detail, using a number of blouse samples, the act of buying one for themselves. Here the moderator took the role of salesman.

A problem involving the factors which are important in home decorating was approached by having groups of married couples go through the actual task of decorating a small-scale model home, using reduced-sized flooring materials, wallpaper prints, drapery fabrics, upholstery fabrics, and a wide variety of miniature furniture of various styles. Each couple decorated in the presence of other couples, and each did so with a conscientiousness that left little doubt that this task had considerable egoinvolvement. These various devices tend to decrease the discrepancy between attitude expression and actual purchasing behavior.

Intensive analysis

A fourth requirement of the group depth interview is that the often voluminous data be *intensively analysed*. Discussion material of this kind defies routine analysis. The method of analyses employed here is similar to that by which group psychotherapy sessions are analysed.

Qualitative analysis of group-interview material focuses on several kinds of data. At the most superficial level are the opinions easily verbalized. They may at times give only some indication of the attitudes that group members are willing to express to others. Subconscious buying motives may be reflected in such data as: what topics are discussed, what kinds of people bring them up and with what degree of intensity, to whom they are said, and, perhaps most important, the temporal sequence in which they are said.

For example, a product that had enjoyed the highest market share in a particular city for fifteen years began to decrease in sales to members of a minority group. The drop in sales did not appear to be attributable to changes in product, package design, or sales policy. In several group sessions, the following sequence of these was discussed: minority and national groups are becoming more alert and militant all over the world; domination by the more powerful majority must stop; sometimes members of minorities are dealt with unfairly by the police; the company in question makes a good product and is the biggest manufacturer of that product; other companies that also produce a good product are entering the field. These themes, in the context of the total group session, suggested an identification of the minority group member with the smaller producer in opposition to the large 'powerful' company. To the extent that their buying behavior was consistent with this psychological identity, the 'big' company was being hurt.

Marketing applicability

The group depth interview is designed to *solve marketing problems*. Even if a study satisfies the other four requirements, it is just an 'academic exercise' if its findings cannot be put to use in the market place.

A variety of marketing problems in which the group depth interview is applicable have already been indicated. As noted above, the group depth interview is most frequently useful and appropriate in the developmental and exploratory phases of research. Here it is used to make it more likely that the correct questions are asked in large sample surveys to follow.

The group depth interview is also helpful in cases where broad sampling is prohibited by security requirements. For example, when used as a complement to new-product development, group sessions are conducted at several points in the process, to aid management in decisions which are not best left for a point later in the process. In this way, management has available consumer reactions *before* large investments of time and money are committed.

For example, development of a new food product may begin with an exploration of several food concepts in order to expose which of several alternative directions would serve the consumers' needs best. Or, perhaps a manufacturer might wish to know which of several kinds of materials are best suited for a home building item before one of them is committed to intensive laboratory development. When one of these materials is selected by the groups and is developed further, the graphic design of the product also is explored by the group method. In a final research phase the progressively refined and elaborated product may be discussed by various kinds of groups in order to help to guide advertising themes, promotional campaigns, and perhaps distribution systems.

The group depth interview has been used to explore attitudes about corporate images, public relations, personnel-turnover rate, recruiting appeals, health problems, container design, political issues, and many other marketing and social problems. The full potential of the method has yet to be realized.

References

LERNER, H. H., and KELMAN, H. C. (1952), 'Group methods in psychotherapy, social work and adult education', *Journal of Social Issues*, vol. 8, whole issue no. 2, pp. 1–88.

MANGOLD, W. (1954), *Gegenstand und Methode des Gruppendiskussions-verfahrens: Aus der Arbeit des Instituts für Sozialforschung*, Europäische Verlagsanstalt, Frankfurt am Main, p. 176.

15 S. Sudman

Consumer Panels

S. Sudman, 'On the accuracy of recording of consumer panels, 1 and 2',
Journal of Marketing Research, vol. 1, 1964, pp. 14–20, 69–83.

Part 1

Consumer panels are household samples that obtain continuous information on household purchases and other consumer behavior. Panels have become a major source of market research information since the end of the Second World War, not only in the United States but all over the world. Today it is estimated that users of panels spend more than fifteen million dollars or the equivalent in foreign currency every year to purchase panel information, with about half of this amount spent in the United States. A substantial literature on the uses of panels is available (Anderson, 1954; Anscombe, 1961; Barclay, 1963; Barton, 1943; Cawl, 1943; Ehrenberg, 1959; Fourt and Woodlock, 1960; Frank, 1962; Kuehn, 1962 and 1958; Lipstein, 1959; Madow, Hyman and Jesseu, 1961; *The National Consumer Panel*, n.d.; Rewoldt, 1953; Telser, 1962; U.S. Department of Agriculture, 1959; Wadsworth, 1952; Webber, 1944; Womer, 1944).

Previous Studies on Panels and Response Errors

A short description of panels that discusses some of their operating problems is found in the American Marketing Association pamphlet by Boyd and Westfall (1960). Quackenbush and Shaffer (1960; 1954) have described their experiences in operating the Lansing Panel for Michigan State University. Two reports prepared by the Market Research Corporation of America for the U.S. Department of Agriculture (1953; 1952) discuss in some detail the problems of sample design, recruiting techniques, and sample selectivity. Ferber (1953) gives another discussion of sample selectivity. A description of a sample maintenance program for a panel is found in an earlier paper of the author (Sudman, 1959). And Ehrenberg (1960) has described the Attwood Company's experiences in operating the British Consumer Panel.

Only in recent years have researchers come to realize the importance of response errors in surveys, but now the literature is growing (Payne, 1951). Neter and Waksberg (1961) measured response errors in a survey of homeowner's expenditures for alterations and repairs and found that respondents overstated expensive repairs while forgetting minor ones. Lansing, Ginsburg and Braaten (1961) in a study of consumer saving behavior observed substantial understatements of amounts in respondents' savings accounts. In earlier studies, Metz (1956) measured the accuracy of response in a study of milk consumption, while Drayton (1954) compared a survey on cheese consumption to a wholesale audit. In both cases, substantial recall overstatements of consumption were observed. A U.S. Department of Agriculture study compared the results of four different recall methods to purchase results obtained from a consumer panel. Four products were studied – butter, oleo-margarine, fresh oranges, and frozen orange concentrate. Again for all four recall methods on all four products, serious overstatements of consumption appeared (U.S. Department of Agriculture, 1957).

In consumer panels, too, recording errors are very important. Previous literature is sparse. Soon after the Second World War, researchers found that a weekly diary gave more complete results than a monthly one for most grocery products (Lewis, 1948; Shaffer, 1955). Except for some recall questions asked by Quackenbush and Shaffer of their Lansing Panel, nothing else seems to have been published on recording of panels.

The Data

During the past twenty years, the Market Research Corporation of America has operated the National Consumer Panel, the largest consumer panel in the United States. The author was privileged to spend seven years with MRCA, primarily in methodological research. These findings are a result of that research.

A brief description of the operation of the panel may be helpful. Households in the National Consumer Panel report their purchases of a selected group of products on a continuing basis. For this purpose they use self-administered forms called diaries. Diaries for grocery products cover one week's purchase behavior and are mailed in at the end of each week.

Diaries for less frequently purchased items, such as clothing and photographic equipment, are kept on a monthly basis. Households are recruited and trained by personal contact, but additional contacts are normally made by mail. During training, the immediate entry system of recording is taught, i.e., diary keepers are told to record their purchases immediately upon returning from the shopping trip. The diary forms developed from the accumulated twenty-year experience of MRCA in operating panels. As the requirements for information were revised, or as data problems arose, the forms were modified. The research studies described were not intended to develop a diary form *de novo* but rather to measure the results obtained with the current forms and to measure the effects of varying these forms.

The remainder of this paper discusses the actual level of recording accuracy at a point in time, and the factors which determine it. Of equal or greater importance is an understanding of just which factors cause changes in the level of recording through time. Unless these changes in recording level can be measured and controlled, a panel cannot accurately reflect changes occurring in the universe it measures. This is the topic of Part 2 of this paper (p. 292).

Factors Determining Accuracy of Recording

Causes of recording error

Record keeping of purchase behavior by consumer households is subject to several kinds of human error. The following difficulties might arise:

1. The record keeper is not aware that the purchase was made by another household member.

2. The record keeper is aware of the purchase but forgets to enter it in the diary.

3. The record keeper enters the purchase in the diary but errs on some detail of the purchase due to either a memory or a recording error.

4. Deliberate falsification of the diary, either by omission of purchases or inclusion of imaginary purchases or purchase details, is also a possibility.

Measurement of recording accuracy

Faced with these possible errors, the operators of consumer panels need methods for measuring recording errors. For these measures of recording error to be useful, the errors in the measurement should be smaller than the recording errors being measured. Thus, it is not appropriate to validate consumer panel results by comparing them to recall survey results which are substantially less accurate, as will be shown in a later paper.

The most direct way to validate consumer panel recording would be to secretly follow all members of a panel household and note all items purchased. These could then be compared to entries made in their diaries for the same date. The cost and difficulty of such detective work have to date prevented any direct validation.

Another way of validating purchase recording is to use the records of the seller. This method was used by Metz (1956) in his study of milk consumption, and by Lansing, Ginsburg and Braaten (1961) in their study of consumer saving behavior. Unfortunately, nearly all of the purchases reported by panel households are made in cash, which leaves no seller's record. This method could be used to validate purchases of durables, particularly if purchased on credit.

Consumer panels generally provide their clients with information on a continuing basis. It is often possible to obtain information on shipments from clients for corresponding periods. Over a sufficiently long period, there should be a high degree of correlation between shipments and reports of consumer purchases.

Even with panel data one must be cautious in validating shipments. The manufacturer generally sells to a broader universe than a consumer panel measures. If a manufacturer has an institutional division, as most do, sales of consumer sizes from warehouses and retail stores will be made to nonhousehold establishments, such as small retail stores (non-foods), offices, factories, etc., as well as to individuals not living in households. Differences between consumer diary reports and shipment data may also be caused by factors other than recording.

Factors determining the accuracy of recording by consumer panel households

Recording accuracy depends on the characteristics of the product and the techniques used to obtain purchase information, as well as on the characteristics of the panel members. For example, comparisons with shipment data indicate that frequently purchased grocery items are recorded very accurately by members of the National Consumer Panel, while up to half the purchases of unusual non-grocery items, such as phonograph records, may be omitted.

Factors affecting all product classes will be discussed in a later paper. The following discussion is limited to those factors which affect products differentially. During 1959 and 1960 seventy-two products were examined for which information was available from National Consumer Panel reports and client shipment data. The list of products included is shown in Appendix 1. The results not only indicated factors important to the accuracy of diary recording, but also quantified the importance of these factors. While it must be stressed that the specific estimates obtained were valid only for the diary format, sample, and training methods on which they were based, the method is of general interest.

Many variables were originally considered related to accuracy of recording. Insufficient data reduced the number examined to eight. Note how they relate to the causes of recording error shown in the first paragraph of this section.

Awareness of purchase
Type of product

Memory errors
Page in diary
Position on page
Prominence on page

Frequency of purchase
Percentage of product class purchased in chain stores
Convenience of product preparation

Deliberate falsification
Complexity of entry

The record keeper is usually the housewife and grocery shopper. She should be more aware of grocery items than of drugs, personal care, or miscellaneous items which are often purchased by other household members.

In learning which product purchases are to be entered in the diary, the record keeper studies the diary from front to rear. The retention of learned behavior is a function of activities occurring before and after learning as described by the 'law of proactive and retroactive inhibitions'.[1] Products in the rear of the diary should be affected by proactive inhibition, while those in the middle are affected by both proactive and retroactive inhibition. One would expect the fewest memory errors for items in the front of the diary, and the most errors in the middle. For the same reason, one would expect that, in general, products at the top of a page would be better remembered than those in the middle or at the bottom.

Learning is related to the strength of the stimulus. Products listed in larger type should be noticed more often and better remembered.

Complexity of entry is related to the possibility of deliberate omission.

Due to reinforcement, the more frequently the item is purchased the better it will be remembered.

Purchases made during major shopping trips, which are likely to be to chains, are more likely to be remembered than are purchases of a few items at small neighborhood stores.

The record keeper's attitudes about a product will influence her memory. Convenience of preparation is one of the factors which determine attitudes toward a product.

1. This law states that retention of learned material is a function of activities occurring prior to and subsequent to the original learning. See for example, Hilgard (1956).

The empirical reporting model

A multiplicative model was developed which related recording accuracy to the eight factors listed above.[2] Recording accuracy for the ith product was defined to be the ratio:

$$\hat{A}_i = \frac{\text{National Consumer Panel recorded purchases}}{\begin{array}{c}\text{Manufacturer shipment data corrected}\\ \text{for non-household usage}\end{array}}$$

Note that $\hat{A}_i$ are pure numbers and have no units of measure attached.

Corrections for non-household use were made using sources independent of National Consumer Panel Reports. These sources included recall surveys of non-household usage; manufacturer estimates of non-household usage; and industry and U.S. Department of Agriculture and Department of Commerce estimates on non-household usage. Frequency distributions of the $\hat{A}_i$ by type of product are given in Appendix 2.

The eight factors examined for their relation to recording accuracy were classified into groups to sort the seventy-two products into approximately equal groups for each factor. The definitions of these groups are included in Table 2.

The general form of the multiplicative model considered was:

$$\hat{A}_i = B_0 \prod_{j=1}^{m} x_{ij} B_j, \qquad \textbf{1}$$

where $\hat{A}_i$ was the fitted accuracy of recording for the ith product,

2. Many people at MRCA played a role in the development of this model. Harlan Mills, Steve Stock and William Allen contributed substantially to the theoretical framework underlying the model. Louis Fourt supervised the initial reports.

The Mathematica group of the Market Research Corporation of America explored other possible criteria for fitting parameters, specifically stratified least squares, minimum chi-square, and a linear programming model. In evaluating alternative criteria the following three factors were considered:

1. Variability of estimates.
2. Simplicity of method (cost).
3. Reasonableness of results.

Considering all three factors, the simple least squares criterion appeared to be most satisfactory for this problem.

$x_{ij} = 1$ if the ith product has property j,

$x_{ij} = 1/B_j$ if the ith product does not have property j (so that $x_{ij}B_j = 1$),

m = total number of properties in a given combination (17 for the combination finally selected),

$i = 1, 2, \ldots, 72$ products,

the B_j were parameters to be estimated.

For computational purposes the logarithmic equivalent of this model was used:

$$\log \hat{A}_i = \log B_0 + \sum_{j=1}^{m} \log x_{ij} B_j \qquad \textbf{2}$$

Note that if the ith product class does not have property x, $\log x_{ij}B_j = \log 1 = 0$. If the ith product class has property jj $\log x_{ij}B_j = \log B_j$. The coefficients of $\log B_j$ are all either zero or one.

For each of the eight factors thought to affect recording accuracy, the B_j for each of the following groups were arbitrarily assigned as 1·00 to reduce the complexity of computations required:

1. Front page in diary.
2. Top half of top page.
3. Main or side listing.
4. Heavy purchase of product class by National Consumer Panel households per month.
5. Heavy percentage of product purchased in chain stores.
6. Food.
7. New, convenience item.

A total of forty-four combinations were tested, of which the more important are shown in Table 1. Many of the remaining cases were variations using different groupings of page numbers. It was impossible to divide page numbers into more than about four groups without running into strong correlation with such other characteristics as product type and purchase frequency. For each combination, the variance estimate was computed using the formula:

$$s^2 = \frac{1}{72-m-1} \sum_{i=1}^{m} (A_i - \hat{A}_i)^2,$$

where m was the number of properties in a particular combination. The combination finally selected was the one which gave the least variance, although there was not much difference between the selected combination and the first few runners-up. This decision resulted in eliminating percentage in chains as a variable. Table 1 shows the standard deviations for the best seven

Table 1
Best Combinations of Factors Tested and Variances

Rank	Page no.	Prod. type	Prominence	Complexity	Factors position on page	Number of purchases	Percent in chains	Standard deviation s*
1	×	×	×	×	×	×	—	4·1%
2	×	×	×	×	×	×	×	4·2
3	×	—	×	×	×	×	×	4·5
4	×	×	×	×	—	×	×	4·5
5	×	×	×	×	×	—	×	4·8
6	×	×	×	×	×	—	—	4·8
7	—	×	×	×	×	×	—	4·8

$$*s = \sqrt{\left[\frac{1}{72 - m - 1} \sum_{1}^{m} (\hat{A}_i - A_i)^2 \right]}, \text{ where the } A_i \text{ and } \hat{A}_i$$

are expressed as percentages.

combinations. An x indicates that a factor was included in a given combination. As can be seen, the convenience of the item and the percentage purchased in chains do not appear in the best combination. For this best combination, the percentage of the variance in coverage which is explained by the model (i.e. the, coefficient of multiple determination or the square of the multiple correlation coefficient) is 75 per cent.

Values of parameters

Table 2 shows the values of the B_js using the least squares criterion from the runs made on the computer in May 1960. These values, in general, agree with the hypotheses on page 282 which were based on experience in areas other than panel operations. Recording is less accurate for products in the rear of the diary and least accurate for products in the middle, although the difference between products in the rear and the middle is slight. Accuracy declines as complexity increases. Infrequently purchased and non-grocery products are less accurately recorded than are frequently purchased grocery products. The more prominently mentioned products are more accurately recorded, and products at the top of a page are recorded better than those at the bottom. It must be remembered that these results were obtained from a specific panel sample using a specific diary format, so that they may not be directly applicable to all panels.

Table 2
Estimated Effects of Variables on Accuracy of Recording

	All Products
A. *Diary page number*	
3–7 (front)	1·00*
8–26 (middle)	0·89
27–34 (rear)	0·91
B. *Complexity*	
Easy (0–1 check boxes)	1·00*
Medium (2 check boxes)	0·91
Complex (3 or more check boxes)	0·87
C. *Product class purchases per month*	
in a panel of 6000 households	
Over 2000	1·00*
Under 2000	0·92
D. *Type of product*	
Food	1·00*
Non-food, grocery	1·00
Non-food, non-grocery	0·56
E. *Prominence of entry*	
Main (1/8 inch heavy type)	1·00*
Subtype ($\frac{1}{16}$ inch heavy type)	0·86
F. *Position of diary page*	
Top half of top page	1·00*
Bottom half of top page	0·87

	All Products
Top half of bottom page	0·99
Bottom half of bottom page	0·95

G. *Percentage of product class purchased in chain stores*
1. 60–100 per cent — —
2. 0–59 per cent — —

H. *Convenience of product preparation*
1. New, convenient — Frozen foods, baking mixes, dry bleach, etc.
2. Old, semi-convenient — Canned foods, breakfast cereals, etc. — —
3. Non-convenient — All other, such as flour, fresh fruit, etc. — —

Constant Term	1·07

* Arbitrarily assigned as 1·00.

The values shown for non-grocery products must be interpreted cautiously. There are only five products in this category since the National Consumer Panel Weekly Diary is very heavily oriented toward food and grocery products. The training of panel households in keeping a weekly diary also stresses food and grocery products. As will be shown in Part 2, moving these non-grocery products to a special monthly diary very substantially improved the levels of recording.

Examples

As examples of how the model operated, two product classes are shown below. Cake mix is a typical grocery item, while shoe polish is a product not purchased very often.

Cake mix		Factor
Diary page:	13	0·89
Complexity:	Easy	1·00
Product class purchases per month in a panel of 6000 households:	4400	1·00
Type of product:	Food	1·00

Cake mix (Contd.)		*Factor*
Prominence of entry:	Main	1·00
Position on diary page:		
Top half of bottom page		0·99
Constant:		1·07

$\hat{A}_i$ = Estimated Accuracy of recording = (0·89) (0·99)
(1·07) = 94 per cent.

Shoe polish		*Factor*
Diary page:	34	0·91
Complexity:	Easy	1·00
Product class purchase per month in a panel of 6000 households:	1250	0·92
Type of product: non-food, non-grocery		0·56
Prominence of entry:	Main	1·00
Position on diary page:		
Bottom half of top page		0·87
Constant:		1·07

$\hat{A}_i$ = Estimated accuracy of recording = (0·91) (0·92) (0·56)
(0·87) (1·07) = 44 per cent.

Verification of results

Since the seventy-two products were not a random sample of any universe, but were rather those products for which information was available, it does not seem wholly appropriate to observe only measures of the variance as indicating the reliability of the method. The model has been tested, though, on all products not included in the original model for which shipment information has since become available, and the results have been generally encouraging.

Table 3 shows these results for fifteen products. To avoid disclosure of confidential information only product type is shown and product names are designated by letters. The empirical model appears slightly biased downward, since the average difference is 2 per cent. The 2 per cent is small, relative to the standard deviation of 6 per cent, and both these values seem satisfactory, considering the possible errors in the shipment data discussed above. Note that this standard deviation of 6 per cent is slightly higher than the estimated standard deviation of 4 per cent shown in Table 1.

Table 3

Comparisons of Estimated Accuracy of Recording for Sixteen Product Classes not Included in Model

| Type of product | Estimated accuracy of recording | | |
	Shipment data	Empirical recording model	Differences
A Food	100%	92%	8%
B Food	100	94	6
C Food	90	82	8
D Non-food, grocery	86	87	− 1
E Food	85	86	− 1
F Non-food, grocery	85	75	10
G Non-food, grocery	85	77	8
H Food	81	80	1
I Non-food, grocery	80	80	0
J Non-food, grocery	78	76	2
K Food	75	76	− 1
L Food	72	82	−10
M Food	62	67	− 5
N Non-food, non-grocery	53	44	9
O Non-food, non-grocery	45	47	− 2
Mean	78·4	76·3	2·1%

$$s = \sqrt{\left[\frac{(A_i - \hat{A}_i)^2}{15}\right]} = 6 \cdot 0\%$$

Summary

During 1959-60, seventy-two products were examined for which information was available from National Consumer Panel reports and client shipment data. Eight variables were selected for testing on accuracy of recording. An empirical model was constructed to relate these factors to accuracy of recording. The form of the model was multiplicative. The fitting of the parameters was performed using a simple least squares criterion. Alternative methods of fitting the parameters were considered and tested, but the least squares criterion appeared to be most satisfactory.

The computed values of the parameters generally agree with experience in areas other than panel operations. Recording is found less accurate for products in the rear and the middle of the diary. Accuracy declines as complexity increases. Infrequently purchased products and those not purchased by the housewife are less accurately recorded. The more prominently mentioned products are more accurately recorded as are products at the top of a page.

The values of the parameters have also been tested on fifteen products not included in the original model. In no case did the difference between the predicted accuracy of recording and the observed accuracy exceed ten per cent.

Appendix 1

Products used in fitting of empirical recording model

Bed sheets	Frozen orange juice
Bird food	Frozen peas
Bleach, dry	Frozen spinach
Bleach, liquid	Gelatin
Cake flour	Gingerbread mix
Cake mixes	Hot Roll and biscuit mix
Canned citrus juices	Instant potatoes
Canned corn	Lemons
Chili	Margarine
Canned fruit cocktail	Mops
Canned macaroni	Mustard
Canned peaches	Packaged soap
Canned peas	Pancake mix
Canned pears	Peanut butter
Canned pineapple	Pectin

Canned spaghetti
Canned tuna
Cocoa, instant
Cocoa, regular
Coffee
Dog food
Dry soup
Facial tissues
Fish sticks
Flour
Frosting mix
Frozen beans
Frozen broccoli
Frozen corn
Frozen french fried
  potatoes
Frozen fruit
Frozen fruit pies
Frozen lemonade
Frozen lemon juice
Frozen meat and poultry
  pies
Frozen mixed vegetables

Pie crust mix
Pizza pie mix
Pudding and pie filling
Ravioli and spaghetti
Ready-to-eat cereal
Records
Refrigerated biscuits
Rice
Salad dressing
Scouring cleansers
Scouring pads
Shirts
Shortening
Starch, dry
Starch liquid
Syrup
Tapioca and tapioca
  puddings
Toilet soap
Tomato paste and sauce
Towels
Waxes

Appendix 2

Observed values of A_i used in fitting of empirical recording model
Food products

Observed values of A_i	Number of products
100 and over	15
90–99	7
80–89	12
70–79	12
60–69	8
50–59	1
	—
Total products	55

Non-food, grocery products

Observed values of A_i	Number of products
90–99	3
80–89	5
70–79	3
60–69	1
	—
Total products	12

Non-food, non-grocery products

Observed values of A_i	Number of products
50–59	3
40–49	1
30–39	1
	—
Total products	5

Part 2

Part 2 continues the discussion of experiments dealing with the accuracy of recording of the National Consumer Panel (NCP) of the Market Research Corporation of America. The paper is divided into two sections. The first section describes a series of experiments conducted by the National Consumer Panel to measure effects on recording behavior resulting from the following changes:

1. Total work load of keeping purchase diary records and recording other special information, such as family classification data, magazine reading and television viewing.
2. Motivation, including financial compensation.
3. Training and/or fatigue.

These controlled experiments require only data from internal records and so avoid the difficulties which were discussed earlier of comparison to outside sources. The second section compares the accuracy of diary recording to the accuracy of consumer survey recall. These two methods are studied and compared since the usefulness of any technique depends on the alternative methods available.

Factors Influencing Changes in Accuracy of Recording

General method for testing changes

The basic statistics measured in recording tests are the number of diary entries per product class and per diary.

Let X_B = Number of entries per diary made by the experimental group in the period before the experiment begins.

X_A = Number of entries per diary made by the experimental group during the experiment.

C_B = Number of diary entries made by the control group in the period before the experiment begins.

C_A = Number of diary entries made by the control group during the experiment.

D = Difference due to diary forms.

$$\text{Then } D = (X_A - X_B) - (C_A - C_B).$$

As can be seen, the measure of recording accuracy is taken to be the number of diary entries made. The experiments have not attempted to measure changes in the accuracy of recording of purchase details, nor have any efforts been made to measure changes in the number of imaginary purchases. These latter two are difficult to measure, and the same problems would arise as those discussed in the previous paper.

Diary changes

As the National Consumer Panel gained new clients, the work load of panel households gradually increased. In 1957, after careful consideration of the NCP Diary, and several small pretests, an experiment was devised to test the effect on recording accuracy of varying the following requirements.

Type of diary. A ledger diary listing the items to be entered had been used by the National Consumer Panel since its inception, and by most other purchase panels. The *Chicago Tribune* Panel, on the other hand, had always used a journal diary in which purchases were entered in time sequence. A journal diary had also been suggested by several panel households. A ledger diary had been found to be easier to code and more satisfactory for picking up details of a purchase such as type and flavor. There was, however, the unresolved question as to which type of diary would be kept most completely by panel households. Pages of the old NCP diary, the experimental journal diary, and the new NCP ledger diary are shown in the Appendix.

Length of diary. Household interviews as well as past experience had strongly indicated that recording accuracy would be affected by length of diary if a ledger diary were used. There were no available data which quantified this effect. Nothing was known about the effects of work load in a journal diary. The diary test was designed to measure the effects of diary length on accuracy of recording.

Product reminders. Past experience had indicated that some diary entries were recalled at the end of the week, rather than being entered immediately. This recall was stimulated in the ledger diaries by requiring the monitors to check 'none' boxes if a product was not purchased in a given week. Since the same method could not be used with a journal diary, a weekly buying record checklist was tried as part of the diary test. In the ledger diaries, the buying record checklist replaced the 'none' boxes.

Frequency of diary. As indicated in the previous paper, a weekly diary gave more complete results than a monthly one for grocery products. Because of its grocery product orientation, recording accuracy in the weekly diary was low for miscellaneous products such as shirts, towels and records (cf. Table 3, Part 1). For these reasons, it seemed sensible to test a special monthly diary which included only miscellaneous products.

Sequence. It was known that items in the front of the ledger diary were better recorded than items in the middle and rear (cf. Part I). The diary test attempted to again measure these effects in the ledger diaries and to discover whether sequence had any effect in journal diary recording.

1958 diary test: method

In a $2^4 \times 3$ factorial design, 432 N C P households were tested on forty-eight different diaries in the period February–April 1958. Table 1 indicates the factorial design used in the experiment.

The sample size used in the experiment was determined subjectively on the basis of need for data from test households in continuing reports, allowable change (1 per cent) in total product class volume, and maximum effect due to the new diary forms. Combining these judgments, it was decided that a sample of about 1/12 of the active National Consumer Panel should be selected. Half of the households received ledger diaries, and half received journal diaries in which purchases were entered in time sequence. Each of these groups was subdivided into equal groups which received either the usual length diary or one approximately 20 per cent shorter. It was not possible to further reduce the smaller diary, since the data from the test families were being used in the continuing reports.

These four basic forms were further equally divided into those containing or not containing the buying record checklist reminder. These eight forms were further equally divided into those in which miscellaneous products (shirts, towels, records) were put into a special monthly diary or were kept at the back of the regular weekly grocery diary.

Finally, these sixteen forms were divided into three diary product sequences:

1. Food first, laundry second, utility and miscellaneous last.
2. Laundry first, utility and miscellaneous second, food last.
3. Utility and miscellaneous first, food second, laundry last.

The journal diaries tested had separate pages for the entry of the three types of products.

Only nine households received any one diary; but for estimation of effects, subsamples were pooled, ignoring higher order interactions.

It is important to note that these results were obtained from panel households which had been trained to keep and had always

Table 1
Factorial Design Used in 1958 Diary Test

| | | | Journal diary | | Ledger diary | |
			Long	Short	Long	Short
With buying record checklist	With separate monthly diary	Sequence	a b c	a b c	a b c	a b c
	Without separate monthly diary	Sequence	a b c	a b c	a b c	a b c
Without buying record checklist	With separate monthly diary	Sequence	a b c	a b c	a b c	a b c
	Without separate monthly diary	Sequence	a b c	a b c	a b c	a b c

kept a ledger diary in the past. In addition, these changes were related to the length of the diary kept by panel households at the start of the experiment. Different results might be obtained from households originally trained to keep a journal diary, but this must remain conjecture, since nothing has been published on households which were originally trained to keep a journal diary and which were then switched to a ledger diary.

The length of the NCP diary at the start of the experiment was thirty-six pages, and included over 100 products. With a substantially smaller diary, changing the length would probably not have produced the same results. For example, Ehrenberg describes an experiment with the Attwood Panel where increasing the number of products to be recorded from thirty to fifty did not affect the accuracy of recording (Ehrenberg, 1960).

Results

Length and type of diary. Table 2 shows total purchase entries on all products common to all diaries for the period February–April 1958 by the four basic groups, long and short diaries and ledger and journal diaries. An analysis of Table 2 indicates that panel households recorded 10 per cent higher on the short ledger diary than on the long ledger or on the journal diaries. The

Table 2
Purchase Entries Per Week, February-April 1958, by Type of Diary, and Indices of Total Purchase Entries (Long Ledger, Current Diary = 100)

Type of diary	Purchase entries			Indices of purchase entries		
	Short diary	Long diary	Combined	Short diary	Long diary	Combined
Ledger	27·6	24·9	26·2	110·5	100	105·2
Journal	25·3	25·4	25·3	101·6	101·7	101·7
Combined				106·1	100·8	

standard error of the differences between the groups was estimated to be about 4 per cent. Clearly, the results of Table 2 cannot be attributed to chance.

Production and cost problems prevented obtaining identical purchase information for all products prior to February to control for possible differences between subsamples. However, information on the purchasing of fifteen products was available for the test households for January 1958. These products were selected to include those both with and without recording problems. Table 3 shows the changes in the four subsamples during February–April as compared to January. These changes are again indexed to the change in the current long ledger diary. The results seem to be in rough agreement with those of Table 2.

Based on these results, the decision was made to continue using the ledger diary, and to keep it as short as possible consistent with client commitments. Fortunately, the ledger diary, which was easiest to code and gave the most detailed information, also gave the most complete recording. Retrospective rationalization suggests that the recall aids in the ledger diary are mostly responsible for this more complete recording.

Table 3
Indices of Changes in Purchase Entries of Fifteen Selected Products February-April 1958 Compared to January 1958 by Type of Diary

Type of diary	Length of diary		
	Short	Long	Combined
Ledger	105·6	100	102·8
Journal	101·5	98·5	100·0
Combined	103·5	99·2	

Position in diary. Table 4 shows the effect of position in the diary on recording. The results indicate that recording of products in the front of ledger diaries is higher than recording of products elsewhere in the diary. The standard error of the differences between the groups was 5 per cent, so the differences in Table 4 are not likely due to chance. This is in agreement with the results of the recording model given in Part 1, and with the laws of proactive and retroactive inhibition. Recording does not seem to be related to position in journal diaries.

Weekly checklist reminder. The effect of a weekly checklist was very small when measured for all products in the February–April period, causing at most a one per cent increase in recording.

Miscellaneous products in monthly diary. Miscellaneous products were recorded substantially higher, by 62 per cent, in the monthly diary than in the weekly diaries.

Note that in all cases increased recording was considered an improvement. This was confirmed by examination of specific products. Those which were known to be under-recorded such as non-food and miscellaneous products (see Part I) had large increases in purchase entries, while those food items already recorded completely were unchanged. These conclusions were further verified by the next experiment to be discussed.

Table 4

Indices of Purchase Entries, February–April 1958, by Type of Product and Position in Diary (Product in Front Section = 100)

Type of product and diary	Product in 1st section	Product in 2nd section	Product in 3rd section	Product in 2nd or 3rd section
Ledger diary				
Food	100	91·6	96·3	93·8
Laundry	100	99·6	98·5	99·0
Utility	100	84·7	98·0	90·9
Combined	100	91·9	96·7	94·3
Journal diary				
Food	100	100·6	100·3	100·4
Laundry	100	96·7	89·8	93·1
Utility	100	114·9	98·2	105·9
Combined	100	101·8	98·8	100·3

Additional tests, 1958–60: method

For two years, October 1958 to October 1960, a new diary based on the results just described was tested on a subsample of six hundred NCP households. The prime purpose of this test was to measure as accurately as possible the effect of the new diary on specific products (which the Diary Forms Test had not been able to do with sufficient accuracy). The sample size was determined by the same considerations as in the Diary Forms Test, that is, maximizing the discrimination of the experimental results while keeping the expected changes in the continuing product volume totals about 1 per cent or less. Finally, in October 1960, the new diary was adopted for all NCP households. Recording on a product-by-product basis was compared for households keeping the new and old diaries, both before and during the experiment. The differences found were used to form links between the old and new series of continuing reports.

Results

Table 5 shows the estimated changes in recording for products ranked in order of the magnitude of the change. The standard error of this estimate, and the number of months on which the estimate is based are also shown. Although the experiment lasted for two years, the number of monthly observations available was less than twenty-four since the products were not tabulated continuously.

These estimates of changes in recording are also compared in Table 5 to those obtained in a different way by comparing the changes in purchase entries for the whole panel between the third and fourth quarters of 1960 to the average changes between these quarters in 1959 and 1958. If seasonal patterns are assumed not to have changed, then the differences can be attributed to the new diary. Symbolically, let:

$A =$ Fourth quarter 1960 purchase entries per diary of households who received new diaries in October, 1960.

$B =$ Third quarter 1960 purchase entries per diary of these households.

$C = A–B.$

$D =$ Fourth quarter 1959 plus fourth quarter 1958 purchase entries/diary.

$E =$ Third quarter 1959 plus fourth quarter 1958 purchase entries/diary.

$F = D–E.$

$G = C–F =$ Estimated change in recording due to new diary.

This is analogous to the general method for testing diary changes.

Measures of variability were not computed individually for the estimate of recording change based on fourth versus third quarter comparisons. Based on past experience, these were assumed to be roughly of about the same order of magnitude as the variability of the estimates based on the sample of six hundred. A quick check on the comparability of the two estimates is to note from Table 5 the magnitude of the differences between the two estimates as compared to $1·5 \times$ standard error of estimate, which product is the rough estimate of the standard error of the difference.

This comparison shows that for thirty-eight products the estimates are these

Less than 1 S.E.(d)   in 16 cases

Between 1 and 2 S.E.(d)	in 11 cases
Between 2 and 3 S.E.(d)	in 4 cases
Over 3 S.E.(d)	in 7 cases

Generally, the two nearly independent estimates were in fair agreement. For some products, comparisons were not possible since the data were not processed and not available for all three years. Of the two methods used, that utilizing the six hundred test households is generally more reliable. The other method is discussed, since it may sometimes be useful when controlled experiments have not been conducted. For the majority of products where the differences between methods were small, the agreement between the methods lent added confidence to the results.

All in all, the new diary improved recording of about half of the products in the diary, and some as much as 50 per cent. This was particularly true of products that had been out of sequence in the old diary, such as foods that were in the drug section. For this reason, the new diary has empty spaces so that new products may be added to the diary in their proper places rather than being put at the end of the diary. No adverse effects on any products were noted

During the two years of this experiment, other changes were occurring due to the normal operating requirements of the panel. Some households left the panel and were replaced by new households. New products were added to both the experimental and regular diaries while some were dropped. The major complication was the experimentation with the monthly diary to obtain purchase information on all textile and clothing purchases. While this provided vital information which led to the establishment of a new textile service by the National Consumer Panel, it made impossible the accurate measurement of the effect of the monthly diary on the miscellaneous products previously in the weekly diary

Effects of small diary changes

Diary changes can be tested on a controlled basis. For example, the National Consumer Panel is divided into four subsamples containing 50 per cent, 25 per cent, 15 per cent and 10 per cent of the households. While a diary change is generally tested on the 50–50 split, it is also possible to test on other subsample combinations. The basic measure used is the difference in entries per diary before and after the test in the control versus the experimental groups. From this control program, in effect for many years, the following generalizations have emerged:

1. *Adding or deleting a check box or changing the wording within a check box will not measurably affect the level of recording.* For example, a new column was added to the dentifrice section of the diary to pick up fluoride toothpastes versus powders and to allow for dentrifices with more than one additive. There was no significant change in recording.

2. *Changing a product heading, especially the specific listing of a type which had been previously included under 'Other', may measurably change the level of recording.* Thus, the main listing 'Polishes, Waxes, and Cleaners' was divided into two main listings: 'Waxes, Polishes and Cleaners for Floors, Furniture, Kitchen Cabinets, Woodwork, etc.' and 'Automobile Waxes, Polishes'. No change in recording occurred for the floor polishes; the added section for auto polishes, however, resulted in a doubling of the recorded purchase entries for those items.

3. *Moving a product listing from one page to another will temporarily reduce the level of recording.* For example, the 'Frozen Fruit and Dessert Pies' section was moved from the top of one page to the middle of the page facing it, to make room for another product. The announcement of this change in the monthly newsletter to panel households produced no change in recording the first month. Apparently, purchasers during the first month saw the announcement in the newsletter of the changed diary location. The next two months, recorded entries by the group receiving the experimental diary declined 14 per cent. Evidently, purchasers in these two months did not see or remember the announcement in the newsletter, and were not able to find its new location. In the next three months, however, recording returned to the old level, suggesting that by then it had been rediscovered at its new location.

Table 5

Estimated Changes in Purchase Entries Due to New NCP Diary 1958-60

Purchase entry	(1) 600 test house-holds 1958-1960	(2) Third to fourth quarter 1960 vs. 1959-1958 average	(3) Difference (1)-(2)	(4) Standard error of estimate in column (1)	(5) Number of monthly observation of estimate in column (1)
	Estimated percent change in purchase entries				
1. Refrigerated dough	54%	41%	13%	2%	10
2. Skin cream	52	NA	—	—	4
3. Food drinks	20	20	0	2	18
4. Mayonnaise	18	NA	—	5	3
5. Cooking and baking chocolate	17	0	17	5	18
6. Instant potatoes	17	8	9	3	18
7. Canned meat	15	NA	—	5	7
8. Frozen dessert pies	15	17	— 2	3	18
9. Tomato products	15	11	4	5	7
10. Window cleaners	15	NA	—	4	4
11. Dry milk & toppings	13	NA	—	4	18
12. Frozen juices	12	19	— 7	2	7
13. Starch	12	NA	—	1	6
14. Canned fish	10	10	0	5	7
15. Mustard	10	13	— 3	6	7
16. Fudge & frost mix	9	0	9	2	18
17. Waxed paper	9	9	0	3	18
18. A.P. cleaning pads	8	1	7	3	18
19. Rice	8	14	— 6	3	7
20. Dentifrice	7	0	7	5	18
21. Peanut butter	7	NA	—	1	3
22. Pet food	7	NA	—	6	7
23. Spaghetti & macaroni	7	15	— 8	4	7
24. Frozen dinners	6	10	— 4	3	18
25. Packaged soap & detergents	6	NA	—	2	17
26. Salad dressing	6	NA	—	3	7
27. Scouring powder	6	15	— 9	2	18
28. Syrup	6	18	—12	2	7
29. Soup	5	0	5	2	7
30. Baking mixes	4	2	2	1	6
31. Canned vegetables	4	0	4	1	7
32. Packaged desserts	4	14	—10	4	7
33. Shortening	4	NA	—	3	17

Purchase entry	(1)	(2)	(3)	(4)	(5)
	Estimated percent change in purchase entries			*Standard error of estimate*	*Number of monthly observation*
	600 test house-holds 1958-1960	*Third to fourth quarter 1960 vs. 1959-1958 average*	*Difference in column (1)-(2)*	*in column (1)*	*of estimate in column (1)*
34. Facial tissue	3	5	— 2	2	18
35. Canned juice	3	0	3	2	7
36. Fresh juice	3	16	—13	6	18
37. Aluminium foil & plastic wrap	2	14	—12	4	7
38. Bleach	2	0	2	2	18
39. Margarine	2	7	— 5	1	7
40. Frozen vegetables	2	5	— 3	2	7
41. Coffee	0	5	— 5	2	7
42. Canned fruit	— 1	NA	—	1	7
43. Fresh fruit	— 1	15	—16	4	18
44. Cold cereal	— 1	0	— 1	2	7
45. Toilet tissue	— 1	4	— 5	1	18
46. Marshmallows	— 2	0	— 2	6	18
47. Toilet soap	— 3	NA	—	1	17
48. Paper cups	— 3	NA	—	5	4
49. Flour	— 3	0	— 3	3	7
50. Bird foods	— 3	1	— 4	4	18
51. Paper towels	— 4	5	— 9	2	18
52. Cake flour	— 5	0	— 5	5	7

4. *Special reminders in the diary such as stickers or inserts result in temporary improvement in the level of recording, but not necessarily in long-term changes.* Thus, a special post card was sent to the experimental group reminding them to list purchases of soft drinks. In addition, diaries for the next two months had yellow stickers on their covers to remind households again about soft drinks. During these three months of special reminders, recording of soft drink purchases rose 30 per cent in the experimental group. In the next two months recording was still up, but only by 15 per cent. In the third month the increase was down to 9 per cent, and after this month recording of the experimental group returned to the normal level.

Effects of work load changes

NCP households not only keep continuing records of purchasing but also fill out special questionnaires from time to time on such subjects as appliance ownership and media receivership. Simple questions on ownership have no effect on recording of purchases, but it is possible that a special survey might influence continuing record-keeping. A special usage study of citrus products in 1955 caused substantial increases in recording of purchasing of citrus products for more than a year after the usage study ended.

This section will describe three major changes in work load due to special surveys. None of these three surveys did, in fact, change recording behavior substantially although it had been feared that they might.

The menu study. In the year which began in July 1956, the National Consumer Panel was used in a massive study to obtain information on how food was prepared and consumed in American homes. Four thousand panel households kept records for two weeks, listed every ingredient of every meal prepared in the home, and reported who in the household ate what. Since the menu study was by far the most difficult reporting assignment ever asked of Panel households, three pretests were conducted to determine whether there would be any effect on NCP diary reporting. Comparisons were made between fifty experimental households and fifty control households in each pretest. Records of diary reporting were obtained for the four weeks preceding the menu study, the two weeks of the study, and the six weeks after the study.

The results were somewhat surprising. They showed that, rather than a decrease which had been feared, the menu study would, if anything, slightly increase reporting of food items during the two weeks of the study. This could have been caused by an increase in purchasing due to the stimulation of the menu study or to an increase in purchases recorded. Since only a small group of panel households were to keep this record at any time during the year, the overall effect on continuing data was expected to be less than 1 per cent. Because of the generality of the menu study stimulus, there was no reason to expect that particular food products would be affected more than others. A slight decrease was observed in the reporting of non-food products during the two weeks of the Study. Again, this indicated an expected difference of less than 1 per cent to continuing data. The results of these pretests were confirmed during the full-scale menu census. There were no indications of any measurable changes in product class recording.

Auto diary effects. During January-June 1961, a sub-sample of 1500 NCP households kept a special monthly diary of purchases of gasoline, oil and auto repairs. To determine whether this added work load affected recording of purchases in the weekly diary, comparisons were made with a control group of other car owners who did not keep an auto diary during this period. The statistic measured was total coded weekly diary entries. An analysis of the results indicated virtually no effect on recording of weekly purchases due to the Auto Diary.

1951 Media diary effects. A large-scale media study was conducted in 1959 for the Magazine Advertising Bureau (1960) of the Magazine Publishers Association using the National Consumer Panel. A pilot test with 1500 NCP households was conducted for seven weeks during the winter of 1959. The MAB Pilot Study was designed to investigate several areas dealing with the accuracy of media measurements obtained from the National Consumer Panel. In addition, there was some concern that keeping very detailed media records would reduce the accuracy of recording in the regular purchase diary. Comparisons were made of the reported products purchased by households who kept media records and products purchased by the remaining panel households. Again, no important differences were observed.

Panel relations effects

Basic work in social psychology leads to the expectation that accuracy of panel recording as well as continued co-operation may be influenced by the relationship between the household and the panel operators (Kretch and Crutchfield, 1948). This relationship develops from such things as the initial contact by the recruiter, the additional contacts (either mail or personal), and the compensation methods used. There have been no experiments to determine the role that the initial contact by the recruiter plays in recording accuracy. Some investigations have been made of the effects on recording of changes in compensation methods and special contacts with panel households. These are discussed in this section. The limited number of these tests and their generally negative results again point up large areas which need further exploration.

Compensation effects

Households keeping NCP diaries receive points redeemable in merchandise. That compensation is necessary to keep households co-operating over long periods of time was first learned in the early 1940s. It is still not clear twenty years later, however, exactly how or why compensation influences recording.

The Panel contains households with no income and households with annual incomes over $50,000. Economic theory would suggest that the prizes received for keeping diary records are of greatest value to lower income households. Yet, upper and middle income households also respond to this compensation as a tangible expression of the importance of their efforts.

Recruiting experience of the National Consumer Panel has indicated that the percentage of households who, when invited, will join a panel is independent of the compensation offered within rather wide limits. Recent indications, although still inconclusive, suggest that long-run willingness to remain in a panel is influenced by the level of compensation.

Technical accounting difficulties, plus the fear of upsetting panel households, prevented until recently the testing of alternative compensation levels. Four tests are described in which compensation of closely matched groups was varied. The first three tests did not involve changing compensation of households, since the differential rates were established at the time the households were recruited. The final experiment was intended to measure changes in recording behavior when compensation is changed after the household has joined the panel.

New household study. The National Consumer Panel continuously recruits newly formed households to represent the new household formation in the United States. These newly formed households are recruited from split-offs of households already in the panel, i.e., households formed when one or more members of a panel household move away and establish a new household.

Beginning with January 1960, two compensation rates were paid to newly recruited split-off households. A small group of twenty households was compensated at six tenths of the rate the remaining 122 households received. In all cases, the split-off households received the same compensation as did their parent households. These differential compensation rates were established at the time the new households were recruited. Both groups kept the regular NCP diary and were very similar in characteristics.

No important differences in the recording levels of the two groups were observed. The groups receiving the lower compensation actually recorded a fraction more purchases than the other group, but this could easily have been due to chance.

Controlled recruiting study. During the fourth quarter of 1961, three hundred new households were recruited as replacements for the National Consumer Panel. Assignments to interviewers were made in groups of ten, of which five households were selected in advance to receive higher compensation and five lower compensation. This design was intended to randomize interviewer effects. As in the previous test, the lower compensation was at six tenths of the rate of the higher compensation. No meaningful differences were observed in the level of recording accuracy. The differences were small and in the opposite direction from what one would expect if compensation influenced recording accuracy; that is, the level of recording of the low compensation households was above that of the high compensation households.

City M test market. During April 1961, a special consumer panel was recruited in a midwestern city by MRCA. Since only purchasing of a single product was to be measured, a short two-page diary was used. The diary did, however, ask for purchases of nine products so that undue emphasis would not cause conditioning on the product measured.

In May, it became necessary to do additional recruiting in this area so that the sample size would not fall below a minimum figure of four hundred households. An additional one hundred households were recruited by the same interviewers in the same area, using the same diary. These additional households were, however, compensated at a rate 50 per cent higher than the households originally recruited.

The households receiving the 50 per cent higher compensation made 12 per cent more purchase entries per diary than did the households receiving the lower compensation. This difference looked real and appeared to indicate a positive relationship between amount of compensation and completeness of recording. This result disagrees with those of the previous two experiments described. It may be due to the special circumstances of this test market, but also suggests that families keeping short diaries and receiving less compensation than regular NCP families may be more sensitive to changes in compensation.

1962 compensation experiment. An experiment conducted in 1962 was intended to measure changes in recording behavior when compensation is changed after the household has joined the panel. The test did not change work load but raised compensation rates by 60 per cent for an experimental group of one hundred households and lowered compensation 60 per cent for the second experimental group of one hundred. Purchase entries per diary of the experimental groups were compared to purchase entries of control households.

There did not appear to be meaningful changes in either the willingness to return the weekly diaries or in the levels of recording as a result of either the increases or decreases in compensation. The group which had its compensation reduced showed no change in purchase entries. The group whose compensation was increased showed a slight decline in entries, which may be due to sampling variability.

Special contacts with panel households

This section will discuss a series of special contacts with panel households and the effects of these contacts on recording. A test of whether a series of indirect reminders to households would stimulate their reporting was conducted during the period from

October 1957 to April 1958. The following reminders were tried:

1. 'Contest' quiz (October–December 1957).
2. Inventory quiz (October–December 1957).
3. Purchase quiz (October–December 1957).
4. Store shopping record insertion in diary (January–April 1958).

The 'Contest' quiz asked families to go through the diary and write down the names of all the product classes in the diary. Special compensation was awarded for filling out this form completely. The thought behind this quiz was to remind families of diary product classes that they might have forgotten.

The Inventory quiz asked for a record of products actually on hand in the home. Twenty products were listed, mainly those which were underreported. Again, the purpose was to remind households of product classes in the diary.

The Purchase quiz asked for a recall of who in the household selected products. The objective was, again, to specifically remind households that selected products were in the diary.

The Store shopping record was an insert added to the front of the diary which asked households to list each trip to a food store and to give the amount spent. The objective was not to remind households of specific items but to insure that the diary was opened after each shopping trip.

Three hundred households participated in these training tests. The three quizzes were rotated among all the families in six different sequences to balance possible order effects. The Store shopping record was kept by 150 households for three months with the other 150 households as control.

Reporting on selected food and non-food products was computed by the product class purchases per month method. The balance of the panel acted as a control group for the three hundred households.

The quizzes had no long-term effect on reporting, although there was a possible short initial effect. The Store shopping record did, however, measurably increase recording, and it was made a part of the new diary. These results again confirmed earlier tests which had shown that periodic training had no discernible long-term effect on diary recording.

Comparison of Accuracy of Diary Recording to Consumer Survey Recall

While earlier studies have shown that survey recall data tend to overstate purchases, another significant error in recall data has not been studied very fully. This error is the tendency to recall the names of well-known brands when, in some cases, the actual purchase may have been of a lesser-known brand.

While sophisticated market researchers have long been aware of this tendency, its magnitude is probably larger than most would suspect. Leading nationally advertised brands often have their brand shares doubled on recall surveys as compared to diary records, while chain brands are almost always understated substantially. Methods are available for improving recall data through screening questions and other aids to the respondent's memory; but these are not often used, perhaps because the magnitude of recall error is not realized.

Suggested hypotheses

Some preliminary comparisons of diary recording and recall of a small sample of panel households and products suggested three hypotheses for refining this relationship:

1. The status of the brand will affect the degree of difference between diary recording and recall:

(a) The brand shares of the best known nationally advertised brand will be overstated the most on recall surveys.

(b) Brand shares of other nationally advertised brands will be overstated on recall surveys.

(c) The brand share of the leading chain brand will be understated more than other chain brands on recall surveys.

(d) Brand shares of other chain brands will be understated on recall surveys.

(e) Brand shares of local brands will be understated, but less than chain brands, in recall surveys as compared to diary recording.

2. The type of product will affect the degree of difference between diary recording and recall:

(a) Differences will be greater for products purchased less frequently.

(b) Differences will be greater for products which are consumed after purchase (*e.g.*, bread) as compared to those which are more durable (*e.g.*, scouring cleanser).

3. Changes in brand shares obtained by recall surveys will lag changes reported in diaries.

A simple measure of the discrepancy between recall and diary recording is the ratio of brand shares on recall to brand shares on diary recording. This ratio is the basic statistic examined here, but the actual brand shares on recall and on diary recording are also shown.

It is possible to consider these hypotheses in the light of elementary psychology:

1. The more a brand is advertised and known by respondents, the more likely it is to be remembered and mentioned, regardless of the question.

2. The emotional content of a brand image will affect brand mentions. There may be guilt feelings connected with purchasing low-price brands, since the shopper may feel that there is a positive relationship between quality and price and that she is in some way depriving her family of the best. In addition, advertising may give a brand a quality image.

3. The accuracy of recall has an inverse relationship to the length of the period of recall.

4. Respondents may tend to recall their usual behavior during a period rather than a specific act. This may result in recall lagging actual behavior.

Fortunately, it has been possible to obtain additional information to test these hypotheses. Information is available on brand shares of thirty-one food and eleven non-food grocery products in the Chicago metropolitan area from the *Chicago Tribune* Consumer Panel.[3] Information is also available from the *Chicago Sun-Times-Chicago Daily News* Consumer Analysis for

3. Information from the *Chicago Tribune* Panel was made available through the co-operation of Mr Leonard Elliott of the *Chicago Tribune*.

Table 6

Distribution of Ratios of Recall Brand Shares to Diary Brand Shares by Brand Groups

A. Nationally advertised

Ratio	Best known brand	Other brands
Under 1·01	6	16
1·01–1·10	6	5
1·11–1·20	2	7
1·21–1·30	1	2
1·31–1·40	4	2
1·41–1·50	4	4
1·51–1·60	2	1
1·61–1·70	1	0
1·71–1·80	5	0
1·81–1·90	3	0
1·91–2·00	3	0
Over 2·00	5	5
Total sample	42	42
Median	1·45	1·10

B. Other brands

Ratio	Local brands	Other chain brands	Leading chain brand
Under 0·11	1	4	0
0·11–0·20	1	0	4
0·21–0·30	1	1	5
0·31–0·40	4	4	8
0·41–0·50	6	2	7
0·51–0·60	6	3	2
0·61–0·70	9	2	2
0·71–0·80	2	3	1
0·81–0·90	3	1	0
0·91–1·00	2	1	0
Over 1·00	5	1	2
Total sample 40	40	22	31
Median 0·62	0·62	0·50	0·38

the same area. The *Tribune* Panel used diary recording; the Consumer Analysis is a recall survey. Data are available for the years 1956, 1957, 1958, and 1959.

Four other reasons, except differences in forms, suggest themselves as possibly responsible for some of the differences between the two services: sampling variability, differences in sample characteristics, conditioning, and differences in brand preferences related to frequency of purchase. None of these, however, appears to have any significant effect.[4]

Brand differences

The results in Table 6 and Figure 1 enable one to test the hypotheses concerning brand differences. Each brand category is distributed by the size of the ratios of recall brand shares to diary recording brand shares. An even simpler summary is to observe that the median values of the ratios for the group is in the order hypothesized.

The brand shares of the best-known nationally advertised brands are overstated the most. Brand shares of other nationally advertised brands are overstated. The brand shares of the leading chain brands are understated the most. Brand shares of chain and local brands are understated, with local brands understated less than chain brands.[5]

The way in which the best-known nationally advertised brands and the leading chain brands are defined could introduce a regression effect, but additional evidence suggests that the differences observed are not due to this. In all but five cases, the leading chain brand was an A & P brand, which agrees with the

4. A detailed analysis of differences between the two services is found in Sudman (1962).

5. Brands are classified as follows:

1. Advertised Brands are those found in the Trade Name Index of the *Standard Advertising Register*.

2. Chain Brands are those manufactured by or for the four leading chains in Chicago: Jewel, A & P, National, and Kroger.

3. Local Brands are all other brands.

4. The Best-Known Nationally Advertised Brand is the one which had the highest brand share among nationally advertised brands in the *Chicago Sun-Times-Chicago Daily News* consumer Analysis Survey.

5. The Leading Chain Brand is the one which ranked highest among chain brands in the *Tribune* Consumer Panel reports.

known leadership of A & P in private label products. During the four-year period there were only three products where the leading chain brand changed.

Similarly, over the four-year period, there were only four products where the best-known nationally advertised brand changed. In addition, while exact advertising figures for Chicago are not available, most of the best-known nationally advertised brands also appear to be the most heavily advertised in the Chicago area.

If there still remains a slight regression effect, it would not change the conclusions of this section, but might tend to overstate the differences between the best-known and other nationally advertised brands, and also the differences between the leading and other chain brands.

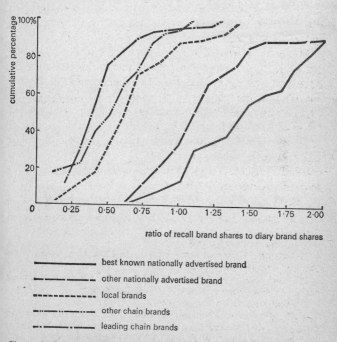

ratio of recall brand shares to diary brand shares

——————— best known nationally advertised brand

— — — — other nationally advertised brand

-------------- local brands

—··—··—··— other chain brands

—·——·——·— leading chain brands

Figure 1 Cumulative percentage of ratios of recall brand shares to diary brand shares

315

Product differences

The forty-two products investigated in these comparisons were grouped into three categories:

1. Grocery – non-food.
2. Food – staples.
3. Food – perishable.

This final category consisted of the following eight items: bacon, bread, butter, frankfurters, frozen fish sticks, frozen orange concentrate, frozen vegetables and margarine.

The data show a clear relation between the durability of the product and the degree of difference between recall and diary recording. To simplify the analysis, a single measure of this difference has been adopted, namely, the ratio of recall brand share to diary brand share of the best-known nationally advertised brand. This measure is shown in Table 7.

Table 7
Ratio of Recall Diary Brand Share for Best-Known Nationally Advertised Brand, by Type of Product and Frequency of Purchase

Rank by frequency of purchase*	Product	Ratio of recall/diary	Rank of ratio
	A. Non-food		
1	Dry bleach	0·90	2
2	Liquid floor wax	1·37	10
3	Dry starch	1·00	5
4	Liquid starch	0·88	1
5	Scouring pads	1·05	6·5
6	Scouring cleanser	1·05	6·5
7	Paper towels	0·98	4
8	Waxed paper	1·08	9
9	Paper napkins	3·57	11
10	Liquid bleach	1·06	8
11	Toilet tissue	0·98	3
Median		1·05	

Rank by frequency of purchase*	Product	Ratio of recall/diary	Ronk of ratio
	B. Perishable food		
1	Frozen fish sticks	0·83	1
2	Frankfurters	1·72	2
3	Bacon	1·79	3
4	Frozen orange juice	2·89	8
5	Frozen vegetables	2·57	7
6	Margarine	1·83	4
7	Butter	2·00	5·5
8	Bread	2·00	5·5
Median		1·83	
	C. Staple foods		
1	Canned luncheon meat	1·17	4
2	Instant potatoes	1·44	10
3	Vegetable shortening	1·80	18
4	Tea	1·77	16·5
5	Dry milk	1·31	6
6	Pancake & waffle mix	1·42	9
7	Hot cereal	1·15	3
8	Fruit cocktail	1·95	21
9	Saltine crackers	1·37	8
10	Salad & cooking oil	1·26	5
11	Syrup	1·90	19
12	Rice	0·64	1
13	Canned peaches	2·38	23
14	Instant coffee	1·03	2
15	Canned tuna	1·90	20
16	Peanut butter	1·77	16·5
17	Canned corn	2·23	22
18	All purpose flour	1·45	11
19	Cake mixes	1·34	7
20	Catsup	1·58	14
21	Canned milk	1·47	12
22	Regular coffee	1·68	15
23	Cold cereal	1·54	13
Median		1·54	

* Least frequently purchased product has rank 1.

Table 7 shows that the median ratio for the three product categories declines from 1·83 for perishable foods to 1·54 for staple foods to 1·05 for non-foods. It seems clear that the more durable the good, the less subject the recall is to memory error. This is further confirmed by studies of appliances, automobiles, and other hard goods.

For the grocery items, only small differences are observed in prices per unit and there is no relationship between durability and prices. This would suggest that it is durability rather than price which improves recall at least for grocery products.

Table 7 also ranks each product by its estimated frequency of purchase with the least frequently purchased product ranked first. The results are mildly surprising. Recall accuracy seems either to increase or remain stable as purchase frequency declines. This contradicts the initial hypothesis suggesting an inverse relationship between frequency of purchase and the ratio of recall to diary recordings.

In retrospect, we see that most heavily advertised grocery products are probably also the most frequently purchased. In any event, there is certainly some correlation between frequency of purchase and strength of 'brand image'. The products are observed in the three categories separately, since it is already known that the durability of the product influences recall.

The results of Table 7 are strongly confirmed when four years of data are examined; that is, each of the years 1956, 1957 and 1959 confirm the results of 1958.

The hypothesis that changes in brand shares obtained by recall

Table 8
Agreement Between Diary Recording and Recall on Changes in Brand Share

Type of comparison	Number of comparisons	Number of agreements	Percentage agreements
Concurrent	283	178	63%
Recall lagged one period	188	99	53
Diary lagged one period	188	110	59

surveys would lag changes reported in diaries is not supported by the data in Table 8. Three changes in brand shares from the previous year are observed for each brand during the four-year period. Comparisons between diary and recall indicate whether the two series agree on a change in brand share from the preceding year. These comparisons are made for concurrent changes recall lagged, and diary lagged, as follows:

Change	Diary	Recall
a. Concurrent	$t_n - t_{n-1}$	$t_n - t_{n-1}$
b. Recall lagged	$t_n - t_{n-1}$	$t_{n-1} - t_{n-2}$
c. Diary lagged	$t_{n-1} - t_{n-2}$	$t_n - t_{n-1}$

Shorter-period comparisons such as month-to-month or quarter-to-quarter may indicate a lead-lag relationship masked by annual data. However, for the annual data there is no evidence that changes in recall are useful predictors of future changes in purchase behavior.

Summary

1. Two major diary tests are discussed. In the first it was found that recording was more complete in a ledger diary listing the items to be entered than in a journal diary in which purchases were entered in time sequence. Length of diary and position in diary also affected recording.

A separate monthly diary for miscellaneous products resulted in substantially higher recording for these products. A weekly checklist reminder appeared to have no significant effect on recording.

2. Using the same methods for testing major changes in diary format to measure small changes, the following results have been observed:

(a) Adding or deleting a check box or changing the wording within a check box will not change recording accuracy.
(b) Changing a product heading may change the level of recording.
(c) Moving a product from one page to another will reduce the level of recording temporarily.

(d) Special reminders result in temporary increases in the level of recording, but not necessarily in long-term changes.

3. The effect of three major changes in work load due to special studies was tested: the menu study, for which households kept records of every meal prepared at home in a two-week period; a special monthly diary of purchases of gasoline, oil and auto repairs; and a seven-week study of magazine receivership and television viewing. None of these three studies had any significant effect on the usual purchase recording behavior. It would appear that, given sufficient compensation, Panel households are willing and able to keep special diaries.

4. Compensation is necessary to keep households co-operating in the National Consumer Panel, but the percentage of households who will keep a continuing record of purchases and the accuracy of their recording seems independent of the level of compensation within rather wide limits, judging by a series of three tests. In a fourth test, however, one not involving the regular National Consumer Panel, a panel kept a short two-page diary and appeared to be sensitive to the level of compensation. Households receiving the higher compensation made 12 per cent more purchase entries per diary than did the households receiving the lower compensation.

5. Four special contacts with Panel households were tested to determine whether accuracy of recording could be improved by training. Three of the contacts required the households to return special quizzes related to purchasing. These three quizzes had no important effects on recording. The final contact was a special store shopping record inserted at the front of the regular diary. The objective of this record was to require the household to open the diary after each shopping trip. This shopping record measurably increased recording.

6. Leading nationally advertised brands have their brand shares overstated an average of 50 per cent on recall surveys as compared to diary records, while chain brands are almost always understated substantially. The data show that the more durable the product, the less subject recall is to memory error. This is further confirmed by studies of appliances, automobiles, and

Figure 2 Old N.C.P. ledger diary

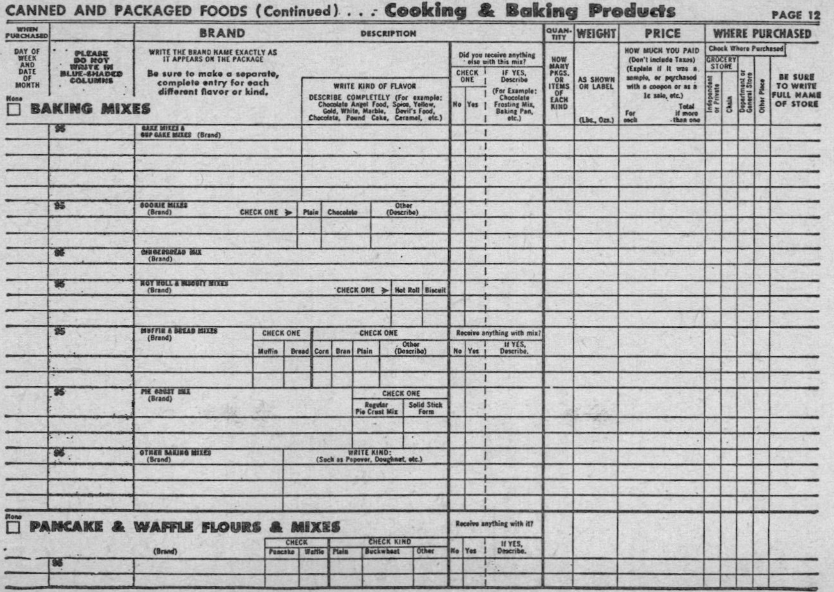

Figure A2

NEW N.C.P. LEDGER DIARY

BAKING MIXES

DAY SOUGHT	BRAND	PRODUCT DETAILS	QUAN-TITY	WEIGHT (SIZE)	PRICE PAID each / Total	SPECIAL PRICE? COUPON? DESCRIBE	WHERE SOUGHT

BAKING MIXES None ☐

WRITE KIND AND FLAVOR DESCRIBE COMPLETELY (For example: Chocolate, Yellow, Spice, Gold, White, Marble, Devil's Food, Pound Cake, Caramel, etc.)

Did you receive anything else with this mix? CHECK ONE No / Yes — IF YES, Describe (For Example: Chocolate Frosting Mix, Baking Pan, etc.)

(Enter Pizza Pie Mix on page 14)
(Enter Pancake and Waffle Mix on page 22)

CAKE MIXES AND CUP CAKE MIXES (Brand)

COOKIE MIXES (Brand) — CHECK KIND: Coconut Macaroon / Oat-Meal / Other (Describe) — WRITE IN FLAVOR

GINGERBREAD MIX (Brand)

HOT ROLL AND BISCUIT MIXES (Brand) CHECK ONE → Hot Roll / Biscuit

MUFFIN AND BREAD MIXES (Brand) CHECK ONE: Muffin / Bread — CHECK ONE: Corn / Bran / Plain / Other (Describe)

PIE CRUST MIX (Brand) CHECK ONE: Regular Pie Crust Mix / Solid Stick Form

CREAM PUFF MIX (Brand)

OTHER BAKING MIXES (Brand) WRITE KIND (Popover, etc.) WRITE FLAVOR

Figure 3 New N.C.P. ledger diary

Figure A3

EXPERIMENTAL N.C.P. JOURNAL DIARY

ALL FOODS AND BEVERAGES – INCLUDING DOG, CAT, AND BIRD FOOD AND SUPPLIES

On these pages, enter all purchases of everything you eat, drink or use in food and beverage preparation.

WHEN PURCHASED	PRODUCT DESCRIPTION	BRAND	QUANTITY	WEIGHT (SIZE)	PRICE PAID		WHERE PURCHASED
Write in Day of Week or Date	KIND OF PRODUCT Fresh, Canned, Frozen, Refrigerated, etc. Type, Flavor, Variety, etc.	Brand Name on Package	No. of Pkgs., Cans, Bottles, Items	Of Each Pkg., Can, Bottle, Item (Lbs., Ozs., Pts., Qts.) etc.	(Don't Include Taxes) Describe if a Special SALE, COUPON, PRICE or OFFER Each	Total	Name of Store or Delivery Company

Figure 4   Experimental N.C.P. journal diary

other hard goods. There does not, however, seem to be any other clear relationship between frequency of purchase and recall error.

7. There was no evidence that annual changes in recall are useful predictors of future changes in purchase behavior, although there might be a shorter lead-lag relationship which is masked by annual data.

References

ANDERSON, T. W. (1954), 'Probability models for analyzing time changes in attitudes', in P. Lazarsfeld (ed.), *Mathematical Thinking in the Social Sciences*, The Free Press, pp. 17–66.

ANSCOMBE, F. (1961), 'Estimating a mixed-exponential response law', *Journal of the American Statistical Association*, vol. 56, pp. 493–502.

BARCLAY, W. (1963), 'A probability model for early prediction of new product market success', *Journal of Marketing*, vol. 27, pp. 63–8.

BARTON, S. (1943), 'The consumption pattern of different economic groups under war changes', *Journal of Marketing*, vol. 8, pp. 50–53.

BOYD, H., and WESTFALL, R. (1960), *An Evaluation of Continuous Consumer Panels as a Source of Marketing Information*, American Marketing Association.

CAWL, F. (1943), 'The continuing panel technique', *Journal of Marketing*, vol. 8, pp. 45–50.

DRAYTON, L. (1954), 'Bias arising in wording consumer questionnaires', *Journal of Marketing*, vol. 19, pp. 140–45.

EHRENBERG, A. S. C. (1959), 'The pattern of consumer purchases', *Applied Statistics*, vol. 8, pp. 26–41.

EHRENBERG, A. S. C. (1960), 'A study of some potential biases in the operation of a consumer panel', *Applied Statistics*, vol. 9, pp. 20–27.

FERBER, R. (1953), 'Observations on a consumer panel operation', *Journal of Marketing*, vol. 17, pp. 246–59.

FOURT, L., and WOODLOCK, J. (1960), 'Early prediction of market success for new grocery products', *Journal of Marketing*, vol. 25, pp. 31–8.

FRANK, R. (1962), 'Brand choice as a probability process', in R. Frank, A. Kuehn and W. Massy (eds.), *Quantitative Techniques in Marketing Analysis*, Irwin, pp. 372–89.

HILGARD, E. (1956), *Theories of Learning*, Appleton-Century-Crofts.

KRETCH, D., and CRUTCHFIELD, R. (1948), *Theory and Problems of Social Psychology*, McGraw-Hill.

KUEHN, A. (1958), 'An analysis of the dynamics of consumer behavior and its implications for marketing management', unpublished Ph.D. dissertation, Carnegie Institute of Technology.

KUEHN, A. (1962), 'Consumer brand choice – a learning process?', in R. Frank, A. Kuehn and W. Massy (eds.), *Quantitative Techniques in Marketing Analysis*, Irwin, pp. 390–403.

LANSING, J., GINSBURG, G., and BRAATEN, K. (1961), *An*

Investigation of Response Error, Bureau of Economics and Business Research, University of Illinois.

LEWIS, H. (1948), 'A comparison of consumer responses to weekly and monthly purchase panels', *Journal of Marketing*, vol. 12, pp. 449–54.

LIPSTEIN, B. (1959). 'The dynamics of brand loyalty and brand switching', *Proceedings of the Fifth Annual Conference, Advertising Research Foundation*, pp. 101–8.

MADOW, W., HYMAN, H., and JESSEU, R. (1961), *Evaluation of Statistical Methods used in Obtaining Broadcast Ratings*, Report of the American Statistical Association Technical Committee on Broadcast Ratings to the House Committee on Interstate and Foreign Commerce, U.S. Government Printing Office.

Magazine Advertising Bureau (1960), *The Profitable Difference*, Magazine Publishers Association.

METZ, J. (1956), *Accuracy of Response Obtained in a Milk Consumption Study*, Cornell University.

The National Consumer Panel, (n.d.), Market Research Corporation of America.

NETER, J., and WAKSBERG, J. (1961), 'Measurement on non-sampling errors in a survey of home owners expenditures on alterations and repairs', *Proceedings of the 121st Annual Meeting, American Statistical Association, Social Statistics Section*, pp. 201–10.

PAYNE, S. (1951), *The Art of Asking Questions*, Princeton University Press.

QUACKENBUSH, C. G., and SHAFFER, J. D. (1954), 'Demand analysis from the M.S.C. consumer panel', *Journal of Farm Economics*, vol. 36, pp. 415.

QUACKENBUSH, C. G., and SHAFFER, J. D. (1960), *Collecting Food Purchase Data by Consumer Panel*, Michigan State University.

REWOLDT, S. (1953), *Economic Effects of Marketing Research*, University of Michigan Press.

SHAFFER, J. (1955), 'The reporting period for a consumer purchase panel', *Journal of Marketing*, vol. 19, pp. 252–7.

SUDMAN, S. (1959), 'Maintaining a consumer panel', *Proceedings of the 42nd Annual Meeting, American Marketing Association*, pp. 326–32.

SUDMAN, S. (1962), 'On the accuracy of recording of consumer panels', unpublished Ph.D. dissertation, University of Chicago.

TELSER., L (1962), 'The demand for branded goods as estimated from consumer panel data', *Review of Economics and Statistics*, vol. 54, pp. 300–325.

U.S. Department of Agriculture (1952), *Problems of Establishing a Consumer Panel in the New York Metropolitan Area*, Marketing Research Report, no. 8.

U.S. Department of Agriculture (1953), *Establishing a National Consumer Panel from a Probability Sample*, Marketing Research Report, no. 40.

U.S. Department of Agriculture (1957), *Response Variations Encountered with Different Questionnaire Forms*, Market Research Report, no. 163.

U.S. Department of Agriculture (1959), *Effects of Coupons and Special Offers on Sales of Margarine, Shortening, Salad and Cooking Oils*, Market Research Report, no. 356.

WADSWORTH, R. D. (1952), 'The experience of a user of a consumer panel', *Applied Statistics*, vol. 1, p. 169.

WEBBER, H. (1944), 'The consumer panel: a method of media evaluation', *Journal of Marketing*, vol. 9, pp. 137–40.

WOMER, S. (1944), 'Some applications of the continuous consumer panel', *Journal of Marketing*, vol. 9, pp. 132–6.

16 J. E. Fothergill

Retail Audits

J. E. Fothergill, 'Retail audit: principles and practice', *Research Paper*, British Market Research Bureau, 1960.

Surprisingly, perhaps, the name describes the form of research accurately. It is carried out amongst *retailers* and, what is more, it is carried out by an *auditing* (or accounting) procedure. The procedure does not involve questioning people or rely upon memory. Indeed, the retailers themselves are scarcely involved in the operation: all that is required fundamentally is their co-operation in allowing the audit to be carried out.

Traditionally, the audit procedure involves the counting of stocks in shops at two consecutive visits, and the inspection of invoices (or delivery notes) for goods delivered during the period between visits. *If* the stocks of any product in a shop are accurately counted at both visits, and *if* the data on deliveries are accurately extracted from the relevant records, then by *calculation*, the sales of the product over the period can be accurately determined, as follows:

First Stock + Deliveries between visits − Second Stock = Sales

If this information is obtained shop by shop, from a representative sample of shops, then an accurate estimate can be made of the sales of the product through all shops in, for example, Great Britain. Normally, the data are collected from a 'panel' of shops (i.e. the *same* shops are visited at every audit)[1] which are selected to be representative of the universe.

You will notice that we have so far introduced two big 'ifs'. 'If' the audit procedure is carried out accurately, and 'if' the sample of shops is representative, then an accurate estimate of

---

1. The reasons for using a 'panel' are partly in order to reduce the costs of the operation, partly because this is the only practicable way of obtaining invoice data and partly because the main use of data collected lies in the study of trends. Trend information is more accurately determined (for a given size of sample) by using the same sample at each visit.

total sales in Great Britain can be made. I will return to these two 'ifs' later.

One may well ask why the traditional method of Retail Audit involves arriving at the sales of each product for each shop by 'residual' methods, rather than by more direct means. The reason for this is mainly historical in as much as the type of shops in which Retail Audit began were those where the direct means (e.g. from sales receipts) are not normally available. Whilst some form of receipt for a customer's *total* expenditure may sometimes be available in, for example, grocer or chemist shops, this receipt is unlikely to contain information in sufficient detail (e.g. brand by brand) to provide the sort of data which can be obtained from the stock and invoice check. This, in general, can be as detailed as one requires (e.g. providing information by individual pack-sizes, by flavour).

However, when considering the application of the Retail Audit technique to certain product fields (e.g. clothing), it is always worthwhile considering whether or not sales receipts are available with sufficient detail to provide a measurement of sales by direct method. Of course, the direct means can only provide data on sales, whilst the indirect method can provide data on other points such as stocks.

This leads to an examination of the kind of information which is available from Retail Audit research.

Information Provided by Retail Audit Research

There are four basic measurements provided by the Retail Audit procedure:

1. *Distribution.* The proportion of shops which were in stock at the time of each audit: the proportion which 'handled' the product at some time during the period between audits.

2. *Consumer Purchases (or Shop Sales).* The sales (in terms of sterling, tonnages or bottles or packs) over-the-counter between audits. Needless to say, if this information is to be provided in sterling or tonnage terms, the original information must be collected in homogeneous units. Thus, each pack size of each brand must be treated separately, and an individual figure for sales calculated for each.

3. *Shop (or Retailer) Purchases.* The purchases (again calculated in various ways) made by the retailer during the period between audits. Frequently, this information is analysed as 'direct' (from the manufacturer) or 'indirect' (from wholesalers).

4. *Stocks.* The actual physical level of stocks as found at each audit. This may be expressed again in sterling, tonnage or other terms. The relation between stocks and consumer purchases (during the current audit period) may also be calculated. Known as 'stock cover', this is a measure of the period of time which current stocks would last at the current rate of sales.

These four measurements provide the basis of all retail audit data. They can, of course, be expressed in many ways. For example, apart from expressing Consumer Purchases in sterling or tonnages, the data can be expressed in terms of averages (per shop checked or per shop handling) or grossed up to give estimates of total Consumer Purchases in Great Britain.

So far, no time period between audits has been considered and, in theory, the foregoing conclusions hold, whatever the time period. However, it is customary to carry out audits at equal intervals of time. This has the double advantage of, on the one hand, making comparisons between two sets of data easier (for the Client) and, on the other, of enabling the production of results to be programmed (for the operating agency). Further, and equally important is consideration of the shopkeeper himself. Visits at regular intervals are likely to become routine and the keeping of requisite invoices etc. for a limited, and known, period does not become arduous.

Usually, the period between audits does not exceed two months. A more lengthy period may, in many types of shop, involve the loss of some invoice data which is, perhaps, the most serious of all problems, in this type of research. Errors in physical stock counts will, in the long run, rectify themselves: lost invoices will always provide a downward bias in estimates of Consumer Purchases. To avoid difficulties due to the variable length of calendar months and, more particularly, the number of shopping days in a calendar month, it is quite common to work to a fixed period, e.g. four weeks.

Theoretically, the ideal arrangement would be to audit all the shops on the same day. Consumer Purchase data would then relate to a particular calendar period. However, for reasons of economy, this is not normally practicable and auditing of shops is spread over a period. Thus, if auditing is carried out at twenty-eight day intervals, the field work may take fourteen days (ten working days) in all. *Each* shop, however, will be audited at exactly twenty-eight day intervals. Data shop-by-shop, therefore, relates to precisely four weeks. The aggregation of the information will then provide, for example, sales over four weeks, but the date to which aggregate information can be ascribed relates to a calendar period somewhere between the date of checking the first shop and the last shop in each cycle of auditing: approximating, in fact, to the half way point. This spread is unfortunate but more or less unavoidable.

Why Carry Out Retail Audit Research

Many of the reasons why this type of research is of interest to manufacturers will have become apparent from the foregoing, e.g. to ascertain the levels of distribution or of stocks. The value of this form of research becomes even more apparent when the following facts are borne in mind:

1. Many of the goods sold by manufacturers pass through 'wholesalers'. In the grocery trade probably some 35 per cent – 40 per cent of total sales pass through wholesalers.

2. It is difficult, if not impossible, for any manufacturer to know how his competitors are faring.

3. Data on the levels of distribution and stocks of a manufacturer's products obtained from his own sales-force are likely to be biased, consciously or unconsciously, and non-systematic.

Manufacturers do, of course, know their own ex-factory sales. However, an increase in ex-factory sales may only be due to an increase in the stocks held by wholesalers or retailers, and may not be due to an increase in the demand by the final buyer (i.e. consumer) at all. A decision, therefore, to buy in extra raw materials or to switch productive capacity as a result of an increase in ex-factory sales, could be incorrect unless the manufacturer can be certain that the rise is due to increased consumer demand. Similarly, since the stocks involved in the 'pipe-line' (through wholesaler and retailer) may be increasing due to a fall in consumer demand, a manufacturer may continue to over-produce until the stocks in the factory and cancelled orders reach alarming proportions. It may well be several months (due to 'pipe-line' stocks) before a manufacturer becomes aware of the falling off in consumer demand.

Knowledge of competitors' sales is also important. The manufacturer who finds ex-factory sales this year 5 per cent up on last year, may well rub his hands in glee. However, if his competitors' sales are up by 10 per cent in the same period, his long term prospects are, to say the least, not rosy. Any manufacturer is not only concerned with increasing his sales, but also in ensuring that, relative to other similar manufacturers, he is improving his position or, at the worst, maintaining it.

The information which comes back from a manufacturer's own sales-force is not to be decried. Frequently this gives an early indication of possible difficulties. It must be remembered however, that the function of a sales-force is to sell – not to collect unbiased information. There seems to be a general tendency for a sales-force to over-emphasize: if things are going well then the sales-force feels that nothing could be better, if things are going badly then nothing could be worse. This is, of course, the salesman's natural reaction to the circumstances he meets on a day-to-day basis. It is not, however, the best basis on which to plan the manufacturer's future production schedule or his future advertising appropriation.

The foregoing considers some of the main reasons for carrying out Retail Audit research on a product which is established. I shall return to discuss this in greater detail at the end of this lecture. There is also the application to the marketing of new products: either entirely new or, alternatively, a new venture for the particular manufacturer. Here, Retail Audit research has another role to play.[2]

These days due to the investment involved, a manufacturer

2. Retail Audit research has a somewhat similar role to play in the case of an established product when major revisions are made in the product itself or in the merchandising of such a product.

who decides to market a new product generally proceeds through various stages. First of all, there is the laboratory stage – just finding the new product. This may then be followed by consumer acceptance tests of various sorts, just to find out whether or not the new product is, in the eye of the consumer, as acceptable (or more so) than other similar products. A consumer survey may be conducted in order to discover the pattern of demand in the existing market. He may well carry out 'motivation' research, in order to find out the best copy platform and to discover just how consumers 'tick' as far as this product is concerned. However, the acid test is 'will the product sell when in competition with similar products, albeit backed by the "right" copy platform with the "right" advertising pressure?'. This can only be discovered by a 'true' experiment: that is to say by putting the product into the shops alongside its competitors, applying the appropriate advertising pressure, and then watching its performance.

All this seems, no doubt, very sensible. However, until the investment in new product formulation became expensive, much was done by 'hunch' and little by science. That is not to say there is no room for hunch in the modern day. Research enables the area in which hunch plays a part to be reduced, but it can never remove its value altogether. There are times, in fact, when so much time is spent in research and development that the 'boat is missed' altogether: some other manufacturer, relying on hunch, having got there first. It is not our purpose here, however, to discuss 'hunches' versus research.

The type of Retail Audit research considered now is normally described as a 'test panel' operation. It is usual to establish a panel in a limited area (e.g. one town, a Television area). On this operation, the object is to measure sales to the consumer before, during and after the introduction of the new product. The introduction will be supported by the appropriate form of advertising (press and possibly TV, couponing etc.) The experiment may become quite elaborate, i.e. different weights or forms of advertising in different town. However, the principles involved are similar to those found in the simplest cases. Here one is concerned with finding out how the new product succeeds in a competitive situation.

The 'before' part of the operation is to establish a base period. The 'during' part is to establish what happens when the new product is actually launched with the appropriate degree of advertising pressure. The 'after' part is to establish the level to which sales of the new product settle down after the initial launch. How long the period 'before' and 'after' should be depends upon individual circumstances. However, one can almost say for both these – 'the longer the better'. The main determining factors are, of course, cost and the period within which the decision to go 'national' has to be made. Frequently, the research worker finds himself with less time than he would like, and less money available than he would like! A compromise between what is desirable and what is possible, is, therefore, usually involved.

The information obtained in the test area, even when based upon a lengthy base period and a lengthy period after introduction, does not cover one important aspect. It is, in fact, an incomplete experiment in as much as no information is obtained on the behaviour of the market under normal conditions (e.g. without the new product). This could be particularly important in a seasonal market.

Frequently, therefore, a corresponding panel is established in another town where the new product is not being introduced (alternatively, data may be obtained from a 'national' panel) in order to provide a 'control'.

Since most operations of this nature are confined to small areas of the country (almost by definition) perhaps the most important information required from the research is the share of the total market achieved by the new product, since this is more likely to be independent of the particular area chosen as a test-market than, for example, absolute sales. Usually, it is the share of the market achieved by the new product some months after the intial launch, rather than immediately after launch, which is most important. Knowing this, the manufacturer can gauge whether or not the new product is worth marketing on a national scale or not. In the test launch of a new product it is also important to discover whether or not there are 'repeat purchases' without which the new product will not have a long term future.

Information on repeat purchasing is best obtained by means

of consumer research. Indeed, when test-marketing a new product a combination of Consumer and Retail Audit research is often desirable, although for reasons of economy not always possible. However, if the Retail Audit panel in the test town is continued long enough, some indications of the pattern of repeat purchases may be ascertained from the shape of the curve taken by the Consumer Purchases.

Sample Selection

I am now returning to one of the big 'ifs' mentioned earlier. Whilst many of the following considerations apply to all forms of Retail Audit research (including test panels), I shall confine our attention to the problems involved in establishing a national panel.

There is, as usual, one basic consideration before the question of sample selection arises, e.g. what 'universe' the panel is to represent. Generally, this question can be asked in a more positive fashion, viz. is the panel to be representative of shops of a given type or is it to be representative of outlets for a given type of product? The difference between 'shops of a given type' and 'outlets for a given product' cannot be over-emphasized. For example, there are probably in Great Britain some 300,000 outlets for groceries and provisions, but only some 150,000 grocers shops. In establishing a panel to cover sales of a grocery product, therefore, the first decision is whether the panel should be representative of the 300,000 or the 150,000.

There are advantages and disadvantages in either procedure. If the panel is based on outlets, the data obtained from, for example, the 150,000 shops which, although they sell groceries, are not grocers shops, may be very scanty. In this particular case, for example, it is estimated that these non-grocer shops account for only some 10 per cent of total sales of groceries and provisions in Great Britain. Further, whilst the Census of Distribution provides considerable basic information on sales etc. by type of shop, it provides no information on an outlet basis. Information by type of *outlet* can, in fact, only be obtained from special sample surveys designed to provide estimates of the numbers of outlets for goods of different types. Since the universe in terms of outlets is subject to much greater likelihood of change than the universe in terms of type of shop (due for example to one manufacturer's decision to expand his merchandising efforts from the traditional into non-traditional types of shops) these special sample surveys may have to be carried out at fairly frequent intervals and appropriate adjustments made to the panel composition.

If the panel is based on type of shop, the data collected, even if there were no problems of non-cooperation, represents only a sector of total trade. In the case of a grocery product, for example, 10 per cent on average (probably considerably more for particular brands) will be sold through shops which are not represented on the panel. If sales through this sector of the trade increase due, for example, to the growing importance of department and variety stores, this would not be apparent from a panel of grocers.

A further, and perhaps more important, consideration enters. The operation of a Retail Audit panel involves considerable expense, normally far in excess of any one manufacturer's budget for research. Therefore, it is usual for the costs of the operating panel to be recovered from a number of manufacturers who pay on a subscription basis: the amount of the subscription varying to some extent according to the amount of information provided. It is obvious that a panel based upon shop-type is more likely to appeal to a wider range of manufacturers than a panel based upon outlets which would appeal only to manufacturers with more or less identical interests. Thus, a panel of grocer shops may be equally of interest to the manufacturer of household polish as to the manufacturer of margarine. A panel of outlets for household polish (including as it would many non-food shops) would not be equally of interest to the margarine manufacturer.

Thus, Retail Audit panels tend to be set-up for different types of shops. However, occasionally, where there is sufficient identity of interest amongst a number of manufacturers, and where sales through the non-traditional types of shop may be important, a Retail Audit panel may be based on 'outlets' rather than 'shops'. A particular example of this is in the Chocolate and Sugar Confectionary field, where it is estimated that there are, in Great Britain, some 275,000 outlets for this type of product although there are only some 80,000 shops in the confectioner, tobacconist and newsagent group.

Having decided the universe which the Retail Audit panel is to represent, the problem then involved is in the selection of individual shops which are to comprise the panel. The immediate suggestion which springs to mind is to select the sample randomly. However, in most cases, the next question will be 'from what?', since generally speaking there are no comprehensive lists available of the addresses of different types of shop.

It would, of course, be possible to carry out an area sample census to provide a sampling frame from which a random sample of shops could be drawn. This method would be costly but, apart from this, would be ideal were it not for one major problem – that of securing the retailer's co-operation. The degree of co-operation is not, unfortunately, constant through all types and sizes of shops. As a general maxim, one can almost say that the larger the organization (i.e. number of branches controlled by one firm) or the larger the shop, the lower the level of co-operation. Consequently, even if the operation is begun with a random sample, the final sample of recruits to the panel would almost certainly be biased towards the smaller organizations and towards the smaller shops. This problem could be overcome, at least to some extent, by stratifying the original sample in the first place so that substitution for refusals to co-operate was made by shops of similar sizes.

This initial level of refusal and subsequent cancellations, together with the high cost involved in carrying out the area sample census in the first place, may cause the rejection of this method of recruiting, although it has been used, I believe, on more than one occasion.

If data on the universe of the particular types of shops which are being recruited to the panel are available (and generally these are available from the Census of Distribution), the panel is often recruited by 'quota' sampling. As you know, this method ensures that the final sample conforms in certain known respects to those of the universe, but the actual choice of shops within any one quota control group is left to the individual person recruiting the shops.

This has the disadvantage that the final sample may deviate

in unknown ways from the universe, and further, that strictly speaking the theory of probability cannot be used to determine the margins of error. All that can be done is to judge the results obtained subjectively, and to make as many checks as possible with other information, from both official sources and ex-factory sales data from the manufacturers subscribing to the panel. In my experience, these independent checks on samples based on adequate controls indicate that panels based on this method of sampling can give accurate information.

The quota controls used in recruiting a panel may well be:

1. Standard region distribution.
2. Town size distribution.
3. Shop size.

Data for setting these quota controls can be obtained from the Census of Distribution. The control on shop size may be operated either on the basis of 'turnover' of each shop or on the basis of the 'number of persons engaged' in each shop. There are arguments for and against each of these two measures: 'turnover' is perhaps closer to what one is trying to measure, but it may be rather more difficult to obtain accurately. However, since the Census of Distribution shows that there is a high association between the two measurements of size, they are largely interchangeable.

Whether or not the three controls mentioned above should be applied independently or interlocking is arguable. However, since there are definite geographical variations to be found in the size of shops, I consider that they should be applied on an interlocking basis.

A fourth control on selection of the sample may also be applied on 'form of organization' (i.e. independent/multiple/co-operative) and, since there is a tendency for the refusal rate to increase with size of organization, the number of branches (or total turnover) of the multiple and co-operative organizations may also be used as a control. In spite of this form of control there is one insuperable difficulty. Certain large multiple chains, e.g. Boots or Woolworths, do not co-operate in this form of enquiry. It is, of course, impossible adequately to recompense this type of organization for any 'nuisance' involved, or to supply them with information of interest to them without upsetting relationships with the subscribers to the panel data. Exclusion of certain sectors of, for example, the chemist or grocery trade is unfortunate and is one of the major problems in Retail Audit research. The gaps may be filled by making estimates using other available data (from Consumer Surveys as well as Retail Audit). However, this is a process of *estimating*, not of *Retail Audit* research.

In spite of the refusal of these very large organizations to co-operate, the data obtained from the Retail Audit panels is of considerable value. The following are the main reasons for this:

1. The Retail Audit research on, for example, a panel confined to 'independent' grocers, covers some 80 per cent of the total number of grocers and some 50 per cent of total grocery sales. This sector of the trade is the section about which the manufacturer has least knowledge, since he normally deals directly with the larger multiple organizations.

2. Much of the value of the Retail Audit data lies in the study of trends over time, rather than arriving at an estimate of total market size etc. for a limited period of time. Whilst the trends as between individual brands in one sector of the trade may not be identical with trends in the whole market, they are unlikely, except in special circumstances, to be markedly different. This is simply due to the fact that such trends in the market fundamentally reflect changes in *consumer* demand and may, therefore, be largely independent of the particular type of shop in which the consumer shops. If there are special circumstances why this should not be so, this will frequently be known from trade and other sources.

Thus, the lack of information about certain sectors of the trade is unfortunate rather than disastrous.

The other main problem which affects the sample design is due to losses from the panel: either temporary or permanent. This is a problem which affects all forms of continuous research. These losses arise for many reasons. Permanent losses are due to death, closure of shop, loss of interest and so on. Temporary losses arise from the shopkeeper being too busy, ill or away on holiday. These losses are kept down partly by adequate supervision, partly by the close relationship which, in time is formed between the shopkeeper and the auditor and, partly by a modest monetary incentive. However, this particular incentive can only be modest if Retail Audit research is not to become far too expensive. In spite of the fact that the shopkeeper himself is not involved in the operation, he does have the 'nuisance' of an outside person poking around his shop, perhaps for a whole day or more.

Permanent losses can, of course, be made up by recruiting new shops but this in itself intrudes certain problems. Since the stocks of any product are unlikely to be identical in both the new and the old shops, and since sales to the consumer are calculated by residual means, the *change* alone from one shop to another is, in itself, likely to provide a component in the estimate of sales.

Temporary losses cause similar difficulties, even though shops from a reserve list are included in order to keep the panel up to strength.

If there were a large number of such changes at any one time, or if the data are examined over a period of time, these additional components to the estimate of sales will tend to cancel, since they are equally likely to be positive or negative.

However, changes in panel composition at any one time, are small in number, and under these conditions, these additional components to sales may well not cancel out absolutely although, of course, they are normally small. However, it is necessary to watch carefully to ensure that any sudden change in sales is 'real' and not just due to a change in panel composition.

The Collection of Data

Following the selection of the sample, the next fundamental operation in Retail Audit research is the actual collection of data in the field.

The shopkeeper does not play a direct part in the collection of the data.[3] The field worker (or checker or auditor) does this alone once the shopkeeper has agreed that the audit may be carried out. The stocks of goods in the shop which are being checked are actually counted brand-by-brand and size-by-size

3. Furthermore, he does not see the data collected: to let him do so would tend to make him become unrepresentative.

and the information recorded on specially prepared stock forms. Next, invoices or other delivery notes are inspected and the relevant information also transferred to the stock form. All of this must be done with meticulous care whatever the conditions under which the information is collected (e.g. poor light, on top of ladders, in a shop full of people). Training and supervision of the field-force is important in ensuring that such care is taken.

The method of collecting the data outlined above suggests that the Retail Audit procedure is most easily applied to branded, packaged goods. This is one reason why much of this type of research has been carried out in grocers and chemists. In many cases, non-branded or non-packaged goods are audited, but this may bring additional problems, both of identification of the stocks in the shop and identifying the corresponding delivery information.[4] The latter may, in many circumstances, be the main stumbling block since the problem of identifying the stock in the shop can often be overcome by adequate training of the field-workers.

It is impossible to obtain information of a greater degree of fineness than the detail given on the invoices. Those from some of the smaller wholesalers tend to provide the least information and, if it is customary in the trade for this information to be recorded only in broad terms (e.g. simply as '7lbs of cheese') it may prove impossible to provide details of sales in finer terms (e.g. by individual variety of cheese – Cheddar, Cheshire, etc.). In some circumstances the relevant data may be obtained by asking the retailers to keep special records, but obviously the amount of information they will be prepared to keep in this way is limited. The lack of detailed information on invoices affects the Retail Audit procedure in some trades more than others. For example, in the textile trade a large proportion of goods are invoiced in very general terms.

You will remember that earlier I described the accurate collection of this data as the second big 'if' without which the information obtained by Retail Audit research could prove worthless or, worse still, positively misleading. The way in which I have so far described the collection of data must sound relatively

4. A further problem may be involved: measuring the stock, for example, of bulk liquids.

easy, if somewhat arduous. It is frequently far less easy than it sounds.

Counting stocks sounds simple and may well be more simple than extracting details of deliveries. However, counting stocks involves counting *all* the stocks of the particular product concerned. That is to say, those in the shop window, on the counters, on the shelves, in show cases, in all the stock rooms (behind as well as in front of other products), and even under the bed if that position is used (as it sometimes is) as spare storage space.[5] Once the habits of each shopkeeper in these respects are known to the field-worker, the problems involved are decreased and it is customary to reduce the chance of 'missed stock' in two ways. Firstly, by using a supervisor who, when recruiting the shop to the panel, carried out a thorough inspection in order to scent out possible future difficulties. Secondly, by 'running the shops in', i.e. by carrying out a few checks on a purely experimental basis before any of the data is used. This helps to ensure that stocks hidden in the unexpected places come to light before the information collected is actually being used.

Dealing with invoices also sounds simple. However, there are always many more invoices to be inspected than those relevant, and they are usually filed in such a way, e.g. by date, that the relevant ones cannot be sorted out. Invoices are not always kept in one place, retailers varying considerably in their tidiness in dealing with paper work. Nevertheless, all must be found and thoroughly scrutinized.

A shopkeeper with more than one branch may have all the goods invoiced to one, and distribute the stock himself to the remaining branches. If only one of his shops is on the Retail Audit panel, special records may be needed to deal with this problem. A similar problem is involved whenever a shop belongs to a voluntary buying group where one retailer buys for a number of others in order to secure better trade terms. Some goods may be bought for cash at the door – again special records are required.

Acting in the opposite direction, goods are sometimes returned

5. Stock is sometimes found in the most unlikely places, e.g. in the bath, in the cellars of an adjacent house, used as a base for some (other) window display.

to the manufacturer either because they are faulty or because of a deliberate policy of the manufacturer in withdrawing old stock. Since consumer sales are calculated by 'residual' there is a considerable possibility that goods returned in this way become treated (quite wrongly) as sales over-the-counter. Again, meticulous care is needed to ensure that this does not occur.

By carrying out a reconciliation, item by item, the problem of missing invoices is kept to a minimum. This check is 'one-way' only, and involves calculating sales as residual whilst the field-worker is in the shop. This calculated sales figure, if truly representing sales over-the-counter, must always be positive (or zero). A negative result shows that some error has been made and can, therefore, be rectified.

These problems are dealt with partly by training and supervision and also become less important as a field-worker gets to know her (or his) shops. We all tend to think of shops as 'impersonal'. In many ways, however, each shop has a personality of its own (perhaps of its owner). Once this personality has been established by constant association with the same field-worker, the problems outlined above are susceptible to solution.

Processing the Data

This represents few theoretical problems and since Retail Audit research is usually continuous, it is possible to handle the processing in such a way as to be efficient and expeditious. The main problem lies in balancing expenditure in processing against speed of reporting. Increasing speed tends to increase costs but, on the other hand, speed in reporting to a manufacturer, particularly when he has a crisis on his hands, may make all the difference between a satisfied and a dissatisfied client.

The main process involved in processing the data is one of re-arranging the information from the order in which it is collected, i.e. shop-by-shop, to the order in which it is presented, i.e. product-by-product. Having made this rearrangement, the information must be accumulated to provide totals etc. These processes are susceptible to punched-card treatment, to the use of computers or, for that matter, to hand posting operations. Which method is 'best', taking into account such factors as the cost and timing involved, depends largely upon individual circumstances.

Presenting the Data

Fundamentally, the information can be provided in two ways, viz. as data relating to the 'universe' or as data relating to the panel itself. The former method provides estimates of, for example, total sales in Great Britain through all the shops of the type represented by the panel or, for example, of the actual numbers of shops in the country of this particular type which stock a given product. When presented as 'panel data', the corresponding information is provided as average sales per shop, or as a percentage of the shops on the panel which were found to be stocking the product. Each method has its own advantages and disadvantages but, of course, either is equally suitable in studying trends over time.

Perhaps the main drawback to providing 'universe data' arises from points already made. Firstly, the necessity of carrying out at intervals sample surveys to establish the size of the universe and, secondly, because the panels are usually confined to a given shop type within which some large chains may not be represented. Thus, the information is only 'universal' in a certain sense, and this may not always be apparent to those who receive the information. If presented as 'panel data', this particular difficulty cannot arise. From time to time the information will, no doubt, be grossed-up to provide 'universe' estimates[6] but, the mere fact that this will involve calculating the grossing-up factor, draws attention to what is and what is not included in the 'universe'. The main drawback to the provision of 'panel data' arises from comparisons between sub-sectors of the panel (e.g. geographical, shop size). Average sales of a given product in one part of the country may differ markedly from those in another, but so may the population, the number of shops of the given type, and so on.

6. On the whole, such estimates are mainly required for year-to-year comparisons, rather than on a month-to-month basis: annual sales in, say, 1958 being a much more useful concept than total sales in each separate month of 1958.

Apart from this fundamental decision on presentation, how the data are presented depends largely upon the individual tastes of the subscriber. Needless to say, the information must be presented in an easily assimilated form using those kinds of layout, graphs and tables, which put over the information clearly and succinctly. Since one object of the Retail Audit operation is the study of trends over time, the provision of an adequate amount of back-data together with the current information is important. The operating agency needs always to bear in mind that the data is generally presented to busy men who have many things to do besides studying Retail Audit research findings. Perhaps this is the main consideration to keep in the fore-front when designing the method of presenting results.

Another important consideration (at least from the client's point of view) is flexibility, and the ability to provide special analyses. No manufacturer has the same problems, or even the same view point, as any other manufacturer, even if they operate in the same product field. Flexibility in presentation so that facts important to the particular client are highlighted and special analyses directed to help meet his particular needs, enable him to draw maximum benefit from the research.

Apart from providing comprehensive data in volume form after each audit has been completed, it is customary with many clients to present the information at regular intervals at a 'visual' presentation. It usually consists of presenting the main items of information, collected in the period since the previous 'visual' presentation was held, in the form of large scale charts and of discussing these findings in detail.

Again, the precise form which these presentations take vary from client to client. However, from the research man's point of view, there are perhaps the following cardinal rules:

1. *Not* to present too much information, but to confine the presentation to *essentials*. Otherwise some listeners are likely to become confused and bored by the whole proceedings.

2. *Not* to have these presentations too *frequently*. The right frequency depends upon whether the market being studied is relatively static or dynamic. Too frequent presentations leave one with little of importance to say at each presentation, and it

then becomes difficult to secure the full attention of the listeners.

3. Have plenty of time available for discussion. If no one wants to discuss any points which arise in the course of the presentation, so well and good. If they do, however, there is more opportunity to ascertain the problems which are worrying the client and, as a result, to ensure that full use is made of the Retail Audit data in answering these problems where possible.

Interpreting the Results

As with all forms of market research, the findings of Retail Audit research must be interpreted with care. It is easy to interpret the data just as they turn out without any consideration, for example, of their method of collection.[7] All the problems already discussed, from those concerning the universe covered by the panel and its method of selection, to the problems involved in collecting the data, must all be borne in mind by those interpreting the information. Too hasty conclusions, based on small shifts in the market, may be proved incorrect by the subsequent audit. There is, of course, no sure way of validating the data. If there were, there would be no need to carry out research in the first place. Validation as such is a slow process and involves comparing the Retail Audit information with external sources of information as and when they become available. Generally, where it has proved possible to make comparisons with external data (particularly on trends) Retail Audit data has proved reliable.

The Use to which Retail Audit Data are Put

Earlier, I have given some indications as to why these data are collected. Perhaps we can discuss this further and some of the reasons can be illustrated by showing you some charts. The use made of this type of research when test marketing a new product has already been described in some detail. Consequently, I shall confine our attention to the uses made of the data provided by regular panels on an established product. The use made, of course, varies enormously both from time-to-time and from

7. Maybe this arises just because it *is* an audit procedure.

client-to-client and, therefore, can only be touched upon in this lecture.

Perhaps the first use to be considered corresponds to an insurance policy. Manufacturers need to ensure that what they are putting into one end of the pipe-line (to wholesalers or directly to the larger retailers) is leaving the other end of the pipe-line, i.e. being bought by the consumer. For example, in Figure 1 is an illustration of what happened when a particular manufacturer gave a bonus offer to the trade. In the period covered by the offer, retailers bought in heavily (as shown by a rapid increase in 'deliveries'). However, the consumer off-take ('sales') remained practically unaltered and, consequently, the stocks of the product in the shops rose rapidly. Subsequently, of course, the shop-keepers cut back their buying until, eventually, stocks returned to a normal level. Apart from illustrating that this particular bonus offer was of little value, this chart indicates that during the period of the offer the increased amount of the product which the manufacturer was putting into one end of the pipe-line was definitely *not* going out of the other.

Manufacturers want to know further whether they are operating in an expanding, static or declining market, since they may be concerned, on one hand, with expanding their production and raw material buying and, on the other, with switching production capacity to other lines. They also need to ensure that their competitors are not stealing a march on them by capturing an additional share of the market by means, for example, of new products, new advertising campaigns or distribution drives. Vice versa, of course, they want to know whether their *own* attempts to secure an increased share of the market by introducing new products, new advertising campaigns or distribution drives are succeeding or not. Compare, for example, the positions of Manufacturers 'A' and 'C' if, instead of having the data illustrated in Figure 2, all they had was the information of their own ex-factory sales. Manufacturer 'A' would have appeared to increase sales by 33 per cent between the two years, but whether or not this were entirely due to his own efforts or to the fact that the total market had expanded, would be unknown. (In fact, he was doing well, having achieved an increased share of an expanding market). On the other hand, Manufacturer 'C' would, on the basis of ex-

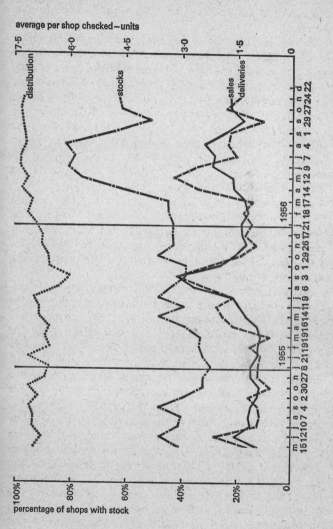

average per shop checked — units

percentage of shops with stock

Figure 1   Brand A sales, deliveries, stocks and distribution — chemists

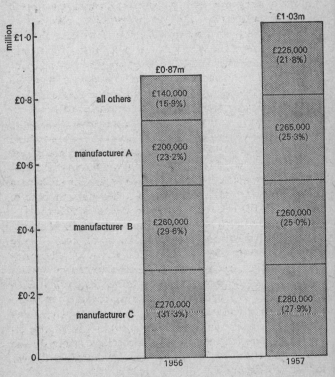

Figure 2 Consumer expenditure – by manufacturer at retail prices

factory sales, possibly feel reasonably content having made a slight increase. However, he is in fact in an unsatisfactory position having expanded sales at a slower rate than the total market. Manufacturer 'B' is, of course, worse off still.

The second use to be considered is in the planning of the activities of the manufacturer's sales force. This may simply take the form of using regional data to encourage certain members of the sales force to greater activity. Alternatively, it may take the form, particularly in a seasonal market, of ensuring that the selling-in-efforts of the sales force take place at the 'right' time, that an out-of-stock position in retail shops does not develop, or that retailers' stocks are kept at a sufficient level to meet consumer demands. Compare the summer of 1956 and that of 1955 in Figure 3. In 1956, the manufacturer brought forward his selling-in (see 'deliveries') so that it preceded the expected peak in consumer off-take ('sales'). Even if off-take in 1956 had reached the same peak level as it did in the summer of 1955 (the poorer summer of 1956 possibly accounts for why it did not) the manufacturer's lines would then still have been available in all shops in the vital peak period, whereas in the earlier year a number of shops ran out of stock at the critical time (see 'distribution').

The third use is involved in the attempt to establish the impact of particular advertising campaigns. This use has become more important since the advent of commercial television. Advertising on ITV can be expensive and there is considerable scope for experiment in the formulation of TV advertising policy. Such considerations as length of advertisement, frequency of transmission, time of transmission and so on, come into play, as well as those of cost. Retail Audit research, which can provide information television area by television area, can help in the comparison of the impact of campaigns conducted in different fashions (see Figure 4).

These are, perhaps, the three main ways in which this type of data can be used. Frequently other particular problems arise which can also be settled by studying the Retail Audit information. Often, of course, the data suggests that the verdict is 'non-proven' but sometimes the movements seen are spectacular and there are no doubts as to the conclusions to be drawn. Perhaps the most important point is that Retail Audit research (in

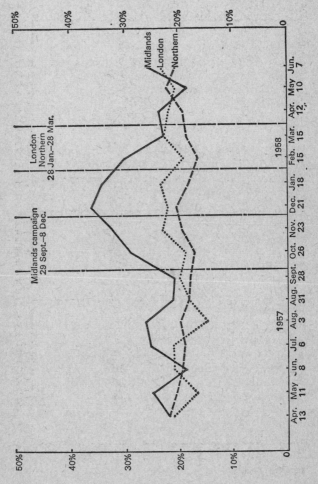

Figure 3 Brand A sales, deliveries, stocks and distribution – grocers

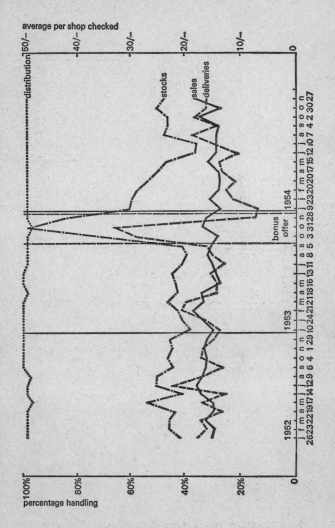

Figure 4 Total consumer expenditure by ITV area — brand A's share

common with all forms of market research) has most value when the market is 'active'. When no such activity exists, Retail Audit research acts more as an insurance against untoward events, and tends to lose tactical significance. In these conditions it provides a framework within which discussion of the client's problems can take place even if it does not affect policy directly.

17 M. Adler

Telephone Surveys

M. Adler, 'The use of the telephone in industrial market research', *Scientific Business* (now *Management Decision*), vol. 1, 1964, pp. 336–42.

The telephone as a means of conducting market research is, of course, not new. For many years it has been used when approaching consumers, or radio listeners or television viewers, and these respondents have accepted the telephone voice asking questions with more or less good grace. But the great disadvantage of this technique in consumer and allied research has always been the fact that telephone ownership has nowhere spread far enough among the population as to yield a complete cross section. 'Even in the U.S.A., telephone ownership is not yet so universal that the entire population could be reached by this means and the results are therefore confined to the middle and upper classes'. Since I wrote these words in 1956, the ownership of telephones has doubled throughout the world, but the statement is still true as far as the general population is concerned. Apart from the United States, the countries with most telephones per 1000 population are Great Britain, Sweden and Switzerland. But even in these countries only certain sections of the community can be exhaustively sampled by telephone and the large majority is still without this means of communication.

Telephone interviewing has therefore been used successfully only when the universe consisted of people belonging to the middle class, e.g. doctors. In industrial market research, however, no such problems exist. There is no business man, large or small, who is not on the telephone. It has become a part of his way of life and he is inconceivable without this instrument. Whatever business men may say about the telephone, they like it. Most of them will overtly show irritation when they are interrupted in a conversation by the ringing of the telephone; in fact, the more often this happens the more pleased they will be covertly, for this proves that they are recognized, that they are an active part of the world, that they are busy people who have a stake in affairs. Nevertheless, the telephone can become a nuisance quite objectively to the man who may be pestered by all sorts of people who want something from him without giving anything in return. This is a very important fact to be taken into consideration when planning to use the telephone in industrial market research, and it will be considered later in more detail. For the well-organized business man has an intermediary between himself and his telephone: this is his secretary whose task, among others, consists of preventing people getting through to the boss whose business is immaterial to him.

There remains, however, the fact – and this is very important – that the whole universe of business men, administrators, engineers, and other categories in the economic life of the nation, is on the telephone. Therefore it can become a very fruitful and accurate means of communication and the use of it is not confined to interviewing itself. It will become abundantly clear why this paper is called 'The use of the telephone in industrial market research' instead of simply discussing it as a tool of interviewing.

For there are many other uses, some confined to the telephone interview, some connected with other techniques.

Sampling

Having established the fact that in industrial market research every member of the universe is on the telephone, we can now go into more details as to the use of this method. It is well-known that most of the random or quota sampling is undertaken in several stages, one of the reasons for this being the fact that the interviews have to be clustered in order to save time and expense when conducting personal interviews. It is true that clustering has other advantages apart from those of cost and time. But more often than not the market researcher would be happier if he could use a sample which is spread widely over the whole country because he would then avoid the additional sampling error which is caused by clustering.

This problem does not arise when the sample is undertaken on the basis of the telephone. Even where certain industries are concentrated in a few areas, as is the case in Great Britain with the textile industry in Lancashire and Yorkshire, or the electronics industry which is mainly concentrated in the South East of the country there are always exceptions and these can prove costly when personal interviews are contemplated. In addition, even where concentration has taken place, some of the firms will be located in places difficult to reach, even if the motor car is used as a means of transport. It happens from time to time that the interviewer arrives at a plant after having been given an appointment, only to be told that the respondent is unavoidably absent. This also has to be considered, for such occasions make another journey necessary, or the interview is abandoned, which means, of course, a loss in the accuracy of the sample.

Many industrial market research surveys are not confined to one industry only. In this case, the spread of the universe becomes a very considerable cost factor, if personal interviews are contemplated. Here the telephone sample has obvious advantages which may outweigh the disadvantages connected with this method. The telephone is ubiquitous, and the cost of using it very small compared with the journeys connected with personal interviews. The market researcher need not feel restrained to produce a nation-wide sample because of cost. In addition, he can reduce expense by locating interviewers in geographically favourable points from where most of the telephoning can be undertaken by paying the fees of local calls only. The expense of distributing interviewers strategically over the country must be carefully considered against the expense of long distance calls; however, even these will have to be used on certain occasions, as will be shown later.

Sampling in industrial market research poses problems quite different from those in consumer research. Very often it is difficult to establish the universe for a survey either because the lists of companies are incomplete or because the product to be surveyed is used in many different industries and to a different extent. In the first case, the telephone can be used in order to establish whether a company comes within the universe at all; it is a simple matter to ask for the names of competitors as well, in this way building up a relevant sampling frame. In the second case, preliminary telephone enquiries can reveal the approximate number or weight of the product used by a company. This information will be invaluable when stratifying the sample by size of usage and later, when the results of the survey are considered, as a means of weighting the results. This is especially important when the quantities used differ very widely and when the actual size of a company does not give any indication as to the use of the particular product.

A sampling frame consists of the names and addresses of companies in the first place. But this information is not sufficient for the successful conduct of a survey because the individuals to be interviewed have to be identified. This is not a simple problem because of the varying job descriptions in industry; in addition, it may be useful sometimes to interview more than one individual in a firm in order to obtain all the information for the survey. The girl answering the telephone will almost every time disclose the name of the chief engineer or buyer, or whoever may be considered to be the correct informant. If she does not know, she will put the caller through to a better informed person. The advantages of knowing the name and title of the prospective respondent are obvious, whether later on a telephone survey or a survey with personal interviews or by mail is undertaken. A letter or call, be it personal or by telephone, is more likely to be favourably accepted if a particular person can be addressed.

Thus in surveys where the universe is not unduly large, as is often the case in industrial market research, all members of the universe can be contacted cheaply by telephone. This action can be considered as the first phase of a two-phase sample. The second phase then consists of selecting the actual sample and this can be stratified according to the information received over the telephone, thus oversampling the especially important companies, and later on reweighting the results. The stratification is dependent on the information received as to the amount of usage of the product concerned, of the size of the companies (very often measured by the number of employees), and other characteristics which will be revealed by the telephone call and which will vary with the object of the survey. The fact that a variable sampling fraction can be used to define the ultimate sample is both time and cost saving, and it increases the accuracy of the survey.

Telephone directories can also be used as sampling frames, but great care is needed because they may be out of date and therefore incorrect. This is especially true of the classified directories which, otherwise, would be ideal means of sampling certain industries. There are twenty-three classified telephone directories available in Great Britain and they include about 80 per cent of industry. The remaining 20 per cent are mainly in rural areas and their omission should not impair unduly the accuracy of the sample. The directories are grouped by areas and within each area by trade. A difficulty arises with the fact that some entries are duplicated when a company produces several different products. In some cases, this may be an advantage because the list of producers of a certain commodity includes also those whose main business is perhaps in another product line. It has also been established that about 5 per cent of the companies have more than one telephone line. If the sampling is undertaken from the directories those companies have a larger chance for being selected than those with only one telephone. However, this difficulty can be overcome by not accepting the company for the sample unless the random selection yields the first entry; if an entry other than the first comes up it can be ignored.

Thus the telephone directories can provide a good sampling frame as long as they are not too much out of date. The ideal case would be to obtain from the General Post Office the names and addresses of the owners of business telephones, either in certain exchanges or in certain industries. There is little doubt that this information is readily available at the Post Office, but no case has been heard of when it was given to a company undertaking market research. In any case, the telephone directories, whether classified or not, can easily be sampled randomly and lists established in this way used as samples.

Interviewing

The telephone interview can be very versatile. It has certain advantages over the personal interview, but it has its own problems as well. A telephone call is an immediate process. Very much depends on the interviewer whether contact is established quickly; but in this respect there is not much difference from the personal interview. Compared with the mail survey, the telephone interview has the advantage that the respondent hears only one question at a time and cannot be biased, therefore, by the subsequent questions. A telephone interview is a quick way of obtaining information, for the questions can be asked in rapid succession. There are, however, limitations with regard to the subject matter of the interview. Only such questions can be asked which do not involve the looking up of documents or need the assistance of somebody else in the company. If the respondent is very pressed for time, another call can be arranged easily and without incurring much additional cost.

Thus telephone interviews are ideally suited for piloting a questionnaire, both with regard to the actual questions asked and to the order in which they should be placed. It happens often in industrial market research that no formal questionnaires are used, but that the information is gathered in the free exchange of a discussion. This also can be piloted and it can be established whether the survey can be conducted at all over the telephone or whether it would not be more advantageous to make personal calls. In the same way as the newcomer to market research finds it difficult to believe what sort of information people are prepared to divulge to a trained interviewer, it is not realized that the respondents will answer frankly and truthfully a large number of questions, even if they appear initially to be unsuited to the telephone interview.

There are market researchers who believe that in industrial market research the face to face interview is more important than in consumer research. They maintain that the respondent, who in most cases belongs to the upper strata of the business hierarchy, wants to see the interviewer in person because he can gauge both his professional knowledge and his sincerity in this way. This is certainly a correct point of view, especially when complicated and highly technical subjects are the aim of the survey. On the other hand, it should not be over-rated. One can obtain information over the telephone about many aspects of a particular product, as long as the information is readily available, one can hear about the company's competitors, and one can even establish the image of the sponsoring company compared with that of its competitors. In this respect the interview by telephone is even better suited than a personal call, because the respondent is likely to be freer in his answers when he does not see the interviewer himself. Also the basic classification data will be divulged over the telephone when a respondent may be likely not to answer in a personal interview enquiry.

The quality of the researcher conducting telephone interviews must be very high indeed. He not only should be an expert in the field of the enquiry (this is true of all interviewers in industrial market research) but should also be a good telephone personality, a qualification which is difficult to describe although most people will know what is meant by this term. He must obviously be sincere and able to explain in a few words why he wants the information he is going to ask about. He must give the impression of a man who knows what he wants: cringing and begging for it is certainly the worst possible policy. Whilst politeness is an obvious ingredient of the good interviewer he must always give the impression that he is in business in his own right and that it is not really a favour he asks for, but that it is normal business procedure to obtain information and that this is to the mutual benefit of both parties concerned. Interviewers of such calibre are pretty rare. Because the telephone interview has the advantage of being less costly in time and expense, a more senior man can be employed to undertake the interviews than would be the case when personal calls are being made.

The methods of interviewing over the telephone can be very flexible and the one best suited to the particular project can be adopted. No matter, whether a completely structured questionnaire is indicated, or a semi-structured one, or whether the interview is completely unstructured and conducted as a free discussion, the telephone is certainly not a worse medium than the personal interview. Here the problem of recording the answers arises. With the formal questionnaire it is obvious that the interviewer will fill it in whilst the interview is carried out. Since the respondent does not see the actual questionnaire form this particular source of embarrassment, which sometimes occurs with personal interviewers, is eliminated. Semi-structured or unstructured interviews pose different problems. The ideal way of registering the answers is the tape recorder attached to the telephone; also in this case the respondent will not become self-conscious because he will not see the machine. It should be emphasised, however, that it is only fair to tell the respondent that his answers are recorded in this particular way. If a tape recorder cannot be used, the interviewer should take down the answers in shorthand or another person should listen in and undertake the actual recording. In this connexion similar problems arise as with the recording of all open-ended questions obtained in consumer or in industrial market research. The personal bias of the interviewer will make it inevitable for him to select those parts of the answer which seem to him to be of importance, whilst he will omit those which he thinks of less or no importance at all. Only by thorough training and an objective way of thinking can he avoid part of this bias, but there will always be doubt as to the completeness of the answers if they are recorded by the interviewer or his helper.

Another advantage is connected with the telephone interview method. If it happens that the person spoken to proves not to be knowledgeable on the subject matter it is not difficult to persuade him to transfer the call to the expert. In many cases the first person will volunteer to do so and in every case he will introduce the interviewer to the expert in this way making the conduct of the interview very much easier. However, those people who are professionally often away from the office are difficult to reach over the telephone; but the same is true of the personal interview situation. This refers to such people as service engineers or members of the sales staff, and it will become necessary in these circumstances to accept an interview with a person other than originally intended.

The real difficulty of the telephone method is not so much the interview itself, but to obtain the connexion with the respondent. It has been pointed out already that an important role is played here by the secretary of the great man, whose responsibility it is to ward off the unwanted caller. However the question is: who is an unwanted caller? If it can be made quite clear to the secretary that the call is to the mutual advantage of both participants she will establish the connexion. It may become necessary to go through the questions with her in order to convince her of the need for the conversation with her superior. In every case it is essential to prove that no selling efforts whatsoever will be made, a matter which is, of course, well-known for not being confined to the telephone interview only. Once the connexion is established, it is a good idea to tell the respondent at the outset how long the conversation is likely to last. Such a statement should be truthful, as all market research should be. If the respondent is genuinely unable to spare the time, he will say so and make another appointment. On the whole, telephone interviews can take quite a time in spite of the attitude expressed at first by most respondents. Interviews of up to fifteen minutes are not impossible if the subject matter is of interest to the respondent. Should the interview have to last longer it is better to use two samples and ask about half the questions of each (Riordon, 1963). Another question is as to whether to use the local telephone system or to conduct the interview over a long distance line. The latter is obviously more expensive, but its advantage is twofold: on the one hand, the country can be covered from headquarters thus eliminating the cost of having interviewers placed strategically over the country; on the other hand, many people are more likely to agree to the interview because they feel flattered for having been called from another town: this is especially true of top people in business organizations who are, of course, the least accessible of all potential respondents.

In spite of this, interviews conducted over the telephone are far less costly than personal interviews. It is generally difficult to give indications of cost in industrial market research because so much depends on the subject matter of a survey. For the same reason, no figures can be given for telephone interviews except for stating that they will be about a quarter of the cost of personal interviews. This figure should, however, be treated as an indication only and not as a firm statement of fact. Obviously, telephone interviews can also be conducted much more quickly than personal interviews because the time taken for travelling is eliminated. Fifteen to twenty telephone interviews per day are feasible when conducted by experienced interviewers (Stacey and Wilson, 1963, p. 150).

Finally, the experienced industrial market researcher states emphatically: 'The partial anonymity of the telephone approach encourages some respondents to speak more openly and frankly, than otherwise. Further, a skilled interviewer can pursue an obscure or ambiguous answer at greater length' (Stacey and Wilson, 1963, p. 151). These are advantages which should be carefully considered before deciding on the type of interview.

Connexion with Other Types of Interviews

Mail surveys are used in industrial market research much more than in consumer research, and rightly so. This is not the place to describe their advantages and disadvantages, but to point out that the telephone can be instrumental in improving mail surveys considerably. Before sending out the questionnaires, with the appropriate letter, it is a great advantage to discover the name of the person within a company who would be most able, and most likely, to fill in the questionnaire and return it. That this can be done over the telephone has been pointed out already. A further improvement can be achieved by talking to the particular person over the telephone and explaining to him briefly that he will receive a questionnaire and to tell him about the aim of the survey. The response rate can be increased in this way very considerably, in a particular survey the increase was from 20 per cent to 85 per cent. It may also become necessary to send more than one questionnaire to the same company; and the need for this can be ascertained by a telephone conversation. Once the mail survey is completed it may happen that some of the questionnaires were returned without all questions being answered. Again, a telephone call may make it possible to obtain the missing information, and the same occasion can be used to verify certain answers and to ask additional questions which do not lend themselves to the technique of the mail survey.

A great deal of time and therefore money can be saved when the personal interview method is used in a survey when appointments are first made over the telephone. The higher rank the respondents are in the business hierarchy the more important and essential it becomes to do so. A business man who may refuse an interview point blank if no appointment has been made beforehand will keep the appointment unless some urgent business prevents him from doing so. He will feel compelled for reasons of politeness and of normal business procedure not to refuse the interview once he has allocated a particular day and time for it. Also, he may be shown certain documents, pictures or lists, during the interview. The telephone call to him can be used to tell him that these documents will be sent to him beforehand and that time at the actual interview will be saved because this will enable him to prepare some of the information or have it prepared for him. When the interviewer arrives, the whole atmosphere of the interview will have changed to his advantage.

In fact, it is possible to conduct a survey by using a mixture of telephone, postal and personal interviews. In this case, the telephone will always be the means of warning the respondent and of putting him in such a frame of mind that he will readily answer questions either in writing or personally.

Other Uses

In our modern civilization the telephone has many uses which have become so much part and parcel of our activities that we are hardly able to visualize a world without it. In market research communication with the interviewers out in the field is indispensable. Most of this two-way communication is over the telephone because a problem can be settled in a conversation easier and quicker than by the use of letters or telegrams. Of course, the good market research organization will brief its interviewers before they start work in such a way that they will be competent with dealing with many situations if and when they occur. But even the best informed market researcher cannot foresee all the circumstances which the interviewer will encounter in the field. In this respect the telephone can play a vital part in the success of the survey.

Also in the relationship to the client the telephone may become vital. A survey will be conducted on the basis of terms of reference agreed upon with the client. The more enlightened the sponsor is the more detailed are the terms of reference. When a survey is in the field, certain facts may be discovered which make a change of the terms of reference necessary in order to give the client the best possible answers to his problems. Very often time is pressing and a telephone conversation with the client when the changed circumstances can be explained can obviously contribute greatly to the success of the survey.

Desk research plays a much larger part in industrial market research than in consumer research. The problem is often not so much the information itself but the sources from which it can be obtained. The telephone is very essential in these cases because libraries and other sources of information can be contacted quickly. It is also often necessary to obtain catalogues or prices from manufacturers which then become an important part of the survey. In these cases the telephone is also of great assistance because it obviates the time lag and the expense of writing letters to the companies concerned.

Thus it could be shown how useful and sometimes indispensable a tool the telephone is when conducting industrial market research. Both are children of our industrial age, the one already so common that we do not think much about it, the other much younger but not less important. As industrial market research grows to maturity it will make increasing use of the telephone, to the advantage of everybody concerned.

References

RIORDON, R. E. (1963), 'Using the telephone in sampling', *Printers' Ink.* vol. 29.

STACEY, N. A. H., and WILSON, A. (1963), *Industrial Marketing Research*, Hutchinson.

18 S. Levine and G. Gordon

Postal Survey Methods

S. Levine and G. Gordon, 'Maximising returns on mail questionnaires', *Public Opinion Quarterly*, vol. 22, 1958–9, pp. 568–75.

Although mail questionnaires are often the most practical and economical method of obtaining data, some investigators hesitate to employ them because they tend to yield a low percentage of returns and relatively incomplete responses (see Wallace, 1954, pp. 40–52). In a recent study of Blue Cross plans sponsored by the Health Information Foundation, experience was obtained in the use of mail questionnaires which may be of interest to other students of survey methods and opinion research. Two different mail questionnaires were sent to each of eighty-five Blue Cross plans (seventy-nine in the United States, five in Canada, and one in Puerto Rico). An elaborate questionnaire requiring from one hour to an hour and one-half for completion was filled out by the enrollment director of each plan, and a relatively brief questionnaire requiring from twenty minutes to a half-hour was to be completed by the executive director of each plan. The enrollment director's questionnaire was designed to elicit extensive data on the enrollment experiences of the plan and an evaluation of various administrative approaches and mechanisms. The questionnaire to the executive director was aimed at obtaining information of a policy nature.

One hundred per cent returns were obtained within two and one-half months from the time the questionnaires were mailed. In general, moreover, they were completed as fully as the average interview schedule. These results exceeded the expectations of the research staff. Although the study had the endorsement of the Blue Cross Commission, the national service organization of the Blue Cross plans, it is important to note that each plan is virtually autonomous. The Commission itself, in seeking less detailed information for its own purposes, rarely obtained comparable cooperation from the plans. In another phase of the study, a questionnaire was sent to the insurance commissioner of each state. While considerably less time was allotted to this phase of the study, 87 per cent of the questionnaires were returned.

The success experienced with the mail questionnaire led us to re-examine the procedures employed and the circumstances surrounding the research situation. It is hoped that the following discussion will provide some pragmatic guides which may help other investigators.[1] While the suggestions presented here were largely derived from experience with a small select universe of respondents, some of them should also obtain for mail questionnaires sent to a larger, more heterogeneous population. Other investigators may work under less favorable circumstances and their respondents may not be as motivated as those of the study under discussion. Nevertheless, if our suggestions are useful, some of them, at least, can be followed by other investigators.

The work involved in utilizing a mail questionnaire may be divided into three phases: (i) respondent preparation and involvement, (ii) questionnaire design and construction, and (iii) follow-up procedures.

Respondent Preparation

Long before the questionnaires were mailed, the staff had developed working relationships with the Blue Cross Commission and five individual Blue Cross plans. The Commission, in collaboration with the research staff, undertook to gather basic information vital to the study. Five Blue Cross plans were studied intensively for a period of four to six weeks. These case studies served various purposes, but the chief purpose was to develop an effective questionnaire.

Letters asking the plans to co-operate in completing the questionnaires made reference to the past co-operation which had already been extended by other Blue Cross organizations.[2] In this way, the plans were made aware that their response to the questionnaires constituted one of the stages in the over-all

1. Some related pragmatic considerations are discussed by Longsworth (1953, pp. 310–13).

2. F. B. Waisanen (1954, pp. 210–12) reports on the successful use of telephone contact before mailing the questionnaires.

study, and the one or two hours they devoted to filling out the questionnaire were made to appear as a relatively minor expenditure of time when compared with that expended by the Commission and the five individual plans which were studied intensively. The strategy was to impress individual plans that they were, in a sense, already committed to the study and that their response to the questionnaire was necessary to complete the study.

To obtain a respondent's involvement and co-operation it is necessary to impress him with the seriousness and importance of the project. Administrators are busy people and understandably jealous of their time. They must be assured that the results will justify the time and effort expended in filling out a questionnaire. The letters to Blue Cross administrators assured them that their assistance was vital and the results would be of great value. Finally, they were reminded of the substantial investment which the research organization had already made in the study.

Not all studies permit promising a 'reward' to respondents, but in some cases a 'reward' may be completely in keeping with the objectives of the study. In this study, the research staff was able to reward the respondent by assuring him that through the study he would make a valuable contribution to the field and by promising him a copy of the final report when it was completed.[3]

Our experience testifies to the importance of preparing the respondent for the questionnaire he is to receive. Letters were sent about a week before the questionnaire was mailed; an additional letter accompanied the questionnaire. Some of the information in these letters was repeated in the instructions at the beginning of the questionnaire. Preparatory letters are especially important when the questionnaires are of considerable length. The form then does not come as a surprise and the respondent's irritation with its length is somewhat mitigated.

Who is to send the preparatory letters? The decision will vary with the status of the respondents and the nature and auspices of the study. In this study, it was decided that the Director of the Blue Cross Commission and the President of the

3. The final report was published in December of 1957 (Levine, Anderson and Gordon, 1957).

Health Information Foundation would write the preparatory letters and the Foundation's Director of Research the letter accompanying the questionnaire. Both men were known to a large number of plan directors as important practitioners or students of the field. The research staff discussed the content of the letters with the persons writing them in order to make sure that the appropriate points were covered.

One way of meeting the problem of returns on a lengthy mail questionnaire addressed to personnel of an organization is to work through the line of formal authority. Instead of sending a questionnaire directly to a member of the administrative staff, it may be desirable to get the head of the organization committed to the study and have him delegate the responsibility of completing the questionnaire to a member of his organization. In this study, separate questionnaires were designed, one for the executive director and one for the enrollment director. Both were mailed to the executive director, who was assigned the responsibility of returning the completed forms. This proved to be preferable to having the enrollment director questionnaire sent directly to the enrollment director. Of course, the choice of working through the head of an organization has to be weighed in each research situation. In some cases, the director of an organization may obstruct rather than facilitate return of the questionnaire.[4]

Questionnaire Design and Construction

Even though we prepared the way by our letters, we tried to construct the questionnaire so that it could 'sell' itself. The questionnaire had to draw and hold the respondent's interest, avoid ambiguity, and hold to a minimum the effort necessary to answer it.

Initial impressions influence respondent co-operation. The appearance of the questionnaire frequently determines whether it is read or discarded. Once the respondent takes the effort to

4. Some writers caution against this use of 'intercession'. They feel that responses may be inaccurate since respondents may resent the pressure placed upon them. See Parten (1950, pp. 366–7). Parten's discussion is based on Davis and Barrow (1935, pp. 137–44).

read it, he has some psychological commitment to complete it. In order to produce the most favorable possible response, we tried to design a cover which would be interesting and decorative, without reducing the questionnaire's air of importance.[5] Furthermore, we decided to print rather than mimeograph, because mimeographed sheets are often treated as throw-aways, and reproduction techniques such as varitype or printing allow more flexibility of design.[6]

Attention was given to specific aspects of format and appearance. The following recommendations may enhance a questionnaire's appearance and effectiveness:

1. Questions should be separated by dotted lines or extra space, distinguishing by boldface type etc., to ensure that the respondent will answer the right question.

2. The type should be varied to emphasize important words, phrases, or instructions.

3. Check lists, fill-ins, or multiple-choice questions should be conveniently arranged. Category designations and space for answers should be placed close together to avoid the possibility of error. Where confusion is possible, a series of dots leading from the category to the answer space is helpful.

4. When the questionnaire is necessarily very long, as in the case of the Blue Cross study, it should look as short as possible. Through printing, use of both sides of the page, and double columns, we were able to make the printed questionnaire appear less than one-third its mimeographed size.

The degree to which a questionnaire elicits the desired information depends considerably upon the manner in which it is

5. Parten and others also point up the importance of colors and pictorial material. She adds the following caution: 'It is important to bear in mind, however, that what appeals to survey designers is usually not the same as what appeals to the public. Market researchers have shown in many studies that the choices of specialists in the advertising offices regarding titles of promotion pieces, colors, or other copy invariably differ from the selections of the public at large' (Parten, 1950, p. 384).

6. Whenever budgetary considerations make mimeographing or some other inexpensive process necessary, care should be taken that the questionnaire is as 'professional' in appearance as possible. An attractive cover for the questionnaire can be constructed at relatively low cost.

constructed. The design, wording, and logical order of the questions influence the degree, quality, and rate of response. The following guides in large part have been stated by students of the field. They are repeated and discussed here to permit a systematic presentation.

1. The questions should be stated simply and clearly in words commonly used by the respondents; they must be relevant and meaningful; the categories to be checked should cover the full range of answers the respondent can give to the questions. These suggestions are especially important in designing a questionnaire inquiring about the policy and operational decisions of administrators. Terminology which is not consistent with that employed by the respondents will tend to convey the impression that the researcher is not familiar with the subject he is investigating and that the questionnaire is not worth answering. In fact it may alienate or even offend the respondent. For example, Blue Cross plans customarily speak of 'enrolling members', not 'selling policies', and refer to their field force as 'representatives' rather than 'salesmen'.

2. The position of a question in relation to other questions frequently affects the responses. It is best to keep the first few questions simple and easy to answer, though not trivial. Respondents tend to be discouraged when they have to answer difficult or relatively personal questions in the initial stage of the questionnaire. Furthermore, the initial questions tend to receive more 'don't knows' than any other portion of the questionnaire. In order to counteract both these tendencies, the initial questions of the non-group questionnaire were concerned with the past work and organizational experience of the respondents. Important questions should not be placed at the very end, especially in long questionnaires, since fatigue factors lead to omissions and errors.

To encourage interest, one may use the 'funnel' type of question, in which the more specific questions follow a general question. Questions dealing with a specific subject should be grouped in one section of the questionnaire and not interspersed throughout. Grouping makes the questionnaire easier to fill out. Interspersing is tiring and disconcerting.

3. Questions should be worded so that it will not be easier for the respondent to answer one way than another. In addition, the wording of questions should avoid any indication of what might constitute the 'proper answer'.

4. Whenever possible, a simple and convenient response system should be used. Check lists, fill-ins, and multiple-choice questions may be used to elicit a wide range of information from the respondent with a minimum of annoyance. When a rating type of question is used, an attempt should be made to counteract the tendency of the respondent to seek a middle ground. In constructing the check list or multiple type of question, care should be taken that each category is separate and does not overlap with the other categories.

5. In some cases, as in the Blue Cross study, it may be advisable to encourage the respondent to supply additional information not adequately tapped or specified by the questionnaire, because adhering to the categories or alternatives of a rigidly structured questionnaire may prove frustrating to some respondents.[7] In the initial instruction section the respondent may be invited to write in comments to clarify some of his checked answers throughout the questionnaire. Or a final question may be provided at the end of the questionnaire, or at the end of specific sections, which invites the respondent to discuss any problem that is important to him. This also elicits information not anticipated when the questionnaire was prepared. Researchers must make sure, however, that the respondent does not interpret these 'safety-valve' questions as substitutes for answering the specific questions.

These suggestions demand care and considerable work. A questionnaire which is clear and meaningful to the respondent, which flows logically and easily, and which contains appropriate and inclusive categories is always the result of extensive preparation. This is particularly true of one which employs simple response systems like check lists and rankings as opposed to the open-end type of response system. To perfect a questionnaire,

7. Irwin Deutcher (1956, pp. 566–604) discusses the resistance of physicians to closed-ended questions.

the researcher must know the subject thoroughly and expend considerable effort in refining and pretesting. In our study, the difficulty of devising a wide range of questions and selecting appropriate items or categories for each question in order to extract the experiences of the eighty-five plans was increased by their marked differences in history, practice, philosophy, and terminology.

Some plans are more successful than others in enrolling specific segments of the population. What factors or variables were the staff to select to help explain differential enrollment success? The dual objective of getting breadth in the questionnaire and locating the independent variables of the over-all study were met by preliminary intensive case studies of five Blue Cross plans. The five plans were chosen on the basis of the range and kinds of data they could be expected to yield. For example, some had long experience in enrolling rural farmers, others had experience with specific techniques or methods of enrollment, and still others had experience with enrolling uncovered elements of the population.

The case studies of the five plans proved valuable in several ways. We were able to ascertain the kinds of data Blue Cross plans could readily supply and those which did not exist or would require an unreasonably long time to obtain. We were able to develop relevant items or categories which we would not have known about otherwise. The case studies sharpened our knowledge of terminological usage in the field and introduced a range of data which had not been previously anticipated. We gained new insights and were able to observe new relationships among our data. Finally, the case studies helped us to order our general categories so that they would be meaningful to a larger number of Blue Cross plans.

On the basis of the five case studies and other data, we constructed the first draft of the questionnaire. The questionnaire was then subjected to intensive criticism by the research staff who had worked on the case studies. On the basis of many suggested revisions, a second draft of the questionnaire was prepared. It was studied by the research staff, personnel in Blue Cross plans, and the Blue Cross Commission. Further criticisms were taken care of in a third draft, which was thoroughly reviewed in a conference consisting of personnel in the Blue Cross

Commission and the head of its research committee.[8] Additional revisions resulted in final form.

Follow-Up Procedures

The questionnaires were sent air mail, special delivery. Air mail, special delivery return envelopes were enclosed. This was intended not only to hasten delivery and return of the questionnaires, but to impress upon the respondents the importance the research staff attached to the questionnaire. Thus it reinforced the accompanying letter from the Research Director of the Foundation emphasizing the significance of the study.[9]

The time the research staff allows before it begins its follow-up procedures will vary with the length and nature of the questionnaire, the characteristics of the respondents, the season of the year, and other factors which may affect the rate of returns. In any case, the research team should have a tentative time schedule and begin follow-ups at the time planned. Despite the most diligent effort in respondent preparation and questionnaire design, a considerable number of respondents will fail to respond to the initial mailing. They may intend to complete the questionnaire but misplace it or forget it. In the Blue Cross study, after

8. The head of the research committee was also the executive director of one of the Blue Cross plans. As a result, one of the respondents was familiar with the content and purposes of the questionnaire before receiving it. As a general principle, of course, researchers should aim at creating a uniform situation of all respondents and should not permit respondents to be familiar with the questionnaire. In this case, practical considerations made it necessary for us to get the approval of the research committee and thus to show the third draft of the questionnaire to one of the would-be respondents. We felt somewhat justified in this departure from strict research procedure by the following considerations: the executive director questionnaire was not nearly so important as that filled out by the enrollment director; the head of the research committee made some valuable contributions to the questionnaire; and the director's approval was essential before the staff could send out the questionnaire. The director was asked not to communicate the content to any of his colleagues. An examination of his final completed questionnaire suggested that his previous exposure to the questionnaire draft did not significantly modify the direction of his responses or those of the enrollment director in his plan.

9. Abbott L. Ferris (1951, pp. 247–8) reports deadlines to be effective in eliciting 'immediate heavy response'.

four weeks elapsed a second wave of questionnaires was sent to dilatory respondents. Accompanying letters indicated awareness of the busy schedule of the respondents but again urged them to give the questionnaire their immediate attention. At the same time, a letter was sent by the Director of the Blue Cross Commission urging a prompt response.

As soon as questionnaires are returned, they should immediately be examined for completeness. The Blue Cross questionnaire was constructed in a manner which permitted the respondent to skip sections of the questionnaire that did not apply to his plan and answer a related series of questions. In cases where pertinent questions were skipped, the questions were clipped and sent to the respondent with an accompanying letter and return envelope. This was done a day or two after the questionnaire was received in the belief that the length of time which elapsed would affect the rate of response to the specific questions. In a few cases, the respondent was reached by telephone and his verbal answers were recorded.

Within three or four weeks after the second wave was sent out, about 90 per cent of the questionnaires had been returned. The remaining 10 per cent of the respondents received telegrams or telephone calls. Though telephoning and telegraphing involve some expense, the cost is still below that of direct interviewing. Respondents were informed that they were among the very last to return their questionnaires and that their plan might be one of the few not included in the final tabulations and analyses. Such 'band-wagon' technique would probably be less effective with a larger and more heterogeneous 'public', but in this case the research staff was in possession of questionnaires from all the respondents within another three weeks.

To the extent that it was possible, a personal touch was maintained in communication between the research organization and the respondents. As Parten states, 'It has been found that a personal touch in the letter of transmittal is quite effective in bringing in returns. A postscript which looks as if it were written by hand or a personal signature of the sender whose name appears on the stationery has proved effective....' (Parten, 1950, p. 386). In addition, the respondents were assured that all the data on a specific plan would be treated as confidential, and that no respondent would be mentioned without permission. In good part, the success of the survey was attributable to the earnestness of Blue Cross leaders to co-operate in a study which might help them serve the public more effectively.

In brief, our experience points to some of the following conclusions:

1. Researchers seeking information through a mail questionnaire should consider the feasibility of first conducting case studies or, at least, intensive interviews to increase their range of information. This information may subsequently define the limits of the questionnaire and the types of question to be used.

2. In developing the questionnaire, the knowledge of the research team as well as that of qualified respondents should be utilized.

3. Pretesting should focus on the range of data and the inclusiveness of the categories of the questions as well as on the clarity and meaningfulness of the individual questions.

4. More than one stage of pretesting may be indicated in constructing a lengthy mail questionnaire.

5. Respondent preparation and follow-up procedures require careful planning and administration. Special delivery return envelopes, deadlines, and tentative time schedules for follow-ups and telephone calls all contribute to maximizing response.

References

DAVIS, R. A., and BARROW, E. L. (1935), 'Critical study of the questionnaire in education', *Educational Administration and Supervision*, vol. 21.

DEUTCHER, I. (1956), 'Physicians' reactions to a mailed questionnaire: a study in "resistentialism"', *Public Opinion Quarterly*, vol. 20.

FERRIS, A. L. (1951), 'A note on stimulating response to questionnaires', *American Sociological Review*, vol. 16.

LEVINE, S., ANDERSON, O. W., and GORDON, G. (1957), *Non-Group Enrolment for Health Insurance*, Harvard University Press.

LONGSWORTH, D. S. (1953), 'Use of a mail questionnaire', *American Sociological Review*, vol. 18.

PARTEN, M. (1950), *Surveys, Polls and Samples: Practical Procedures*, Harper.

WAISANEN, F. B. (1954), 'A note on the response to a mailed questionnaire', *Public Opinion Quarterly*, vol. 18.

WALLACE, D. (1954), 'A case for and against mail questionnaires', *Public Opinion Quarterly*, vol. 18.

Further Reading

J. P. ALEVIZOS, *Marketing Research: Applications, Procedures and Cases*, Prentice-Hall, 1965.

S. BANKS, *Experimentation in Marketing*, McGraw-Hill, 1965.

H. C. BARKSDALE and W. M. WEILBACHER, *Marketing Research: Selected Readings with Analytical Commentaries*, Ronald Press, 1966.

F. M. BASS, C. W. KING and E. A. PESSEMIER (eds.), *Applications of the Sciences in Marketing Management*, Wiley, 1968.

L. BOGART (ed.), *Current Controversies in Marketing Research*, Markham, 1969.

H. W. BOYD and R. WESTFALL, *Marketing Research*, Irwin, 1964.

British Market Research Bureau, *Readings in Marketing Research*, B.M.R.B., 1956.

T. CORAM (ed.), *Cases in Marketing and Marketing Research*, Crosby Lockwood, 1969.

K. K. COX and B. M. ENIS, *Experimentation for Marketing Decisions*, International Textbook, 1969.

R. CRISP, *Marketing Research*, Irwin, 1964.

A. DAVIES and O. PALMER, *Market Research and Scientific Distribution*, Blandford Press, 1957.

A. H. DELENS, *Principles of Market Research*, Crosby Lockwood, 1950.

R. FERBER, D. BLANKERTZ and S. HOLLANDER, *Marketing Research*, Ronald Press, 1964.

M. HEIDINGSFIELD and F. EBY, *Marketing and Business Research*, Holt, Rinehart Winston, 1961.

H. HENRY, *Motivation Research*, Crosby Lockwood, 1957.

P. M. HOLMES, *Marketing Research: Principles and Readings*, Arnold, 1966.

W. R. KING, *Quantitative Analysis for Marketing Management*, McGraw-Hill, 1967.

E. KONRAD and R. ERIKSON (eds.), *Marketing Research: A Management Overview*, American Management Association, 1966.

D. B. LUCAS and S. H. BRITT, *Measuring Advertising Effectiveness*, McGraw-Hill, 1963.

D. J. LUCK, H. G. WALES and D. TAYLOR, *Marketing Research*, Prentice-Hall, 1961.

D. B. MONTGOMERY and G. L. URBAN, *Management Science in Marketing*, Prentice-Hall, 1969.

K. S. PALDA, *The Measurement of Cumulative Advertising Effects*, Prentice-Hall, 1962.

R. S. REICHARD, *Practical Techniques of Sales Forecasting*, McGraw-Hill, 1966.

B. TAYLOR and G. S. C. WILLS (eds.), *Pricing Strategy*, Staples Press, 1969.

Further Reading

Thomson Organisation, *Roy Thomson Medals and Awards for Media Research* (annually from 1963 onwards).

K. P. UHL and B. SCHONER, *Marketing Research*, Wiley, 1969.

C. R. WASSON, *Research Analysis for Marketing Decision*, Appleton-Century-Crofts, 1965.

G. S. C. WILLS, *Marketing Through Research*, Pergamon, 1967.

G. S. C. WILLS (ed.), *Sources of U.K. Marketing Information*, Nelson, 1969.

G. S. C. WILLS, D. ASHTON and B. TAYLOR, *Technological Forecasting and Corporate Strategy*, Crosby Lockwood for Bradford University Press, 1969.

G. S. C. WILLS, *Exploration in Marketing Thought*, Crosby Lockwood for Bradford University Press, 1970.

A. WILSON, *The Assessment of Industrial Markets*, Hutchinson, 1969.

Readers will find the most useful learned journals to consult in this field are as follows:

Journal of the Market Research Society (previously *Commentary*)
Journal of Advertising Research
Journal of Marketing Research
British Journal of Marketing
I.M.R.A. Journal
Journal of Marketing
European Marketing Research Review
Revue Française du Marketing

Acknowledgements

Permission to reprint the papers published in this volume is acknowledged from the following sources:

Reading 1 McGraw-Hill Book Company
Reading 2 The Market Research Society
Reading 3 American Marketing Association and C. S. Mayer
Reading 4 British Institute of Management
Reading 5 *Business Horizons*, V. E. Harder and F. R. Lindell
Reading 6 American Management Association Inc., A. B. Blankenship and J. B. Doyle
Reading 7 European Society for Opinion and Marketing Research and I. R. Haldane
Reading 8 *Journal of the Market Research Society* and K. Rogers
Reading 9 *Journal of the Market Research Society* and R. M. Blunden
Reading 10 *Journal of the Market Research Society* and B. P. Emmett
Reading 11 *Behavioral Science* and P. Kotler
Reading 12 Princeton University Press
Reading 13 American Marketing Association and L. J. Rothman
Reading 14 American Marketing Association and A. E. Goldman
Reading 15 American Marketing Association and S. Sudman
Reading 16 British Market Research Bureau Ltd and J. E. Fothergill
Reading 17 Engineering, Chemical & Marine Press Ltd and M. K. Adler
Reading 18 *Public Opinion Quarterly*, S. Levine and G. Gordon

Author Index

References to Bibliographies are in Italic

Author Index

Subject Index

Subject Index